Hare, Hare, What You Doing There?

Hare, Hare, What You Doing There?

A Memoir of Growing Up in the Thirties

Robert M. Twedt

For my very good friend and counselor, Beth from

Robert Twedt

Writers Club Press
San Jose New York Lincoln Shanghai

Hare, Hare, What You Doing There?
A Memoir of Growing Up in the Thirties

Writers Club Press
an imprint of iUniverse, Inc.

For information address:
iUniverse, Inc.
5220 S. 16th St., Suite 200
Lincoln, NE 68512
www.iuniverse.com

ISBN: 0-595-23927-7

For My Parents

Contents

Author's Note

This is an autobiography. Rochester, its institutions, and environs are real, and so was my family. Some events have been expanded, and some names have been changed, without compromising family history.

I am very grateful for the invaluable assistance of everyone who helped me resurrect Rochester and the period of the thirties from historical records and from personal memory. Thanks to the Reference Staff, Rochester Public Library; Marilyn Hensley, Assistant Archivist, Olmsted County Historical Society; Bettina Somerville, Library Director, Owen County, Kentucky; Ruth Ehmcke, St. Paul Pioneer Press Library; Joe Piersen, Archivist, Chicago & Northwestern Railway Historical Society; Timothy Reynolds, Kodak Information Center; Rev. Diane Harvey, Rochester Congregational Church; Berdine Erickson, retired employee, Rochester State Hospital; Horace Heidt, Jr.; Roger Meier, Collector of Leinenkugel Memorabilia; Customer Service Staff, Jacob Leinenkugel Brewing Company; Peter Boulay, Minnesota Climatology Office; Minnesota Department of Motor Vehicles; Minnesota Office of Tourism; and the Rochester Department of Parks.

Thanks to Kay Bush, Owen County, Kentucky High School, for help with the reproduction and placement of images. Most of the photographs in this work are from my personal collection. The views of the Plummer Building, the Congregational Church, Edison School, the Chicago and North Western Railway station, and Rochester City Hall are used here with the permission of the Olmsted County Historical Society.

I also thank Nancy Horton Bragdon, Mary Kepler Wolter, Barbara Berkman Withers, and David M. Pennington, Chairperson of Rochester's Sesquicentennial for their helpful advice. I am deeply grateful to my sister, Nancy Twedt Randall, for sharing her memories of our family, and to my dear wife, Pat, for her patient editing of many drafts and for her unshakable belief that the manuscript had merit.

ON THE WARPATH

E dison Elementary School, my first alma mater, posed in frumpish respectability at the epicenter of a city block, surrounded by a worn and battered lawn, a girdle of spirea, and gravelly playing fields. It was named for the well-known American tinkerer and inventor of the incandescent electric bulb, which encouraged an easy association between the role of light at the Creation, and as symbol of Truth for the budding scholar. Edison School was a three-story brick structure that had been haphazardly adorned with Greco-Roman embellishments to ennoble its purpose and hide its architectural mediocrity. The main entrance cringed between a pair of Neo-Corinthian pillars, and was lit by globe lamps atop cast iron columns. A great overhanging cornice of shaped and painted sheet metal crowned the building. Above the cornice over the entrance perched a stamped-metal, heraldic pediment that had not yet been besmirched with a date, motto, or name of benefactor, an oversight of which I was unaware.

Edison was only a few city blocks away from our home by the circuitous sidewalk route approved by my mother. The walk to school could be halved, if I struck out directly through alleys and yards. Nevertheless, I rarely took the shorter route, because I relished the potential encounters with the neighborhood residents.

We Twedts, my father Nels, mother Stella, younger sister Nancy and I lived in a carriage house behind the stately residence belonging to my father's employer, Dr. Donald C. Balfour, a surgeon and an early partner of the famous Mayo brothers. The Mayo Clinic had its beginnings in 1883 when Dr. William J. Mayo and later Dr. Charles H. Mayo joined their father's medical practice. Dr. William Worrall Mayo had come to Rochester, Minnesota in 1863 as surgeon examiner of federal recruits, and begun private practice there when the Civil War ended.

Dad, Nancy, Mother and I in 1930

Directly across the street from us was a stucco residence with wide, overhanging eaves that resembled the *Prairie* houses of Frank Lloyd Wright. It was home to the Berkman family, whose numerous younger members included my best friend, Johnny Berkman. Johnny's father was a physician on the staff of the esteemed Mayo Clinic, and a descendant of its founder. The Berkmans could thus claim membership in Rochester's most privileged social stratum. Johnny and I had been friends for as long as I could remember, and were oblivious to such fine distinctions.

Johnny bounded down the few front steps, a milk mustache on his upper lip, still munching his breakfast Wheaties. He was carrying his schoolbooks slung over his shoulder with a leather strap. His auburn hair, combed straight across his forehead, framed warm brown eyes, and an infectious smile.

"Hi, Johnny" I said. "We're late. We better hurry, or we'll catch it from Miss Leonard." Miss Mabel Leonard was the school principal and my first grade teacher. Johnny was a year older than I was and in the second grade.

"Naw, Bobby, we've still got lots of time," he replied. "Ten minutes by our kitchen clock."

"Well, okay. But let's get started anyway," I said, not trusting his confidence or his accuracy.

On this warm September morning in 1930 both of us still wore short sleeved, cotton broadcloth shirts and knee length trousers. Freshly starched and ironed, these garments had not yet acquired the inevitable wrinkles and stains that my mother claimed "would be the death of me yet."

On the corner stood a three-story frame structure whose aging wood bulk had been gracelessly covered in gray asbestos shingles. A large screened porch enclosing its two street sides softened its banal four-square appearance. From this vantage point, hidden from the street by a screen of morning glories, passers-by could be scrutinized by Mrs. Hansen. She could scowl at them in secret, only the tortured groans emanating from her long-suffering wooden rocker revealing her presence. This morning we could hear her palm-leaf fan already flapping; though the day's Indian summer heat was still merely a premonition. Mrs. Hansen's two sons, Leck and Mike, no longer attended school but were apprenticed to a house-builder, to learn the carpentry trade. Johnny and I viewed these two dour, but handsome, blonde brothers with the wonder and awe that a later generation would ascribe to Superman. For the past week, they had perched precariously, shirtless and muscular, atop the Hansen home reshingling the roof. Shading our eyes against the morning sun, we measured their progress, concerned about the risky nature of their work. In fearful whispers we discussed the likelihood of either brother falling from such a great height, abandoning this macabre speculation because we had to go on to school!

A few houses beyond the Hansen residence stood the diminutive white bungalow that was the retirement refuge of Dr. and Mrs. C. Edward Prendergast. Old Doc Prendergast had cared for the rural residents of Olmsted County for almost fifty years until arthritis compelled him to give up driving his buggy on house calls. He had arrived at the ford of the Zumbro River early enough to attend the birth pangs of Rochester. Fresh from his medical training, he set up a practice among the Scandinavian homesteaders hereabouts. He had treated all the practical ills that farm folk were ever likely to suffer, and was still the preferred source of medical advice among the elderly. In the beginning, he had chosen not to join the Mayo brothers and their father, which was just as well, for he had never been asked.

Doc and his wife retired to the bungalow in town, where the two old people enjoyed the easy communion with neighbors that their cozy front porch afforded. They were seated there this morning. Doc was attired in overalls, a tan corduroy vest and badly worn velour carpet slippers. His uncombed white hair and beard wafted gently in the morning air, giving him the appearance of an overweight Mark Twain. Ma, her iron gray hair in braids, wore a green and white chenille robe that was missing many of its decorative tufts. She had the merry, inquisitive eyes and thin body frame of a sandpiper.

When Ma was not present to curb his excesses, Doc often regaled us with his masterfully embellished stories of the "pioneer days," when he first began his practice. Replete with renegade Indians, brawling cowboys, and half-civilized fur trappers, these fanciful, hair-raising tales were bearable only because they were told in daylight.

Crossing the intervening alley we came to a frowning, two-story house with attic dormer windows, and a cheerless, glass-enclosed front stoop. It was the childhood home of the reclusive Teasdale twins, Thelma and Velma, who had continued to live in the house long after the death of their parents, the Right Reverend Horace and Mrs. Minnie Teasdale. On each side of their entrance walk the spinsters had constructed small pedestals of stones and mortar, embellished with cheap costume jewelry. On this bright morning they had been transformed into two garish, sparkling pylons. Inspired by Doc's tales of the *old West*, Johnny and I regarded the glittering shafts much like prospectors striking it rich. Hammering wildly with stones from the alley, we attempted to release the precious gems from the mother lode before being discovered, which was not long in coming. After only a few blows to the mortar, the apoplectic countenance of first one and then the other harridan appeared at the open front doorway, screeching imprecations that threatened parental retribution.

"Come on, Bobby, let's get away from here," Johnny exclaimed.

"Yeah, we'd better scram before they call the cops," I replied, and we both ran as fast as our legs could carry us down the sidewalk toward school.

At the next corner, and directly across the street from Edison, stood a multi-gabled brick bungalow with wide eaves and knee bracing that was home to the Faust family. Young Bobby Faust, a chubby, moon-faced, asthmatic child a year younger than I, attended kindergarten later in the morning. He had a querulous, disagreeable personality that had earned him a well-deserved ostracism by all of us kids.

On the previous day, Bobby Faust had waylaid us as we passed his wide yard, rushing out from behind a lilac bush, whooping in a scratchy falsetto. He wore a shapeless, baggy, sand colored Indian suit of a thin cotton material, that had been ordered from Sears and Roebuck. The trousers and short sleeves were fringed, the neck trimmed in red flannel. At the rear of his headband, garishly decorated with red glass beads, a dejected turkey feather clung precariously. Aiming a toy bow with surprising skill, his wooden arrows had narrowly missed us. We had raced past the Faust home and crossed the street.

"That was a dirty trick, Bobby Faust," I had called from the safety of the schoolyard.

"We're gonna get you yet, Bobby," Johnny had echoed. "No one wants to play with you. You're a stinky rotten egg!"

"Fraidy cats," Bobby Faust had replied, at the same time waving his hand in dismissal. "I don't want to play with no ol' fraidy cats anyway. You better watch your step next time you go past my house. I'll be ready for you with more of these here arrers." He held his weapons high in his right hand. We had ambled off contemptuously, the interview at an end.

Today, despite his previous imprecations, Bobby Faust was nowhere to be seen. Johnny and I made a cautious and thorough search for our costumed nemesis without success.

"Boy oh boy, I don't like this at all," said Johnny. "Those darn arrows could puncture us good. I hope he's in his house, or somewheres else besides on the warpath."

"So do I. That Bobby Faust, he's a holy terrier!" I replied.

At the front of the Faust home a smiling woman wearing a peach colored, quilted satin, breakfast robe, seated on the veranda greeted us with affectionate enthusiasm. Mrs. Faust's thick, dark hair had been loosely combed and pinned in a bun atop her head. "You had better step lively," she called to us. "I heard the first bell ring already. Miss Leonard will be out on the steps looking for you," she warned, with a merry laugh.

I was glad to see Mrs. Faust this morning. I recognized in her a natural ally. She was one of those rare adults who had never relinquished the ability to perceive the world through the eyes of a child. Her rapport with children was instantaneous and complete. I wondered how such a wonderful woman could harbor a holy terrier for a son.

"Where's Bobby, Mrs. Faust?" I asked warily, using the savage's Christian name.

"Oh dear, boys," she replied, and her face assumed a worried expression. "Bobby hurt himself yesterday playing in the yard. I still don't quite know how it happened. He was climbing on the back fence when he fell and broke his arm, poor little thing."

I imagined the accident. Chubby Bobby trying to balance himself, tight-rope-fashion, on the top fence rail in his Indian suit, catching the bow in a low-hanging apple tree limb, and tumbling clumsily to the hard turf below.

"Golly, that's too bad," Johnny said in feigned concern.

"Would you boys like to see him?" I heard Mrs. Faust say. "I know he'd be really pleased to see you and it would cheer him so much to have a visit from his friends."

Friends she called us. He's no friend of ours!

"Sure, Mrs. Faust, we'd like to see him" Johnny said, in a rush. "And we'll only stay a minute 'cause it's almost time for the second bell." Awash in a sea of conflicting thoughts, Johnny and I looked at each.

Mrs. Faust opened the front door and ushered us into the hall, from which an overly ambitious central stairway rose grandiosely to a second floor mezzanine. Stepping before us, she led the way to Bobby's bedroom. Within that chamber the hapless victim lay in a walnut four-poster, propped against billowing down pillows. His arm lay outstretched, cozily encased from elbow to fingertips in blazing white plaster. There were already a few signatures scrawled on the latter, "Dad"—"Mom"—"Love, Sis."

Slowly and deliberately, shoulder to shoulder, Johnny and I walked across the figured rug, from the doorway to the footboard of Bobby's bed. Staring into his face for a full minute, we spoke with determination, emphasis, and in unison, "Bobby Faust, it serves you right!"

Turning abruptly, we marched sedately past the gaping Mrs. Faust, down the staircase, and out into the bright sunshine to the joyful sound of the second bell.

Johnny (right) and I in 1929

THE SHOOTING LESSON

I was never able to keep up with my father's long strides, but today my effort to do so was made more difficult by a dragging fear of failure. I doubted that I would understand his instructions, the words cascading erratically in loud, lip-pursing mispronunciations. Knowing from painful experience that a listener who showed insufficient attention or wit to comprehend would receive little sympathy, I dreaded the consequences of my own failure. A feeble sunset heralded an early winter and swathed the view ahead in dingy saffron. Fingers of cold stealthily slipped under my light corduroy coat, adding to my discomfort.

Ahead, my father's lank frame moved up the driveway with resolute purpose. A long, straight nose preceded a narrow, angular face, wide thin lips, and a lean jaw. Silver-rimmed spectacles saddled his nose and outlined green-flecked, hazel eyes. His vested serge suit managed, despite its frayed and shiny blackness, to convey his undisguised self-confidence. A nondescript dark fedora sat squarely forward upon his balding head. He rarely dressed in other than a suit and, even when working, simply drew coveralls over trousers, shirt and tie. A single-shot, bolt-action, small caliber rifle was cradled in his lean right arm. I understood that he intended to explain the intricacies of its workings, and that the importance of the lesson was the reason for his determination.

I knew the rifle's history in outline. It had seen use in the Great War that had burnt out in Europe over a decade earlier. Identical weapons had been issued in great numbers in a vain attempt to eradicate trench rats and contain the spread of typhus. However, returning servicemen, like my father, valued these battlefield souvenirs for hunting small game. As historic symbol, it had joined other nebulous artifacts like the sword Excalibur, the Trojan horse, and the Mayflower that were stored in timeless disarray within my mental attic. A household fixture, it had always hung on a garage wall in the carriage house that was home to my family. I had often seen my father remove the rifle from its pegs for cleaning, occasionally witnessing its use, but had no real interest in its operation. By 1931 it was only used for ridding the Balfour residence of feathered pests.

Dad in the Balfour driveway

On a gable-brace three stories above us, a pigeon peered and craned, turning occasionally for a better view, all the while endlessly muttering to itself. My father looked with disgust at the driveway beneath, coated now with a lumpy patina of pigeon droppings, and complained, "Look at the dirty mess he made." The mottled gray and white material marring the otherwise imposing approach to the porte-cochere did not look like dirt to me, and I puzzled over the comparison.

Squinting against the pewter sky, he studied the bird, reached into his right-hand coat pocket, and retrieved a short metal cartridge. He pointed to the bullet, and in a stern, deliberate manner announced, "We'll change his tune with this." Pulling back the rifle's bolt, he placed the cartridge into its chamber. "Watch me now! You got to push the shell forwards as far as she will go and then close the breech, like this." I watched, mystified, as the shell was rammed home and the bolt closed.

"Hare, Bobby, I'll show you how to hold her," he said. Taking hold of my arms, he placed the rifle in firing position. "Now you got to aim at that bird right!" He knelt next to me, and squinted through his spectacles along the barrel. "Close your left eye and look with your right along the barrel at that dirty cuss. You got to put the front sight between the slots of the rear sight and make them both line up with him." He had given the offending pigeon a gender although I had no idea how that was possible at this or any distance. Pigeons, girl or boy, all looked alike to me.

I squinted down the length of the rifle's brown steel barrel. My father's lean encircling arms steadied and reassured me. His rough serge sleeve scratched my cheek, and his odor, bearing faint traces of gasoline and oily metal, filled my nostrils. *If only I can do this thing right!*

Meanwhile the pigeon ambled back and forth on the gable-brace. Looking through the slits of the rear sight, I watched the bird waltz and preen. I was more certain of the movements of the pigeon, cooing softly so far above, than I was of the front sight. That tiny knob wavered in and out of view between the bird and the rear slits. I could not seem to get all three objects aligned and, losing confidence, felt my throat tighten.

In the gray light of the fading day it became ever more difficult to locate the pigeon by the iridescent sheen of his pewter colored feathers. I felt the touch of my father's bony cheek, the warm pungency of his breath. "I'll check your aim, Bobby. When I tell you, pull the trigger." I groped for the curved steel trigger in its circular guard, while he held me firmly. With his strong arms about me, I felt secure and proud.

"Pull the trigger!" With astonishment at the ease with which this could be done, I squeezed my finger tightly. The explosion deafened me, and the stench of burned powder stuffed my nostrils.

When I opened my eyes, nothing appeared changed. Then from the gable above, a shapeless pearlescent mass fluttered downwards. In the gray dusk I stared as the droplets trickling from the beak collected on the driveway in a slowly enlarging, brilliant-scarlet pool. My father's tall, black-suited figure loomed above me, his face a steel-eyed, sardonic mask. "You got that fella dead to rights, Bobby!" he exulted.

What have I done? It's my fault the pigeon's hurt! Why is Dad yelling and laughing about it? The bird didn't do anything to him, only pooped on the drive! I couldn't understand why my father had needed to kill the bird for just being a bird, and I couldn't comprehend his pride and pleasure in doing so. My calm and kind father, our family's supporter and protector, our champion, had suddenly become a frightening stranger who scared me to death. I felt the hot tears coming even before I began to cry. Then I ran down the driveway, toward home and safety.

FLAG DAY

I knew that the day would be warm and sunny even before I climbed out of bed. The previous night's thunderstorm had ended. The ochre window shades curled in musty protest against the bright light of a June morning in 1932; I was nearly eight years old. Excited by thoughts of the outdoors, I hurriedly donned the light summer clothing that my mother had laid out the night before.

Breakfast smells and the familiar sound of my parents' subdued conversation beckoned. They were speaking Norwegian, a language that both baffled and fascinated me. In deference to his adopted homeland, my father was reluctant to teach his children the speech and culture of the old country, an attitude not at all uncommon among Norwegian immigrants. The costly, often-dangerous venture to the new land burdened most of them with abiding homesickness, and many with disappointment that their hopes and dreams stood in such sharp contrast to the reality of prairie America; a place often coarse, crude, and prejudiced. Most of them worked extremely hard to adapt to the ways of their new country. Many, like my father, adopted a practiced reticence about the homeland and relationships that they had left behind.

Entering the kitchen, I saw my father bent over the sink counter, segmenting grapefruit. Peering through his bifocals, he applied deliberate precision to each sawing motion of the serrated grapefruit knife. He had often reminded us that, "Any yob worth doing is worth doing well." We accepted the homily without question. Restaurant grapefruit was never sectioned merely severed from the rind. His preparation was certainly easier to eat. Only the brewing of coffee outranked the cutting of fruit among the breakfast preparations in our home. The primacy of coffee at every meal was sacrosanct; its aroma, body, and taste the subjects of constant and enthusiastic discussion, and its consumption a religious rite.

My parents were already fully dressed. Dad wore the familiar uniform of his employment, long sleeve white shirt and tie, black serge trousers and vest. His sleeves were rolled above the elbow, his tie tucked deftly inside the shirt. Mother wore a short sleeve, printed cotton housedress, starched and neatly ironed, as was the apron, which covered bodice and waist. Her thick, black hair was combed in waves, her lips rouged in the Cupid's-arc smile of Clara Bow. Though the warmth of a June morning could already be felt, neither of them showed the least trace of perspiration.

"Sit down, Bob, and eat your grapefruit," Dad said. There was, of course, no mention of coffee for a boy of eight. Only adults qualified for that rare honor. When that day came for me, I could be assured of manhood.

"We're having soft-boiled eggs and toast today," Mother announced. "It's much too warm to make oatmeal." Although I wasn't too keen on soft-boiled eggs, inwardly I rejoiced because I disliked oatmeal intensely. Its taste, unless thoroughly doctored with sugar, was boring, and its lumpy, bumpy appearance disgusting.

"Vare is Nancy?" Dad said. My sister, a pretty towheaded child of three, was four years younger than I.

"I haven't seen her." This was untrue. I had spotted her tiptoeing past the kitchen door.

"Bobby," commanded Mother. "Go find your sister before she runs outside, and bring her to the breakfast table." I was used to such orders and took pride in them. My parents, recognizing my protective concern for my small sister, took advantage of it.

Nancy and I in the yard

Outdoors, the grass sparkled under the bright sky, and the air tingled with a freshly washed smell. Nancy was in the small family garden, standing barefoot in the damp grass. Her blonde hair, cut in the current page boy fashion, had seen neither brush nor ribbon that morning. Her loose pink jumper was carelessly buttoned, and mirrored her haste and inattention to such mundane details. I hurriedly corrected her inept costuming, and cajoled her into replacing her shoes and socks with the news that we were not having the hateful oatmeal for breakfast. Taking her hand, I led her into the kitchen where my parents were discussing the coming day's activities. Neither of us was consulted, of course. At table my parents expected us to be seen but not heard!

Serving eggs at any meal was considered a treat. Eggs purchased from the grocery store were quite expensive. My parents usually bought fresh farm eggs that were mixed sizes and not candled; some were fertilized.

Nancy and I took our seats at the kitchen table. Before each place there was a sectioned half-grapefruit, and Mother had cracked and served the soft-boiled eggs in thick green porcelain eggcups. Finishing my fruit, I placed the eggcup on my plate and examined its contents with a skeptical eye.

"I can see the eyes," I exclaimed, half in jest.

"Bobby! I will not have any of your foolishness here at the table." Mother looked stern but there was a sparkle in her eye and a suppressed smile tugging at the corners of her mouth.

It was like a goad to an already running horse. I stared deeper into the cup, and after a pause for scientific analysis said, "There are feet on the bottom, too!"

Nancy, who thought I was wise beyond my eight years, began to examine her eggs with suspicion.

Spying the small telltale brown spot, I delivered the coup de grace, "It's bleeding!"

"I'm not eating mine," Nancy said, pushing away from the table with disgust written all over her face.

"Bleeding, my foot! Now you be quiet, and eat those eggs, you hare!" my father ordered.

Mother laughed merrily, put her arm around Nancy and said to me, "Aren't you ashamed, teasing your sister like that?" But she was smiling.

It happened that today was a holiday, so my father would not be required to put in a full day's work. Many businesses, including the Clinic, would suspend activities or be on shortened hours for the day. My parents were discussing a family reunion at the farm homestead of

Mother's cousin. There would be a picnic social and we were invited. I was pleased with this development. Farm life was strange and exotic; a trip to my cousins' farm rivaled going to a zoo, or even a circus! Being a relative, I could enjoy all the wonders of this curious world like a tourist with a temporary visa. I thought that seeing, touching, and smelling odd and scary animals and birds were not only interesting but also very exciting activities. *I'll have to keep a sharp eye on Nancy. She can do some pretty dumb things. After all, she's just a girl!*

"Now you kids will have to stay out of the kitchen," directed Mother. "I'll be cooking for the picnic most of the morning. I'm going to bake a cherry pie!"

I loved cherry pie more than any other dish that she prepared and would not let anything stand in the way of this enjoyment. Taking Nancy's hand, I headed for the yard. "Come on, Nancy, we'll play in the sandbox."

"Nels, why don't you take Nance and Bobby downtown and look at the decorations. When you get back, I should be finished in the kitchen and we can get started for the farm."

"That ware a good idea, Stella," Dad agreed with ill-concealed relief. He had no wish to remain in an atmosphere of harried culinary preparation, particularly when his own skills in that domain were so very rudimentary.

"Come on, you kids. We go take in the sights."

We enthusiastically embraced this surprising opportunity to accompany him on a journey of exploration that had been blessed, even inspired, by my mother, and bounced happily downstairs to the brick-floored cavern that was my father's domain. It contained four automobile bays, and maintenance space for the various Balfour motor cars. Dutifully towing my sister, I scampered toward an aging sedan that my father utilized for domestic errands. Occasionally it doubled as our quasi-family car, for my parents could not afford such a luxury. Mounting the wide running board and tugging open the ponderous rear door, Nancy and I settled ourselves amidst the fading splendors. I sniffed with pleasure and delight the pungent odor of stale cigar smoke, face powder, and musty velour that resembled the smell of my elderly great aunt, Tante Sine's, home. My sister and I rode with the magnificent pomposity of those unused to luxury, peering out at familiar scenes and hoping that we would be seen and envied by our less fortunate friends. I watched my father's careful and confident motions behind the wheel of the great car with awe. I had already forgotten the cruel, heartless individual who had introduced me to the game of killing.

We came to a stop, all too soon, in a parking lot reserved for Clinic physicians. My father opened the rear door and called, "Come on, you two, step lively, we got lots of things to see." The three of us walked hand-in-hand around the corner of the tall Clinic building, and beheld a breathtaking sight.

The full length of Broadway, the principal avenue of business in Rochester, was festooned with red, white and blue decorations. Banners that hung from storefronts proclaimed the virtues of the Republic, and exhorted citizens to show patriotic zeal by displaying their national emblem. Each lamppost was festooned with bunting from globe to base. Streamers swooped in great billowing arcs, from lamppost to lamppost on opposite sides of the street. Midway of each arc, an enraged heraldic eagle, beak beribboned, its lunch in one claw, hunting arrows in the other, perched atop a gilt-edged shield. But the most exciting thing of all, a sight that brought tingling and goose flesh to the nape of my neck, was the great American flag mounted on a bracket high upon each lamppost. Just now a light breeze was blowing, whipping each flag into full display. I was speechless with awe and delight.

"How do you like that," said Dad. His voice was strong, yet strangely soft and gentle, even proud.

We stood there, mesmerized by the wonder and magic of the civic transformation that lay before us. What had been, at least to my mind, a humdrum mercantile avenue, had become an esplanade of glorious national pride.

"Hold me up high, Daddy," Nancy begged, reaching upward.

Dad bent down and lifted her to his shoulders, holding her legs in his firm grip. She circled his forehead with one small arm and reached high with the other to touch the bedazzling bunting. I stood in front of Dad, leaning against him slightly, taking comfort from the closeness of his strong body.

"Well, well, what do you think of that? Hare it's my birthday, and the whole town has hung out flags on every post to celebrate it for me," laughed my father. Completely ignorant of the existence of Flag Day, and unaware of its coincidence with his birthday, June 14, I misinterpreted his affectionate joking. I truly believed that my father was admired by everyone who met him, that he was probably a friend of everyone in Rochester, and was delighted that the whole town would honor my Dad.

NOTHING BUT A
HOODLUM

Though I had been a healthy, even chubby infant, I suffered from a laundry list of childhood illnesses during the first years of elementary school. In fact, my absences had become sufficiently notorious that my schoolmates had given me the nickname, "Old Man Sick." By the fall of my fourth year at Edison I was a decidedly thin, pale and wan child. Mother, who had received training in both nursing and dietetics, was worried about me and trying all manner of restoratives. She revealed her concerns in a tearful telephone conversation with her brother Leo, a physician living in California. His effusively generous response was to take immediate charge of my nutritional recovery himself, inviting Mother, Nancy and me to be houseguests at his new home in Santa Monica.

Leo John Madsen, born in 1897, was Niels and Laura Madsen's eldest son. He was well built and somewhat short, like his father, but had his mother's wavy, blonde hair and blue eyes. He had grown a mustache during his college days and continued to wear one as long as he lived.

Leo was a go-getter. From a cannily chosen sidewalk spot in front of Furnstahl and Swanger's Barber Shop that he commandeered each day, he had solicited the shoeshine business of Rochester's more stylish males. His hustling enterprise had persuaded old Mr. Weber, the founder of Weber and Judd Drugstore, to hire him as part-time prescription delivery boy. The heavy demands that these responsibilities placed upon his time, only seemed to spur Leo's determination even more, and he graduated valedictorian of his high school class. With the encouragement and financial aid of his employer, Leo entered the College of Pharmacy at the University of Minnesota, working nights in a Minneapolis drugstore. In due time he collected a degree, as well as a wife; she was a charming beautician named Carmen.

Leo's disenchantment with the pharmacist's calling was not long in coming. He worked only one summer behind the prescription counter before heeding the siren call of Hippocrates. A small inheritance upon the death of his widowed father in 1920, the loan of her inheritance from his older sister, my mother Stella, and the aid of a working wife enabled Leo to enroll in the College of Medicine, later to graduate near the top of his class. After an internship at University Hospital, Leo received a residency appointment at the prestigious Mayo Clinic. Despite his exceptional skill in surgery, he was passed over for a coveted post on Dr. Will Mayo's surgical staff. Leo resigned in high dudgeon before the completion of his final residency year. He gathered his modest possessions and decamped with the lovely Carmen for sunny California, where he established a medical practice that would soon become very successful

Fortuitous events brought Leo's medical and surgical skills to the attention of the film colony. Ever since the birth of her two sons, who were then already teen-agers, Mrs. Gertrude Temple had longed for a daughter. That precious gift had eluded her until she sought professional advice at the Madsen Medical Clinic. After the requisite nine months had passed, America's princess, the curly-topped child-star, Shirley Temple, was born unto her ecstatic parents. Years later, Leo told his sister, my Aunt Mary, that he had performed a relatively simple surgical procedure that had done the trick. With the passage of time, the news of this and similar curative miracles spread until eventually most of Hollywood's aristocracy had become patients of my uncle.

Leo gave far more than health care to filmdom's rich and famous. For many of Hollywood's most glamorous citizens Leo's honesty and integrity offered a haven of reality and confidentiality in a world that was often mendacious, tenuous, and bizarre.

When the introduction of "talkies" revealed that John Gilbert, romantic idol of the silent screen, possessed the harsh, unlovely voice of a baseball umpire, he was abandoned by studio and fans alike, but not by his physician. Distraught and ill, the fallen star died of a massive heart attack, his handsome head cradled in his friend Leo's arms.

Greta Garbo retained Leo, her physician and confidante, long after she had become isolated by her own design, and fading stardom. Pressed for any revelations about the mysterious recluse by his sister Mary, Leo merely shrugged. "She's just a big Swede with a size 11 shoe, and don't ask me anything more."

Leo was summoned to New York to treat Yale's adored alumnus, Rudy Vallee, who was suffering throat problems while on tour. Leo told the crooner that his dulcet tones would vanish if he underwent the needed adenoidal surgery. Rudy avoided the surgery but remained Leo's patient, much to the delight of Carmen, who was a Rudy Vallee fan!

Marlene Dietrich, Lionel Barrymore, and Lionel's brother John, the Great Profile, all were long-time patients and friends of Leo. One of Lionel's own oil paintings was hung with understandable pride over the fireplace in the Madsen residence.

In 1927, my Uncle Leo and Aunt Carmen had invited my mother and me to spend the month of August in their Santa Monica home. I could identify myself, a child of three wearing a tank top bathing suit and a sailor hat, seated on a dusty beach with Mother, and Aunt Carmen, in the fading sepia tone snapshots that enshrined the trip. However, my only memories are of arriving in Rochester by train: a gray-white landscape filled with the dancing gauze of an early winter snowstorm, clouds of smoke and steam from the locomotive, greasy rivulets of sooty water angling across the paired windows, the heady aroma of starch, laundry soap, and cinders filling the green and dark mahogany confines of the Pullman berth.

The plan for the present recuperative trip to California was that we three would make the trip to Santa Monica in my Aunt Carmen's big

LaSalle. She and my two young cousins, John and Loralou Madsen were visiting Aunt Carmen's folks in Minneapolis and would stop in Rochester on their way home. Making the trip by automobile was probably Uncle Leo's effort to economize. After all, even for someone as comfortably well off as he there was a limit, and perhaps six Pullman fares had been his. The trip took many days.

At a long, low adobe hotel where we had stopped after a grueling drive through the eastern New Mexico desert, I awakened to a chilly dawn. On the veranda outside our room I watched the sunrise bathe the crumbling adobe houses, tumbleweeds, semaphore-straight cacti, and the endlessly flat desert in waves of lavender, peach and rose. A wonderful feeling of happiness suddenly filled my heart.

We three Twedts remained with Uncle Leo, Aunt Carmen and my cousins for many months, in fact for most of my fourth year in elementary school. Nancy was in kindergarten. The possibility that the long separation from my father was the result of a rift between my parents had never occurred to me. I had never thought of them as romantic or even loving, but accepted their union as comfortable, inevitable and incapable of dissolution.

I hated the school that I had to attend, located many blocks distant from my uncle's home, and I dreaded the long walk to reach it. San Vicente Boulevard ran past the gate at the bottom of the garden. The speeding automobiles on the busy divided roadway were fearsome enough, but the big red, electric, interurban cars that ran to Los Angeles and hurtled down the median, horns blaring, daring me to venture out on the tracks, terrified me. Once across, I had to trudge past endlessly identical pseudo-Spanish bungalows of glaring white stucco with roofs of orange tile. Most had tiny low-walled courtyards behind arched grills, through which dogs barked at my passage. On my first day a Great Dane leapt its containing wall and bounded out with hoarse roar and slobbered fangs. I stood paralyzed with fright.

"Brutus! Come back here at once!" commanded a tiny soprano voice. The monster turned, ambled back across the boulevard, and disappeared.

"Naughty boy! What have I told you about going out without your Mommy! There, now you lie down like a good doggie."

After that I made a daily, three-block detour!

Almost from the first my schooldays were a cruel torture. My schoolmates, a tanned and breezy lot, avoided the frail newcomer. My clumsiness and lack of skill at games was immediately evident on the playground where, instead of receiving encouragement, I was scorned. The daily lessons in the classroom left me feeling confused and inadequate. They centered upon the practical application rather than the nature and extent of knowledge. They weren't at all like the staid, often rote, approaches to reading, writing, and arithmetic prescribed as proper by the Rochester school board. My seeming ignorance, not only on the athletic field but also in the intellectual arena, left me feeling lonely and inferior. When I mentioned these feelings to Uncle Leo, who had scrapped his way to manhood on the prairie streets of Rochester, I was told to stop being a crybaby!

Nancy and I played on the sidewalk in front of my uncle's house. We rode together on a scooter that I had made by nailing a single discarded roller skate, an anchovy crate, and a few short boards together. I propelled the contraption furiously. Nancy crouched inside the crate that formed the steering handle, her arms wrapped about her knees, shrieking with excitement.

Laurel Canyon sloped down to the Pacific Ocean behind the houses across the street. The Santa Monica Polo Club lay within its walls. I frequently descended the canyon wall, through a small eucalyptus copse, to watch the exotic action and frenzied play from the sidelines. Struggling home with splintered, wooden polo balls, trophies from the afternoon's match, I crossed the lawn opposite my uncle's home. Aunt Carmen had said that the property belonged to Myrna Loy, star of a host of movies in which she, her film-spouse, William Powell, and their film-Scotty, Asta, played carefree, socialite sleuths. Suddenly, a shrill voice cut through my daydreaming.

"Young man, get off my lawn and don't cross it again! This is not a public thoroughfare! I know who you are. I've seen you speeding down the sidewalk on that ridiculous scooter affair of yours, endangering the life of your sister. The very idea! You're nothing but a hoodlum! I'm going to tell your Uncle Leo, do you hear?"

She shouted so loud that all the neighbors could surely hear her. I dropped the polo balls and stood dumbfounded as I watched her retreating figure. Hurrying across the street, I skulked into my uncle's house, hoping that her imprecations were hollow.

After that, I made my way to the Club by following the sidewalk that kinked about the bungalow home of Arthur Lake, who was known for his depiction of the bumbling comic-strip figure Dagwood Bumstead. Arthur, who continually smoked a pipe, even off-screen, was often in his diminutive garden, planting, pruning, and weeding. I never once laid eyes on Arthur's wife, whom I felt quite sure was the ineffable Blondie!

My health improved during the stay with Uncle Leo; I was heftier and stronger. All three of us were excited and pleased when my father came west and drove Mother, Nancy and me home to Rochester. We arrived just a few weeks prior to the end of my fourth year at Edison and to my astonishment all my old school friends seemed overjoyed at my return.

My Aunt Carmen had given me a small Bakelite camera that took postage-stamp size photographs. Being the first to own such a curiosity, I became an instant celebrity. When I asked my schoolmates and teachers to pose on the Edison steps for a group picture, they happily complied.

FALLING LEAVES

For most students at Edison Elementary, the novelty of a new school year invited adventure, excitement, and future promise. In those days, the children of Scandinavian immigrants implicitly believed that the pathway to a better life led straight to the school doorway. For my parents, it was essential that Nancy and I get an education if we were to "amount to a hill of beans." I failed to understand what going to school had to do with such an unpleasant dish. Like most of my classmates, I was quite ignorant of the intellectual and economic struggle that my educational pursuit would eventually require, and that saved me from being overwhelmed with premonitions and reluctance.

The warm days of summer seemed to continue despite the fact that we were now unable to enjoy them. The dusty green air of approaching fall beckoned my senses, distracting me from the rote demands of the daily lessons. However, I could easily memorize facts, particularly numbers, and that ability enabled me to stay abreast of my teacher's insistent demands with only minimal effort.

At parent-teacher meetings, Miss Leonard regularly accosted my father in foghorn tones from deep within her ample bosom. "Nels, your boy *definitely* is not using his God-given talents as he should. It's up to you, Nels. If he's to amount to something, it's up to you!" These conversations only served to increase the sense of urgency with which my parents plied me with academic nostrums.

The virtues of music appreciation, as a proper subject for elementary school students, were being widely touted among parents and teachers alike. In consequence, musical programs that would elevate and enlighten were introduced that fall in all grades at Edison. Most often

these consisted of *classical* music that emanated from a decrepit porta-
ble record player. The records were largely the donations of well-mean-
ing but musically illiterate parents; the fact that they were of poor
quality, and in atrocious condition, did not help the concept.

A small minority of my fifth grade classmates found these moments
of musical exposure interesting, even enjoyable. My attentiveness was
paradoxical for there were no musical instruments in my home at that
time and my parents could not afford a Victrola. My musical knowledge, prior to the music appreciation sessions at school, was mostly
limited to the hymns, which my mother sang to lighten the dreariness
of dishwashing.

On hearing the music in the classroom, my ability to recall previously played compositions, including titles, composer's names, and
musical styles, astonished even me. Possibly this stemmed from my
ready association of the music with numbers, real or fanciful: the number of the piece in a composers repertoire, the number of the movement, a number correlated with rhythm, or simply a fanciful
association that some music raised in my mind. I could not have
explained this ability if asked, and probably did not even recognize it as
unusual.

Our teacher, Miss Sadie Suutala, soon learned who the most atten-
tive scholars were. Priscilla Dunbar, a very pretty ash-blonde girl, who
sat on my left in the first row, was probably the most often correct. The
youngest of numerous siblings, she lived a block from our house in a
large pseudo Tudor home. She had a silvery, tinkling laugh that crin-
kled the corners of her eyes, and showed her even, snowy teeth. Her
blue eyes challenged me when she turned to hear my answers to Miss
Suutala's questions. I was sure that with each small smile she was daring me to outdo her. I blushed with joy and anger when this happened.

In tones that were friendly but firm, Miss Suutala admonished her
charges that these musical experiences were not presented as entertainment, or even as uplift, but were necessary to the proper education of

the whole human being! Only the most mediocre scholars could fail to catch the warning of an impending danger—a written test!

"Class, let me have your attention," called Miss Suutala one bright fall morning, clapping her hands for emphasis. She was shorter than average, not much taller than most of her fifth grade students. A light blue knit dress contained her softly rounded figure in a manner that her male charges were not yet old enough to appreciate. Her wavy blond hair framed an open face and guileless smile. She gained willing compliance from even the most recalcitrant and dull-witted among her students.

"This morning, as promised, we will take an examination of our progress in music appreciation," announced Miss Suutala, simultaneously giving each of the students in the front row blank sheets of paper, with instructions to pass them, one to a student, to those seated behind. When Priscilla turned, her smile disarmed and angered me. *Grin at me, will ya. I'm going to show you this time. I betcha that I get a higher score than you do!*

"Listen carefully, each of you," said Miss Suutala. "I shall play short passages from musical compositions that you have all heard in this room before. I shall announce each passage by number only. At its conclusion I shall call 'Time' and allow you a minute to identify what has been played. All right, let's begin with number one."

She placed a record on the phonograph and let down the needle to release a scratchy, cacophonous orchestral rendering. I recognized the piece immediately, the sixth dance, the "Chinese Dance," from Tchaikovsky's *Nutcracker Suite*. I could easily imagine the number sixes, looking like fat little men in brightly colored pajamas, arms crossed in front of their bellies, hands tucked into sleeves. They swayed in unison with the music. Quickly I wrote the answer, and looked up to see Priscilla doing the same. Most of the others were staring at the ceiling for inspiration, or simply looking blankly toward the blackboard.

The music of the seventh dance, of the "Reed Flutes," trembled in soft, sweet thinness. I imagined the number seven with hole-stops along its long leg and a mouthpiece on the shorter one. The number fours of the "Russian Dance" stomped so furiously with their arms crossed and their knees bent in the odd way that Russians knelt to dance that I almost laughed aloud. I always wondered how Russian men and women danced together, if the men were always kneeling and flailing to keep from falling over backwards. My parents never assumed such posture to dance but rather held each other upright, at arms length, turning soberly to the rhythm as if they were taking one of Miss Suutala's examinations!

The rest of the examination continued in the same fashion. At last, I heard Miss Suutala call, "Time!" She did not lower the Victrola arm for another passage. The test was over!

"Please exchange your answer sheet with the person on your left," she instructed. "Each question correctly answered is worth five points. As I read the answers, place a check before each one that is not correct. When we are finished, please pass all papers forward so that I may record the grades. I will return them tomorrow."

As she listed the correct responses, I graded Priscilla's paper, anxiously holding my breath. When we had finished I had only made one check mark on her answer sheet, a score of ninety-five! *Darn it, she must have beaten me for sure!*

I worried all through recess, finding no interest in a dumb game of Pum Pum Pullaway. Finally the bell rang and Priscilla disengaged herself from a knot of girls to talk to me as we climbed the front stairs. She knew that I had corrected her paper and asked boldly, "Tell me how I did on the test, Bobby. I think I beat you," she teased, with a friendly smile.

"Oh rats, I suppose so. You only had one wrong, of course," I said in dejection.

I walked home amidst a shower of yellow gold. The previous night's rain, combined with steadily dropping temperatures, had brought autumn with it. I scuffled along, flipping the fallen leaves with my shoes, and wondered why the most beautiful leaves were the ones that had to drop from the trees in the fall. *Why can't these beautiful shades of red, orange, and golden-yellow be the colors of spring?* I stooped to examine them and then joyfully began gathering a cluster of the most perfect ones as a bouquet that I could carry home to my mother. Picking and choosing, dropping all but the loveliest, I proudly carried my offering up the driveway.

The tall folding doors were open when I entered the garage below our carriage house. My father was bent over the fender of a black four-door Cadillac sedan, peering into its largely disemboweled hood. He wore coveralls over his street clothes, and a mechanic's cap that advertised Perfect Circle piston rings. Straightening quickly when he saw me, he pointed a greasy finger at my bouquet.

"Hare, hare, what you doing there? You're dropping those things everyvare."

"I'm going to give these to Mother," I hesitated.

"What! Those dead leaves! Well, go ahead, but you be careful you don't drop anymore in the house, you hare!" With that he turned his back and bent once more into the hood, like a coroner at an autopsy.

I bounced up the stairs, coming first to the kitchen in an excited search for my mother. At my tread, she came into the room and exclaimed in delight over my proffered bouquet.

"For me, Bobby," she beamed. "Oh, they're so lovely. I must put them in water right away so they won't die. Thank you, dear. You were sweet to think of your mother." She hummed with happiness as she arranged the colorful display on the kitchen table.

"Dinner won't be ready for another hour, Bobby. Why don't you go out and play a while. I saw some of your friends over on Dunbar's front lawn raking leaves."

I hurried out of doors, proud and pleased that my bouquet had so charmed Mother. I wondered if she thought the bright colors of fall were the best, as I did. On Dunbar's lawn I saw a large leaf pile with kids continually adding to it. They were already lining up to jump into the pile. With high-pitched squeals the girls leaped forward, their skirts flaring to reveal exciting flashes of white skin. Boys, on the other hand, affected nonchalance and hurled their bodies forward. Some, including Johnny Berkman, even climbed the maple tree above the pile, to drop down with feigned bravado like parachutists. After a time I tired of this activity, mostly because Priscilla seemed not to notice me. I went home to dinner.

The next day Miss Suutala returned the music test papers, and I was startled to discover that I had received a grade of an hundred, a perfect score. I had done better than Priscilla, whose desk was empty! I wished that she had come to school today so that I could have enjoyed her defeat.

For the next ten days Priscilla was not in school. Miss Suutala said that she had been hurt while jumping in the leaves—fallen on the tines of a rake. They said that she had blood poisoning. I didn't understand how a rake could be poisoned!

Monday morning I took my seat, waiting for class to begin, and looked out the window at the bright yellow leaves still clinging to the sugar maples. Freed by the wind, the leaves floated downward, fluttering and dancing.

"Class, may I have your attention," said Miss Suutala. "I'm sorry to have to tell you all that our dear Priscilla will not be with us anymore. She has gone to Heaven to live with Jesus."

There was more but I didn't hear. I was stunned! Priscilla would not be in class again. She would not turn and look at me with that teasing smile. She wouldn't ever learn that I had gotten a perfect score in the music test. I watched the golden leaves drift past the deep blue of the morning sky and thought of her.

Suddenly, the sunlight burst through the multipaned windows in a glittering cloud of loveliness.

THE NEW FRIEND

In Minnesota it was not uncommon for the season's first snowfall, even a severe blizzard, to occur before Thanksgiving Day. But for me, the true herald of the coming Christmas season was snow that accumulated, not melting until spring. From mid-December until late March, each successive winter storm transformed the familiar compass of my world beneath a patina of dazzling whiteness edged with sun-limned brilliance. A coating of greasy soot that continually sifted from every chimney often corrupted this magical landscape. The ledger of winter's progress could be read easily in the zebra stripes etched upon every snowbank.

Shorter winter days meant that I awakened before dawn. The first sound that I recognized, while still snuggling under the warm blankets, was the methodical "scurrruumph" of a snowshovel rising from the driveway beneath my bedroom window. The shoveler, John Tewes, a rough hewn, taciturn Norwegian, was responsible for all seasonal ground keeping tasks that the Doctor's city mansion and country estate required. On winter mornings his first duty was to clear the driveway of fresh snow so that my father could drive Dr. Balfour to the Mayo Clinic, precisely at 9 o'clock.

Emerging from my cocoon, I trotted over to the frosted window, and sat on the warm radiator. I put my hand to the glass, melted a peephole in the ice, and searched for the moving tracery of pipe smoke that trailed John's fur-capped head. John applied his shovel with plodding, methodical precision, and the cleared driveway resembled a long swath of gray corduroy.

"Bobby, wake up!" Dad called, in mild exasperation from the bedroom doorway. "Why aren't you getting dressed for school? Do you always got to daydream?"

In confusion and with regret, I turned from the lovely scene. The frigidly dull white foreground was tinged at the horizon with a roseate dawn sending fingers of pale pink and peach over the sparkling crests of snowbanks. Reluctantly, I began to dress.

Over my school clothing I donned a heavy wool jacket and trousers of a dreary green color. Nonetheless, I considered myself lucky that these garments were made of the same material. The often flamboyantly mismatched raiment worn by many of my less fortunate classmates proved them the youngest siblings in a large family.

My high-top overshoes of thick rubber with heavily ribbed soles were closed by four clumsy clasps that became rigidly locked during wear by finger-numbing layers of ice. My outsized, leather mittens looked like much used, baseball gloves, and contained liners of loosely knit, coarse gray wool. These mittens never supplied with wear during the winter, but became increasingly stiff, scratchy, and smelly with daily rewetting. My cap, a knit affair mysteriously called a stocking cap, bore no resemblance whatever to a stocking that I could see. *And why would you wear a stocking on your head anyway, for gosh sake?* I envied those boys whose up-to-date parents had outfitted them with nifty, flannel-lined, leather aviator's helmets with isinglass goggles and earflaps that snapped under the chin. A wool scarf was mandatory, not simply to insulate the neck but to veil the nose and mouth. My sister and I issued forth for the walk to school looking, I thought, like those veiled harem girls I had seen in my *Stories from the Arabian Nights. Did their mothers make them wear scarves over their faces, even when everyone knew it never snowed in Arabia?*

When my classmates and I arrived at Edison School, our wintry armor had to be removed and hung on alphabetically assigned hooks in the cloakroom. The school administration assumed that this arrangement would promote a modicum of orderliness at dismissal. For the most part this was a vain hope and served to prove, I suspected, that school principals had never been children, and had probably never attended elementary school. Arrayed in soggy mimicry of their owners seated in the classroom, the garments resembled a dispirited band of refugees puddling the hardwood floor.

To the normal odors of chalk dust, wood varnish, hot radiator paint, and floor sweeping compound that normally characterized my schoolroom, new aromas now appeared. The powder-sweet evidence of well-scrubbed flesh commingled democratically with the pungency of the rarely washed. Hints of too-long-delayed visits to the lavatory hung just outside of consciousness. The garments hanging in the cloakroom gave off a moldy, acrid smell, as they stiffened and dried.

The sourest odors wafted from a rear corner desk where Harold Weinberg sat, dripping, steaming and drying, apparently oblivious to the unpleasant effluvium. Harold, a ruddy blonde child, with outsized ears and a continual face-splitting grin that besought friendship, was the youngest in a family of twelve. Keeping such a crowd adequately fed demanded an all out effort by both parents. His father worked for one of those lettered, federal aid agencies that were popularly considered demeaning make-work outfits, little better than the dole. His mother took in washing for the rich doctors who lived on "Pill Hill," the residential address of distinction in Rochester. Needless to say, in Harold's family new clothing for the eldest child passed through the gamut of many siblings before consignment to the ragbag. His costume, unchanged through the seasons, was a shapeless faded gray shirt, bib overalls, and tennis shoes. Worn without socks, the latter were black high-tops, devoid of tongues, and tied with grocery string. Harold had acquired the nickname "Stink."

The arrival of winter converted what little pleasure I derived from school recess periods into orchestrated misery. Now, the midmorning bell announced sessions of indoor calisthenics and organized games carried out in the school gymnasium. My classmates and I marched down two steep flights of terrazzo stairs into a low-ceilinged basement room. The concrete floor and walls were painted a dreary battleship gray, heavily pock marked to reveal the numerous layers of equally dreadful paint that had preceded this. The heavy wire screens that protected the high, small windows from the ineptly tossed ball only served to increase my gloomy sense that I had been imprisoned. The gymnasium's equatorial temperature betrayed its location next to the boiler room, and necessitated the removal of sweaters and such other garments that etiquette would allow. But the most dismaying aspect of these obligatory exercise sessions was that there was no longer any escape for the physically bumbling, athletically unskilled, like myself. In fair weather I could simply walk off into a world of daydreams where the humiliating catcalls of those with greater athletic prowess could not penetrate.

In January, the sun was already near the horizon when the school day ended in late afternoon. Even on rare cloudless days, further outdoor play took place in the gathering gloom of evening. The universal after school activity was ice skating on the rink prepared over the playground baseball diamond. With the help of city firemen, whose pumper truck made short work of the initial flooding, Mr. Fred Klampe, the Edison School custodian, strung lines of bare electric bulbs overhead. Within this glittering oasis all the students who owned skates of any kind teetered and circled to the tinny sounds of Strauss dribbling from amplifiers atop the building. Many of them managed, through frenetic whirling, to stave off the gathering chill until the lights were extinguished at 6 o'clock. And once the sun had set, the increasing cold, both physical and emotional, sent most children to their homes and the daily radio adventures of *Jack Armstrong, the All-American Boy!*

When played on the relatively soft surface of the summer playground, the game of Pum Pum Pullaway was a fairly innocuous form of team tag. Transferred to the unyielding mirror of the ice rink, where its speed and danger were multiplied, it was a favorite sport for the older boys. The frigid version of the game had been expressly forbidden by Miss Leonard, who gave Mr. Klampe strict orders to be on the lookout for malefactors who would defy her. The game could only surface in the early evening when the good custodian had gone to his home for supper. Consisting, as it did, in the challenge issued by one team maneuvering upon the ice to the other poised upon the bank, tripping and falling were inevitable. The participants' outer garments were usually sufficient padding to prevent severe injury. Nevertheless, smaller children and the less skillful skaters abandoned the ice when the call "Pum pum pullaway, come or I'll pull you away," announced the beginning of a game.

Determined to avoid being ridiculed by my older and more skillful peers, I often remained to play the daringly stupid game, courting personal calamity in addition to parental disapproval. Idly circling under the glimmering bulbs, toying with hockey sticks, and shooting pucks at the unwary, the manipulators gradually seduced the naive, the timid, and the foolish to trade prudence for glory. They gathered on the sidelines, awaiting the ominous call to come out on the ice and dash for the opposite bank, all the while artfully dodging any and all human interference.

I was a reasonably good skater. My father had taken me to the public skating rink as soon as I could walk. There, while sedately circling on his Norwegian skates, the blades curiously curved, he gently guided me on my double-bladed strap-ons. To the onlooker we resembled an unusually tall Arabian prince magically gliding upon the silvery moonlit surface of the Tigris with a pudgy dwarf attendant in tow. With his tutelage and continued practice, I could skate as well as older schoolboys

This evening I was untouchable. Flashing forth from the safety of the side embankment, I sped across, easily escaping the increasingly angry taggers. Like a flea, hopping about the shiny nose of King Kong without being swatted, I felt invincible. Then, from just without the extreme edge of my consciousness I recognized danger. Dick Weber, a big solidly built boy, drove toward me. His wide set eyes, squinting against the rush of cold, gazed down at the shimmering ice. He did not see me silently screaming.

The collision shook Dick to his knees and sent me sprawling, my left arm flailing. *It must be snowing, and the melting flakes are running down my face.* This was odd, since I lay on my stomach. Searing knives pressed down from my shoulder to the pit of my stomach. I bit my lip to keep from being sick and to blot out the pain.

I heard Dick speaking from far, far away, "Boy, that was one hellofa smackup! You okay, kid?"

"Yeah. Yeah, sure," I lied. With that reassurance, Dick stood up and skated away.

I had a terrible time getting to my feet. My left arm was useless; just flopped by my side. I muddled my way off the ice by skating as I had when toddling behind my father. At the embankment where I had left my shoes and overshoes, I slumped down in the snow. I wished that I'd never disobeyed my parents, knew they would be very angry, and besides that I'd probably be punished. I could not unlace my skates. The pain in my left arm took my breath away. *I'll have to walk home in my skates. I could put my shoes in my coat pockets but what on earth will I do with the overshoes. If I leave them they'll be gone for sure in the morning.*

"Gosh, Bobby, that was a nawful crash you and Dick Weber had just now. Did ya break somethin? Does it hurt ya? I felt it way over here on the bank. Gosh, don't cry, Bobby. Let me help ya." The words tumbled over my head from just behind me. I turned to see the troubled countenance of Stink, who bent over me surrounded by his noxious aura.

"I think I can make it home, Harold, but I can't untie my skates. I guess I'll have to walk home with them on. There's room in my coat pockets for my shoes, but I just can't carry my overshoes." I looked into the worried eyes of the only one at the rink who had offered help.

Harold was shivering in his light denim jacket. The skin at his ankles, where the tongues of his sopping-wet tennis shoes were missing, was blood red, blotched with white.

"Tell you what, Harold. Will you take care of these overshoes for me? You wear them home." And then I blurted in a rush, "You keep them 'til spring, okay."

"Gosh, you mean it, Bobby. You betcha, I'll keep 'em for ya. I'll take real good care of 'em. You'll see. I'll have 'em for ya good as new in the spring, all right," he said, in unrestrained excitement, as he ecstatically pulled the boots over his wet sneakers. He helped me to stand up and then grasped my hand in nervous gratitude. The cracked red fingers trembled in my palm.

"I can't wear mittens and hold onto these shoes in my pockets at the same time," I lied, blushing. "You take them home with you, Harold. Mights' well watch over them until spring, too."

Harold was speechless. Then it began to snow hard and I began the tortuously slow walk home. I teetered along keeping mostly to the walk fearful of the toll this was taking on my skate blades and what Dad would say when he saw them.

When I reached our house and climbed the stairs, no one was home. I collapsed fully clothed across the living room sofa, held my throbbing arm tight to my side, and fell into a painful slumber.

"Bobby, whatever is the matter? Are you hurt, dear?" I dimly heard my mother saying, her voice trembling in fear. "Nels, there's something wrong with Bobby." Then my worried parents took me to the hospital where my broken clavicle was set, and I was strapped into a brace that I wore for the next six weeks. There were no questions about missing overshoes or gloves, and never a word spoken about punishment!

PAYING THE PIPER

My startling achievements in music appreciation during the fall of 1934 encouraged my parents' belief that their son was a musical prodigy who should learn to play the violin. Its low cost and portability determined the choice of instrument. They purchased a cheap, student violin from the parents of a failed musical scholar. It had an execrable tone, and loose pegs that destroyed its pitch when it was played.

I hated my violin lessons. My instrument had a mind of its own, struggling to slip from under my chin, stretching its neck beyond any hope of effective fingering, and swayed dangerously, yowling the while, as I oared my bow across the bridge. I was convinced that I had little talent and less ability, felt trapped and longed to be free of the whole business. The walk from our house to the Conservatory of Music was long and lonely, gloomy and cold on winter afternoons. I usually ran most of the way home in the dark. I detested my teacher, Sister Mary Cecilia, a demanding crone who had the sensitivity of a cactus. She was tall and thin with a reddish, windblown complexion, the result of years spent on a Red River valley potato farm. Her scowling countenance betrayed her resentment of teaching duties that robbed her of the peaceful life of a contemplative nun. In the traditional brown and black Franciscan habit, with white-lined cowl and wood rosary, she resembled nothing so much as a hungry buzzard. As I fumbled my way through each weekly assignment, verifying my dilatory practice and debatable talent, her body cringed with every wrong note, and every rhythmic irregularity.

"Sweet Mother of God!" she exploded when the tension raised by my ineptitude became unbearable. "If you cannot manage the music, just try reproducing the notes!"

I devised an ingenious plan to reduce the agony of sessions with her to a minimum. Surrounding the city block occupied by the Sisters' Convent and the Conservatory, was a high iron picket fence, with two gates on the north side, one for the nuns and the other for the budding musicians. By dragging its case against the pickets along my route, my violin would be quite out of tune when I arrived for my lesson. Perhaps five, even ten minutes were consumed by the retuning activity, which frequently earned a stinging blow across my knuckles from the edge of her ruler. But the pain was bearable in light of the significant reduction in the length of my lesson.

"Master Robert," cried the pious harpy, in undisguised exasperation, "I cannot conceive how it is possible for you to arrive for every lesson with a violin that is totally out of tune! How can you ever practice on such an instrument? *Do* you practice, Master Robert?"

"Yes, Sister, but…"

"Surely, you must understand the carelessness that you display. You waste my time as well as your own!"

"I know, Sister, but…"

"It is disrespectful, not only to me but also to your dear parents who, I feel sure, are praying for you and for your success."

Her countenance while pronouncing this last sentiment simulated commiseration, but her eyes were quite vacant, Little Orphan Annie eyes. During her weekly tirades I put on a contrite appearance, feigned dullness, and only succeeded in looking guilty.

"I don't know, Sister. It was all right when I left home. Maybe it just doesn't like the cold!"

At the termination of each semester, the Sisters held a commencement exercise to display their pupils' musical accomplishments to a doting parental audience. These affairs consisted of a parade of inept amateurs mangling works of increasing difficulty, and were held in the reception rooms of the Conservatory. For the spring commencement of 1935, however, it had been decided that all students, regardless of the extent of their talent and training, should participate in a joint musical production. To give this extravaganza proper staging, and provide for a larger audience, the venue was changed to the auditorium of St. Mary's Hospital School of Nursing.

The hospital was opened in 1889 by a tiny group of Franciscan nuns in the aftermath of severe tornadoes that struck Olmsted County in 1883, leaving more than thirty dead and scores of injured. Then occupied solely with teaching, the Sisters prevailed upon Dr. W. W. Mayo, to help them establish a hospital that ultimately became one of the world's largest and most famous.

The auditorium had a large stage with dressing rooms sufficient to produce an opera. And that was just what the sisters did attempt. At least it was an operetta, whose hackneyed score was the product of a disappointed diva among the novitiate. The opus took its inspiration from the early life of Mozart, when the child prodigy was dragged about the courts of Europe by his father, on exhibit like a marvelous trained poodle. The libretto called for a huge cast and was so amorphous that the more talented children could be given roles to showcase their singing or instrumental ability, while the dullards could appear as supernumeraries. I was assigned to this last group.

I did not include this humiliation when I revealed to my mother the Sisters' requirement that each child's costume would have to be sewn at home according to the pattern provided. Sister Mary Cecilia had given me the pattern during my regular lesson period, announcing, with a withering smile, that I would play the part of a page. There were two pages whose walk-on roles required only that they announce the approach of royalty with a flourish, upon long, valve-less horns.

"But Sister," I protested in alarm, "I can't play the trumpet!"

"Nor the violin," replied the tutor, wearily. "All you need to do is walk to center stage, raise the horn to your lips and hold the pose while a *real* musician plays the flourish offstage. Surely you can do that!"

The pages would simply mime their playing. *What if the trumpeter forgets to blow? What then? A silent flourish! How humiliating!*

But there was more. I would have to wear long white cotton stockings, beribboned garters, and a pair of goofy puffed out shorts. *On my skinny legs they'll look like marshmallows on toothpicks!* There was a sleeveless smock that went over my head. And the whole loony outfit was topped off by a big floppy tam!

The pattern called for blue and yellow satin material, but my mother, recoiling at the expense, purchased sateen instead. The result was a pitiful mockery of courtly attire. It was too small for my tall frame and allowed ludicrous gaps to appear at the top of my stockings. I did not dare sit down for fear of wrinkling the flimsy material that my mother had so carefully pressed.

"A sheep thing," commented my father, and he shook his head in astonishment. My parents struggled to keep from laughing when I tried it on. Even so, he gave me a beautiful, long pheasant's tail feather to accent the tam.

During the weeks of rehearsal, fascinated with this newly discovered world of the theater, I forgot my reservations. My partner and I soon became adept at the rudiments of our minimal roles, learning how to walk, stand, and gesture in a courtly manner. We enjoyed the unusual privilege of acceptance as equals among the older members of the acting company, even with the adults. With the passage of time, I was seduced by the fanciful 18th Century milieu, and began to entertain dizzying thoughts of personal triumph in the movies or on the stage. But the very best thing about the operetta was that my violin lessons were very often cut short, or excused altogether in the face of more pressing operatic needs.

Eventually, the piper, or in this case the behind-the-scenes trumpeter, must be paid! The costume was finished, and the nip and tuck alterations put in place in the privacy of my mother's kitchen. The opening night of the Conservatory students' musical venture was at hand.

Backstage, the cast was in a nervous frenzy. The excitement affected everyone. The students with starring roles whispered their arias while staring with perspiring faces that threatened to undo hours of powdering and mascara. Some were struck dumb with fright. I went to the bathroom four times in the final fifteen minutes!

And then Sister Mary Cecilia clapped for our attention and spoke to the cast. "Everyone," she enthused. "You have all worked very hard these last weeks to learn your roles and the music. At last, you can justify all that effort by giving the audience and yourselves a wonderful evening at the opera. Tonight you can make your parents, and the Sisters who have been your teachers, proud of each one of you."

There it is again. Make some adult proud of you. And how can I do that without being proud of myself? Good gosh! How can I ever be proud of myself in this sissy outfit? Recognizing the sense of this, my confidence drained completely away. My instructions and hours of practice vanished as the Overture commenced!

The audience, expectantly awaiting the aural and visual delights that had been described at home by their offspring, completely filled the auditorium. All the blue velour upholstered seats, and all the wooden, folding chairs lining the walls and crowding the orchestra pit, were taken. Parents, relatives, and acquaintances lacking a credible excuse, sat nervously anticipating or dreading the coming event. Before them a massive white-marble proscenium arch framed a deep blue velvet curtain, decorated with gold braid and bearing the school's monogram, St.M.S.N. At the center of the arch was a marble escutcheon embellished with the keys and miter of St. Peter and the scepter of Aesculapius that together betokened the healing power of faith to which the hospital was dedicated. Eggshell colored walls soared up to marble corbels, supporting the robin's-egg blue ceiling. Large marble urns guarded the entrances and flanked the stage. The vaguely sepulchral tone of the whole was relieved by several paintings hanging on the sidewalls that depicted the healing miracles of Christ.

As the last strains of the Overture faded and the lights dimmed, the curtain slowly separated to reveal a royal court of pastel and papier-mâché. The audience gasped with astonishment at the transformation of the familiar Rochester landmark into a royal fairyland. Out of view of the audience, waiting for the cue that would signal the pages' entrance, I saw my parents, Mother's cousin Violet, and Violet's husband, Darryl, sitting in the middle of the third row of seats! I blanched and then Sister Mary Cecilia poked me in the ribs. It was time to go on. I moved mechanically through the paces I had learned. The mock flourish was next! The long horn trembled in my left hand but, thank goodness, I heard the distant muffled trumpet. Beneath my left elbow I could see my parents staring in astonishment. Violet wore a fixed smile. Darryl was already asleep.

I stood at stage rear for the rest of the first act, my mind whirling far from the present site. At intermission, my walk-on part finished, I ran to the dressing room to remove the hated costume. I spent the time that remained before the final curtain, waiting at the front of the auditorium for my parents to come out.

On the drive home I sat, encased in a cocoon of silence; I was neither seen nor addressed. It was just as well. My discomfort was exquisite.

"What was that all about," my father demanded, when we had all reached home. "I thought you ware learning to play the violin. Do you realize that your mother spent hours making that monkey suit because we thought you would play a tune! Why do you stand making no noise on a horn when you could yust as easy play your violin?"

"Gee whiz, Dad," I spluttered "Way back in those olden days they didn't announce folks on the violin. Besides, not many people owned violins then, just troubadours and traveling musicians, I guess," I mumbled at my shoes.

"Why waren't you in the orchestra with the musicians, then?" he interjected.

"Oh, Nels! Leave the boy alone," Mother pleaded. "He can play for us now, can't you, Bobby?"

"I don't think I can. That old thing is always getting out of tune." *Boy, I'm in for it now. Dad will never accept a lame excuse like that!*

"You get your violin right now, and then you play something for Violet and Darryl, and your mother," he commanded. "No more excuses."

And so came the agonizing moment that I had dreaded for so long. I slunk off to my room to get the hateful thing. It was still in tune from yesterday, but I made a show of making final adjustments, anyway. I searched frantically through my beginner books for a piece of music that I could play all the way through without mistakes. Unfortunately, nothing to fit that description existed! In panic, I grabbed the music that had been the subject of my last lesson and of the most recent of Sister Mary Cecilia's exasperated harangues. It was an arrangement for violin of "Fur Elise" by Beethoven. Returning to the living room, I set up my music rack with fingers that slipped from perspiration. Placing the selection on the rack and assuming my best posture, I began to bow.

The heartrending squawks that I managed to wrench from the tortured fiddle were agonizing, even to a musically unsophisticated audience. Mother had taken piano lessons as a child, and was a reasonably accomplished pianist. She recognized my lack of progress at once and was both bewildered and vexed. I played on, face flushed, and body wet with perspiration. The lines of music blurred and my mistakes multiplied. Finally, unable to bear this humiliation, I threw down my violin, and rushed to the haven of my own room. Slamming the door shut, I flung myself upon my bed to sob in shame.

No further interrogation was undertaken until the following Monday when an unforeseen telephone call made the whole matter moot. From the Conservatory came a summons that was honored by my mother and me. She wore her Sunday best to the audience with both Sister Mary Cecilia and the Mother Superior. Attendance by the latter was in response to special pleading by my instructor, who had determined to be rid of her awkward charge. And so the litany of my incompetence was read out in full. My failure to pay attention, to practice, to exhibit an interest in learning the instrument, was laid before my mother in painful detail. No mention was made of a lack of talent or intelligence, but it was not difficult to infer that these, too, were constituents of the bitter pill that my parents were to swallow. During this indictment I sat mute in the dock of disfavor. Mother apologized to the two nuns in polite tones, giving no sign that she agreed or disagreed, although she indicated that she would speak sternly to her son of these matters. The interview was at an end. She bade the two worthies goodbye, and taking me by the hand, with a reassuring squeeze, we left the Conservatory.

As we walked home, Mother's eyes welled with tears, but she made no sound. Overwhelmed with guilt, I struggled to reassure her without bringing myself any further into ignominy.

"I'm sorry, Mama. Please don't cry. I'll really do my best. I'll listen to Sister, and I'll practice, and…"

"Your father and I have done without in order to give you music lessons," my mother interrupted. "We didn't do it so that you could be a lazy lummox. And if you aren't going to care enough to do your best, then I think that we'll call a halt right now."

My heart leapt at these words. Here was an escape from my predicament, and handed to me on a platter at that. Words tumbled from my lips. I told her about Sister Mary Cecilia's peremptoriness, her contemptuous manner, and her ruler. As I spoke her expression changed from disappointment to sympathetic concern. She seemed to understand when I described my fearfulness during the cold and dark of early evening, which encouraged me to explain my fence dragging method.

After that she laughed out loud and said, "Oh my goodness! Bobby, dear, I don't think we'd better tell you father about that! Let's just let it be our secret." We walked the rest of the way hand-in-hand and Mother sang songs that had by now become very familiar and dear to me.

That night, after my sister and I had both been sent off to bed, I lay awake listening to my parents' voices, coming from the living room.

My mother spoke of her afternoon interview at the Conservatory, leaving out those pertinent parts that we had agreed upon during our walk.

"Nels, it doesn't make sense to put the boy through that misery, particularly when we can barely afford the lessons anyway."

"Well, I certainly hope to tell you that ware right," replied my father. And that seemed to conclude my musical career.

PEANUT BUTTER

Awakening to the quiet, I knew it was Sunday. I was nearly 12, just a month short of finishing my last year at Edison Elementary. I had that familiar, and vaguely uncomfortable, feeling of disorganization occasioned by the absence of familiar routine. Going to the kitchen in my pajamas, I found Nancy seated at the breakfast table toying with her oatmeal. Mother was eating grapefruit, with dainty plunging of the narrow, pointed spoon that correct etiquette demanded for the purpose. My father was absent.

"Where is Dad?" I asked.

"You know very well, Bobby. He's gone to get the paper. Now sit down and eat your breakfast. It'll soon be time for Sunday school."

I sighed, and took my place at the table. The grapefruit was always a treat, tangy and refreshing. As I scooped each wedge I thought of white sandy beaches lined with grapefruit trees, the sun gleaming upon frolicking children, with blue, blue waves lapping at their feet. The oatmeal, always a disappointment after that, looked like a lump of wet newspaper.

"Stop dawdling, Bobby, and please don't stick your tongue out at the table."

"I'm not! It's just so hot!" I lied.

Nancy wasn't fooled. She looked over at me, her chin cradled in her hand, and made a puking face to indicate her complete agreement.

My father was never at the breakfast table on Sunday. After his culinary efforts with the grapefruit knife, he had his coffee, put on his coat, and went downstairs to the garage, telling my mother, "I go get the paper."

My parents subscribed to the *Rochester Post-Bulletin*, the local daily, delivered late each afternoon. Ordinarily, my father read the paper while my mother was preparing the evening meal. He sat in his red plush, overstuffed chair, his long legs crossed on a footstool, whispering the words under his breath and following the print with his finger. After the meal, while my sister and I were washing dishes, my mother took her turn.

But on Sunday things were different. My father drove our new, forest green, Oldsmobile sedan downtown, and parked in front of Huey's Cigar Store on South Broadway. There, he bought the Sunday edition of the *Minneapolis Tribune*, and perused the doings of the world beyond Rochester in the peaceful solitude of the front seat. The routine never varied, and he never subscribed to the Tribune.

Apparently reinvigorated by this brief vacation from his family, Dad reappeared at the door of the kitchen shortly before 9:45 AM.

"Are you kids all ready for Sunday school?" he asked Nancy and me.

"Nance, Bobby, come here. Let me look at you," said Mother. I suffered her last minute sartorial adjustments without complaint. Nancy, already a confirmed tomboy, did so with obvious distaste.

The Rochester Congregational Church turned a wary eye on a perverse world from a formidable sanctuary on the corner of Second Street and Second Avenue Southwest. The building, Maltese cruciform in shape, had a front entrance within a portico atop a long flight of steps, and resembled a miniature Pantheon with vaguely fortress like overtones. Built just after the First World War of glazed, ivory brick with limestone lintels and corbels, it was termed The White Temple by its detractors and the faithful, alike The Arts and Crafts movement, popular at the time inspired its interior decor. Wainscoting of shoulder-high, rectangular, oak panels surrounded the auditorium that sloped on a diagonal axis toward the green-carpeted dais. Morning sunlight filtered through a huge leaded-glass dome and tall side windows of beige glass edged in narrow rectangles of light yellow and green, filling the auditorium with a comforting, golden radiance. The organ pipes were discreetly hidden behind the choir loft on the right. From his vantage point at the lectern, the Reverend George Phillip Sheridan, DD, a native of England, kept figurative watch on the continual expansion of the Mayo Clinic, whose newest building towered twenty stories above his church, just across the intersection.

The White Temple

After dropping us off, Dad returned an hour later to bring my mother to morning worship, and to retrieve his children. He rarely attended church, and then only for some special religious holiday.

"Nels, be sure and watch the roast. Don't let it burn! And put the vegetables that are in the dish on the table, into the roaster at 11:30," Mother said when he let her out of the car.

"Stella, do you think I don't know nothing? Don't worry about a thing," he said, with a smile. He sounded like someone dealing with a child.

The Sunday school lesson, like the sermon I would hear if I were to attend the morning service with my mother, usually involved some aspect of eternal life, the glorious reward for those who achieved it, and the dreadful consequences for those who did not. These exhortations were vague, tedious, and incomprehensible to me, and I could not for the life of me understand why they seemed so satisfying to Mother, or anyone else for that matter. The place of glorious reward sounded nearly as dreadful as its opposite. People in sheets fluttering about, eyes downcast, smiling and whispering compliments to each other, and nothing is going on—except harp concerts.

Sunday dinner was the most elaborate of the weekly meals. The entree was intact, the side dishes varied and delicious, but it was all downhill from there—ample, but less exciting. As the days wore on, today's beef roast, would become tomorrow's beef sandwiches, then beef stew, and then vegetable beef soup. The soup was thinned until, by Saturday noon, you could read a newspaper through it.

My mother was always the last to actually sit down at the dinner table. Wanting this, of all the weekly meals, to be just right, she was continually getting up and returning to the kitchen.

"Would anyone like more hot rolls? There are more sweet potatoes." None of the rest of us thought to get our own refills, much less to wait upon her.

"Sit down, Stella," Dad said, in frustration. Nancy and I knew how to remain silent at table and said nothing.

Dad's inevitable, "Goss, Stella, that ware fine," was the signal that the meal was over.

After dinner, the leftovers were put away, the dishes done, and the table scraped clean of crumbs. The last was my father's job, and it never occurred to anyone to inquire where he was placing the scrapings.

But, today Mother returned to the dining room, and suddenly exclaimed, "Nels, look what has happened to my ivy!"

"What do you mean?" He looked where she was pointing.

In the short wall space between the two dining room windows Dad had installed a black iron, flower pot bracket. Mother's variegated ivy lived there, carefully tended, and twining a full six feet along the curtain rods. Crowding the ivy in the pot, one could clearly make out long thin green shoots, unmistakably corn.

Looking startled and sheepish, Dad said, "Well, goss, I didn't think the darned things would grow. They ware cooked, waren't they!"

"Of course, but you had no business putting your scraps in my plant!" Mother had raised her voice, but she was smiling.

"I'm sorry, my dare." He was thoroughly chastised; but I was still puzzled. *How does corn that has been through the hellish heat of cooking live to grow again?*

Turning to us, Mother said, "Why don't you two go do something. Go outside and play!" Now that was a bleak prospect; there would be no children outside at that hour on Sunday. Nevertheless, we obediently trotted off to make a stab at it.

In short order, shorter for Nancy, we were back. "There's nothing to do," we whined to our somnolent parents.

"Oh, I wish I could have a little peace for a change, on Sunday anyway," Mother complained.

"All right, get your things. We go for a ride," Dad decided, getting up from his chair.

Nancy and I greeted his announcement with mixed feelings. On the one hand, it did provide us with an organized activity to fill the afternoon void. On the other, we had no control over the objective that could range all the way from dull to just plain boring!

Dad stuffed a trowel, pruning shears, a rake, and work gloves into the trunk of the Olds. Meanwhile, Mother came into the garage with a basket of spring flowers: iris, peonies, and daisies that she had cut from our garden. We all piled in the car, Dad and Mother in the front seat, Nancy and I in back, as always.

Heading eastward, we passed through town and headed out Center Street. Dad turned left on Seventh Avenue, and headed north. *Oh, no! We're going to the cemetery!* As we slowed and crossed the Chicago and North Western Railway line from the east, I looked in both directions for a telltale column of smoke but saw nothing. *Rats, no train! Just my luck! Whenever we go for a ride I never see anything worth looking at.* I slumped down in my seat, disappointed.

The cemetery was surrounded by a high, wrought iron picket fence. Automobile traffic entered through a monumental gateway arch of pinkish-gray granite topped by a cut-stone frieze. Wrought iron pedestrian gates on either side of the arch complemented the design of the fence. At the roadside, a few feet before the entrance, there was a discreet bronze sign whose polished letters read OAKWOOD CEME-TERY, and gave the closing hour—dusk. The sign was completely accurate; the cemetery was heavily wooded.

Passing beneath the arch, we went up a small rise, and took one of the circuitous roads that led through the grounds. Nancy and I paid little attention to the tombstones, most of which were predictably rectangular and Spartan, but we remembered the exceptions. When we came to a large circular fountain, in the center of a traffic circle, we knew that our landmark was near. Sure enough, at a sharp right hand corner an angel stood on a pedestal. She was forever dropping limestone flowers from her limestone basket onto her bare limestone feet. Her eyes were downcast, heavy with a great sorrow.

"All right, you kids, hare we are. You can get out of the car, but no noise now, you hare. And don't get dirty."

Nancy and I got out of the back seat without much enthusiasm. *How can we get dirty?* I thought. *We can't do anything. How can we get dirty just standing around?* "C'mon, Nancy, let's go see the fountain," I said, taking her hand.

"Bobby. Watch for out for cars, dear."

"Yes, Mother." *What cars? There's no one else in the whole place!* We dawdled along past the angel, who towered over us, and there was "In Remembrance" carved on the pedestal. I didn't know the person's name. We crossed the macadam toward the melodic splashing of the white marble fountain. Water fell from three fluted tiers, rising in the center of a large lily-filled pool. Goldfish moved lazily through the rare patches of sunlight. We sat on the broad stone lip and watched.

"Do the fish eat those pennies?" Nancy asked.

"Well, I've never seen one do it. I think they mostly eat worms. But Dr. Sheridan said a whale ate Jonah, and he wasn't a worm."

"He wasn't a penny either," she said, firmly. She put a stick into the water and started to splash about. "I'm gonna stir 'em up."

"Cut it out, will you. You're getting water on your dress—and on me. Stop it, I tell you."

She stopped, and we looked across the road at the parents. My father was pruning some small decorative yews that grew on either side of the tombstone. The single word carved on the stone read MAD-SEN. My mother was putting the fresh flowers into green iron vases that stood in front of it. She stood up, placed one hand on the small of her back, and with the other brushed a fallen lock of hair out of her eyes.

"Bobby, Nance, come back, we're ready to go," Mother called when she spied us at the fountain.

Gosh, that's a relief. This place is peaceful all right, so peaceful you can't have any fun at all! As we walked back, I continued to wonder about all the people who had been buried here. Rev. Sheridan had said their souls were in heaven. *Boy, I hope heaven is not as boring as this place!*

When we came up to them, my father was just raking a few yew clippings off the thin grass, struggling to grow in the deep shade of an overhanging burr oak. He put them into a woven-wire trash basket that stood nearby, and replaced all his tools in the trunk. I looked over at the MADSEN monument, at the brass markers: Father—Niels Madsen and Mother—Laura Madsen, and wondered if they were enjoying all that peace and quiet.

"All right, we go," Dad said, and we returned to the car. I wondered why we had never been to the TWEDT tombstone, not realizing that my Dad had no relatives in this part of the United States.

Once out of the cemetery, Dad turned left on Center, heading for open country. Soon we were passing through the grounds of the Rochester State Hospital. It was a campus of gloomy, multistoried red brick buildings that was, according to common knowledge, a place for the incarceration of the insane! There was little to suggest that this was a facility for treatment of any kind, only an occasional scurrying white-coated figure. There was no sign of visitors, either cars, or people.

Dad slowed the car, and pointed upwards. "See them, Stella."

"Yes, poor things," she said in a hush.

On the rear of the largest buildings, self-contained balconies rose, one above another. They were enclosed in heavy metal screening, bolted flush to the building walls from foundation to roof. The balconies were crowded with ghostly figures, many clinging to the wire mesh. These imprisoned wretches were the patients!

How can they stand to be cooped up like that? They look just like animals in a zoo. I'd rather be dead!

Once in the country, Nancy and I entertained ourselves with the letter game. Each of us searched for the letters of the alphabet found in roadside signs, in order, one letter to a sign. Q was a hard letter, only Quaker State Motor Oil had that one. The X and Z were almost as scarce. Nancy usually won. And we loved the Burma Shave signs. Jingles, one word or phrase following another each in white letters on a red background, the boards were nailed to fence posts in sequence along the roadside.

In the front seat, my parents talked endlessly of the weather, the quality of the field crops, the people living on the farms that we passed, particularly who had recently died. Now and then Mother removed a butterscotch drop from the bag kept in the glove compartment. Removing the wrapping, she would thrust it toward Dad's mouth, often at totally inappropriate moments, such as when we were passing another vehicle. At this he would fend her off with his upraised right hand, and yell, "Stellaaah! Not now!"

Neither of us liked butterscotch, but the front seat activity whetted Nancy's interest in food. She spotted the EAT sign first. It hung outside the St. Charles Hotel, a two-story, wooden structure in a small farming community twenty-two miles east of Rochester.

"I'm hungry," she cried with just a hint of the whining that could be readily cranked up if she were ignored.

"Me too," I echoed, with the timid vigor used by every fainthearted follower who reassured his leader with 'I'm right behind you.'

"Oh goss, you kids are never satisfied," Dad said with a sigh. The euphemism was as close as he ever came to blaspheming the name of the Almighty.

The hotel was a white clapboard box, entirely surrounded by a wide, screened porch. Dad pulled the Olds to an abrupt stop before a neat row of whitewashed bricks angled into the ground around a bed of bedraggled flowers. A cracked, uneven sidewalk stumbled toward the porch steps across a weedy lawn where whitewashed tires encircled petunias. My parents were in the lead, Nancy followed, skipping in unobserved triumph, and I brought up the rear. Grasping the china spool that served as a handle, Dad opened the sagging screen door, and ushered us inside.

On the left wall of the otherwise empty entrance lobby there was a key rack, and reception desk covered in brown linoleum. A bell with a PLEASE RING sign sat on its dusty surface. Through an archway at the rear was a large dining room decorated in faded blue with curled tapes of flypaper hanging from the ceiling. It appeared to occupy the most of the hotel's first floor.

When we were seated at a wobbly, white wooden table with chairs to match, a skinny, pallid woman, wiping her hands on her apron, came through swinging doors from the kitchen. Blotches of perspiration darkened the armpits of her dress, and a hair net came down almost to her eyebrows. My parents each ordered a toasted cheese sandwich, apple pie with ice cream, and iced tea. Nancy got a glass of milk with graham crackers.

"Tell the girl what you want, Bob. And be quick about it, we don't have all day." Dad was vexed and I knew I was on dangerous ground.

"I'll have a peanut butter sandwich," I hesitated, looking all the while at the menu.

"What! You can have stuff like that at home!"

"That's what I want. A peanut butter sandwich," I said, sheepishly.

Dad had turned away, realizing that further talk would only degenerate into argument. He hated to have disharmony surface, particularly at table.

In due time, the waitress brought our order. My sandwich lay centered on a chipped, white china dinner plate. From between thick slices of homemade white bread a viscous, lumpy, brown substance peeped over a drooping leaf of exhausted lettuce. Reassured by the comforting peanutty aroma, I took a large bite. Almost at once the pulpy mass of dissolving bread, thready lettuce and rancid peanut paste glued my tongue and palate, effectively preventing speech, mastication, or swallowing. Rivulets of peanut oil dribbled from the down-turned corners of my lips. Tears welled in my eyes but I could make no sound. Nauseous and gagging, I felt like I would suffocate.

Nancy took in this scene of utter misery with sympathy, and tried without success to suppress a giggle.

Dad had no sympathy for my distress. "You made your bed, Bob, now you yust lie in it!" he said, and passed me his glass of water. Slowly, I finished the sandwich.

When we left the St. Charles Hotel, I felt simply stuffed. I didn't care if I ever ate again. I sat in the back seat and stared, without interest, at the passing scenery, hoping that the miserable ride would soon come to an end. Two railroad lines passed through St. Charles. Ordinarily I would have scanned their tracks eagerly in each direction for any sign of trains, but today I just didn't care.

"What's the matter, Bob?" my father asked. "You ware so quiet I didn't know you ware hare. You want something to eat?" he smiled at me in the rear view mirror.

"Nosirree," I answered. "I'm fine."

"You look a little peaked, dear," Mother said, turning to look at me.

"I'm just fine, Mother." And I was beginning to feel normal again, the result of the breeze blowing in the rear window.

Coming in from the south, my father decided to make a brief detour past the new airport. Windy pasture, a droopy windsock, and a single hanger of gray metal, it was mostly promise with little to see except a sign boldly proclaiming the wonders of air travel. Ever since his service in the infant Army Air Corps during the First World War, Dad had understood that air travel would be the way of the future.

Nancy, Dad and I got out of the car and walked over to the low wire fence with its DANGER—KEEP OUT sign.

"Some day you kids will see those big Douglas planes coming to Rochester," my father said. We looked out over the waving grass, listened to the wind sighing and tried to imagine the unimaginable.

"You see those people over there," Dad said, pointing across the landing field to a gloomy, peeling, clapboard house on a slight rise. A decrepit porch clung to its front wall. We could just make out the figures of aged men and women, some in rockers, staring out at the future through eyes as unseeing as our own.

"Who are those people, Daddy?" Nancy said.

"What is that place, Dad?" I added.

"There is vare you kids are driving me," he said, and turned to go. "That's the poor farm!" And he chuckled at his own joke.

"Come on, you two. Let's go home," he commanded.

The sun was close to setting, as we drove up Sixth Avenue, SW and turned into our driveway. The neighborhood was aglow with a pale orange light, the homes, and every shrub and tree, were transformed by it. Everything looked different, distant, and odd, as if it were a foreign country, seen for the first time. I saw no one I knew, and though I saw our house, it was a stranger to me. All that I laid eyes on was lifeless. I wondered if my family had driven so long that we had passed into a new dimension—an afterlife. I shivered and could not wait to leave the car and go upstairs.

"Oh, I'm so glad to be home again. Aren't you, Bobby," Mother said, removing her scarf and hanging her purse and gloves in the hall closet.

"Yes, Mother, I am."

Dad turned on the lamp over his red chair, and sat down with a sigh to read his paper.

"Would you two kids like popcorn for supper?" Mother asked.

"Yay! Yay!" Nancy was happy.

"How about you, Nels?"

"Fine."

"You kids go in the living room and listen to the radio if you want to. But keep it low, your father is reading."

Nancy and I settled on our stomachs before the Atwater-Kent, and watched the dial brighten with a familiar yellow incandescent glow. With eyes mesmerized by the pattern in our fringed Oriental-style rug, the dialog and music of our favorite radio shows transported me.

"Come to the table, Bobby, Nance. Nels, supper's ready!"

A LITTLE PEACE AND QUIET

My schoolmates and I received no diplomas to mark the completion of an elementary education at Edison School. There was no ceremony to celebrate the six years that we had spent together, an intimate circle of close friends, learning how to live in the world. Transition to Rochester Junior High School with its citywide mix of students was still a distant hurdle that would be tragic for some, difficult for most.

The last few weeks were busy ones for us sixth graders. There were projects to complete, tests to take, and the agony of waiting for report cards. Eventually, the long-awaited final day came, with farewells and promises exchanged.

At the dismissal bell I left the schoolroom carrying a large, unwieldy bundle of my assignment and test papers, collected during the past year. My teacher, Miss Nelson, noted that her talented pupil was apparently going to maintain a record of the knowledge that she had inculcated.

"I'm glad to see that you intend keeping your papers, Bobby," she beamed. "That is a very wise thing to do. No doubt you'll find it most useful to review some of the things we've learned together before you start Junior High next fall." She seemed comforted by this thought.

"Yes, Ma'am," I replied, without commitment. I smiled, thinking of the actual contribution that these papers soon would make to my future educational experience.

Running down the main stairs and out the front door as fast as the bundle would allow, I ran the several blocks to the alleyway behind the

Berkman residence, where Johnny was already waiting. He too had an accumulation of papers from his first year in Junior High School. He carried a square cardboard box into which he had cut windows and a door. The sign drawn in black crayon over the doorway read "Edison School."

"Hi, Bobby. Are you all set?"

"You betcha," I replied.

"I sure hope the box is big enough this year," worried Johnny.

"It looks it. Here's my stuff."

We silently crumpled our papers, and crammed them into the box. Johnny thrust a short tube from a roll of toilet paper into a hole in the top of the box to serve as the chimney. The coup de grace was a small cardboard-cutout figure labeled "Miss Nelson" that we leaned against the chimney.

"She's gone up there to escape," laughed Johnny.

"Fat chance," I said.

Each of us struck a kitchen match, and simultaneously put the torch to Edison School. Amid the alarming crackling sounds of the ensuing conflagration, we marched solemnly around the fearful scene ritually chanting, "Good riddance to bad rubbish. Good riddance to bad rubbish. It serves you right!"

◆   ◆   ◆

In the first days of the vacation that followed, the delightful freedom from the strictures of daily school attendance was a sweet opiate that washed most serious thought from my head. That feeling soon gave way to the necessity of devising some new activity to fill each day. At first I joined with my neighborhood friends to initiate games and create new playtime activities. But as the summer wore on many of them including Johnny left Rochester to live with their families at lakeside vacation cottages. When only a few children whose parents were unable to afford such luxuries remained, I was hard pressed for something to do. My parents would hardly tolerate any complaint after my late musical misadventure.

I sought out menial odd jobs, first from my parents and then from sympathetic neighbors. I did not expect, nor always receive, remuneration for these occasional tasks. Gradually, I accumulated a small number of coins that I placed in a cigar box in my closet. Like the king in "Sing a Song of Sixpence," I began to frequent my counting closet to reassess my hoard, and on one of these occasions came across a Brownie box camera. It had been a Christmas present from a childless aunt, who could not appreciate the disinterest such a gift would inspire in a six-year old boy who had just received his first electric train set. Turning the camera over in my hands, I imagined myself the ace newspaper reporter, accumulating Pulitzer prizes for his keen photographic acumen.

At Weber and Judd's Drugstore, I purchased two rolls of film for the Brownie with coins from my closet-store. I stalked Rochester for a week snapping twenty-four nifty action-shots of local citizens at work. When I returned the exposed film to the drugstore for development, I was shocked to discover that more of my hard-earned cash was required. In fact, very few coins now remained in my cigar box.

On the day that the prints were promised, I hurried the seven blocks to the drugstore. I couldn't wait to examine my efforts, and did so right there at the perfume counter, while Marie Kvam, the clerk, looked on, disinterestedly.

"Why on earth did you photograph the rump of Oscar Pederson's horse?" she asked finally. Oscar was the milkman whose daily activities I had been trying to highlight.

"Mr. Pederson gave me a lift home, that's all," I lied.

"So why did you take snapshots of his horse?"

"I aimed at the scenery along his route! I guess I missed," I mumbled, sheepishly. I gathered up the remaining prints. None were any better. As I left the store, Marie's loud laughter marked the death knell to my action-reporter's career. It was just as well. I couldn't afford the film anyway.

A few days later a miracle occurred! I discovered that my friend Martin Adson harbored unfulfilled aspirations in photography.

"Hey, Bob, where'd you get the camera? Is it any good?" Martin asked.

"I've been trying it out, using it for action shots," I said. "But it's kinda slow for newspaper work. That's what I'm aiming to do in life, report action news!"

"Does it take good pictures of people standing or sitting still?"

"Gosh, yes, Marty! This is a keen picture taking camera!" *It is if you want to take pictures of horses' rumps.* "What'll you give me for it?"

"All I got with me is my 'llowance—that's fifty cents. I'll have another seventy-five cents tonight, though. I'm going to caddie for my dad at the Country Club this afternoon. Take a dollar 'n a quarter?"

"Nope, this is a swell camera. You have anything to trade?"

"Hey, I know! You've taken music lessons. How'd you like a clarinet?"

"It's a deal!" I said with delight. The now useless camera went home with Marty and I acquired his clarinet!

There were no instructions with the instrument, but I still had my beginner workbooks for the violin. With a talent previously unrecognized either by Sister Mary Cecilia or myself, I began to teach myself to play the licorice stick. As my familiarity with the finger holes improved I even began to imagine a revitalized musical career, as soloist with one of the Dorsey brothers, or even with the great Benny Goodman! *Then that rotten old Sister Mary Cecilia, who said that I had no musical talent, would have to eat her words!*

To my parents, unacquainted with my high-flown daydreams, the horrid screeching that I produced from my new possession was nerve-racking. I squawked and honked by the hour, forcing my father to evict me from the precincts of his garage. Upstairs, Mother was just as adamant. So, I practiced on the stairway, in negligible light. Eventually, as autumn approached and with it my first day in Junior High School, my father put his foot down.

"You can't toot on that fool thing day in and day out and still manage your school work," he said. "You get your camera back from Martin, and you give him back his horn-pipe! You had no business trading off your aunt's gift in the first place! Your mother and I could use a little peace and quiet around here!" Though his last sentence was uttered as an afterthought, I knew it was the heart of the matter. My musical career was once again on the decline!

◆　　　◆　　　◆

The Junior High School drew its students from all of Rochester's elementary schools. There were many more students in the seventh grade than had attended all of Edison School, and I knew very few of them. I found myself in a fast-paced and bewildering new world of learning. For one of my elective subjects I chose Chorus because many of my Edison friends had done so. The subject was considered more refined and befitting of students from Pill Hill than were typing, shop, home economics, or band.

At the first meeting of the Chorus class, all of us awaited our teacher's arrival with considerable curiosity. There were many stories going around concerning Miss Helen Church. None prepared me for the events of that afternoon. Miss Church swam slightly sideways through the door, a nimble behemoth, with a radiant smile and twinkling kindly eyes. Her pince-nez roiled upon her bosom like a cork upon the waters, but most remarkably, remained ready for instant use.

She had spent most of her adult life caring for her late mother, a personage who had enjoyed a minor operatic career during her youth. Miss Church lived alone in an apartment filled with her mother's musical mementos: a cravat worn by Caruso when singing the lead in *Cavalleria Rusticana*, a fan dropped by Nellie Melba when assuming the role of *Carmen*, a program signed by Majewska. Posters, playbills and fading photographs of yesterday's operatic luminaries adorned the walls.

Miss Church went briskly and quite daintily to the piano and, played several bars of music. She turned swiftly around on her piano stool and smiled with mischievous innocence. "Who can identify that composition and name the composer?"

Mine was the only hand raised. The piece had, after all, been my nemesis! "It is 'Fur Elise' by Ludwig van Beethoven," I answered, confidently.

"You're quite correct. Can you tell me anything more?"

"It was composed for his little daughter to play. It is in the key of C and is in 3/8 time," I said. The other students looked on, astonished.

"Bravo, Bravo," cried Miss Church, clapping her hands with delight, as if at the conclusion of an artistic performance. Some of the others clapped limply as well, in idle imitation of her.

"You must love music," she said. "What is your name?"

"Yes, I do," I answered. "My name is Robert Twedt."

"Are you Nels Twedt's son, Robert?"

"Yes, Ma'am."

"Well, then I am not at all surprised at your knowledge of the classics. Your father is a smart man, Robert, a brilliant man. He is the kind of man who would encourage his children to appreciate art!"

With that she turned her attention to the lesson at hand, but she had already won my adoration, and relaunched my musical training. This time it would never falter. I had found my voice! I enrolled in Chorus every year after that, and sought out extracurricular choral activities as well, particularly if Miss Helen Church was the director. I was delighted to be able to sing with others who loved music as much as I had learned to!

THE WORLD OF
OUTDOORSMANSHIP

In the fall of 1936, soon after entering Junior High School, I discovered that a troop of Boy Scouts meeting at the Presbyterian Church near our home was made up largely of boys from my neighborhood. Giving in to their repeated cajoling, I trailed along one evening—and was promptly hooked. The meetings taught civic responsibility and personal virtue in a cohesive atmosphere that focused upon outdoor skills, and controlled athletics. The latter, conducted in the church basement, were very tolerant of my bumbling ineptness. I felt comfortable with my friends of Troop 26 and did my best to succeed in scouting.

The Scoutmaster, Mr. Ed Fiksdal, the owner of Fiksdal Flowers, was tall, hollow-chested, with thinning straw-colored hair, and a pleasant, toothy smile. He was a talented flower arranger, but seemed an unlikely candidate to lead a group of boisterous youngsters into the world of outdoorsmanship. But, his unceasing enthusiasm sold us boys on the privilege of being a Scout, the strength of teamwork, and pride in our own accomplishments.

My schoolwork improved in proportion with my involvement in Scouting. As a result, my parents supported my activities with delight. Without complaint, they bought me a uniform and many camping accessories. My mother took all her trade in floral arrangements to Mr. Fiksdal's shop. My father invited Ed to join an informal men's kaffe klatch that met weekly at the Woolworth counter.

The following summer every scout from Troop 26 spent two weeks at Kamp Kahler, a local Boy Scout facility that had been given to the regional organization by a wealthy Rochester hotel magnate. By the time I started eighth grade in the fall, I had conquered the first two levels of scouting, acquiring the skills prescribed for each, and was well on the way to completing the requirements for a third, First Class Scout. The ranks beyond these first three were achieved by proficiency in a variety of disciplines sufficient to satisfy any boy's interests, each marked by a merit badge. Many focused on activities associated with camping and campcraft, and could be practiced only at a campsite. Opportunities for acquiring these skills were mainly restricted to the summer season at Kamp Kahler.

I determined to remedy that situation by building a weatherproof shelter where my friends and I could continue camping activities. It was an ambitious undertaking! I shared my intentions with Robert Seaman, a friend from my troop. Bob's family was less fortunate than most in our neighborhood. His father, a timekeeper with the WPA, seemed oddly out of place, walking past the homes of affluent Clinic physicians each morning, carrying his black lunch pail. I concluded that his most valuable possession must be his pocket watch, and that it was this that he used on the job! Bob's mother did domestic service in Pill Hill homes, trudging to work with a hamper containing her employer's laundry that she had washed at home. There were three Seaman children; Bob, his younger brother, and an older sister, Shirley, who had long reddish hair, a fiery Irish temper, and a slim waist that looked well on the dance floor.

"Jeez, how ya gonna get the boards 'n stuff?" my friend asked.

"Maybe we could pick up scraps offa lots where houses are being built."

"Okay, maybe, but how're ya gonna get the boards to wherever yer planning on putting up this shack of yours?"

"It's gonna be better'n a shack, for criminy sake," I said, miffed.

"Okay, okay, excuse me for living. But how?"

"How about using our bikes?" I replied, without conviction.

Bob's ordinarily smiling, chubby face twisted in contempt, and he assailed me with an angry outburst that brought him close to tears. "That's the dumbest thing I've heard of yet! Have you ever in your life scrounged for stove wood? Well I do it all the time. It's hard work! And, believe me; you can't carry boards on a bike!"

"Gosh, Bob, I guess I just didn't think straight. I'm sorry. Let's think of something else then."

We sat on our bicycles, steadying them with one foot, hunched over the handlebars, and stared at the ground.

"I've got it! We'll build our *cabin* on the island out at Balfour's farm. I've seen a pile of old boards out there, next to the boathouse. Let's go and scout it out!"

The next morning we hitched a ride with John Tewes.

◆   ◆   ◆

Dr. Donald Balfour was born in 1882 in Ontario, of Scotch-Canadian parents, and had come to Rochester in 1907, to accept an assistantship in pathology with the Mayo brothers. By 1909, he had become their surgical assistant, and in 1915 he became the sixth and last member of the original Mayo partnership. In spring of 1910, Donald married Dr. Will's daughter Carrie. For a wedding present, the Mayos gave the couple the house on Sixth Avenue, SW that had been the childhood home of Mrs. Mayo. The newlyweds began at once to greatly enlarge their new home, and constructed an adjacent carriage house in the rear.

After the First World War, the Balfours decided to build a country retreat, choosing a half-section adjacent to Dr. Charlie's estate, "Mayowood". The South Fork, a meandering tributary of the Zumbro River, divided the two properties. Situated on a rocky hillside about a quarter mile from the river, the Balfour house was constructed of stone quarried on the site. It had a slate roof, copper gutters, mullioned windows, and a massive fireplace opening into a two-story living room.

The room's huge exposed beams originally supported a covered bridge in northern Minnesota. The home was furnished in the style termed Southwestern that was a pleasing mix of Spanish, Anglo, and Native American cultures. Decorative artifacts from the latter: blankets, arms, headdress, pottery and basketry lay in every room.

The lovely view from a long window seat in the living room looked southward down a long sloping lawn to lush fields that ended at the river's edge. To enhance that picture, a low earthen dam strengthened with center piles had been built across the stream, creating a shallow lake with a small central island. In 1934 this dam had been breached to hasten the filling of a larger lake forming behind a permanent dam newly-constructed a mile or so downstream at Mayowood. Since then the South Branch had meandered freely through the Balfour property, encircling the island and lending a bucolic quality to the living room vista. An unused green boathouse slumbered unobtrusively on the river bank near the breached dam. Leftover lumber from its construction was piled neatly against its far side.

"See, what did I tell you. There's plenty of stuff here to build a swell cabin," I bragged to Bob when we reached the lake.

"I got to hand it to you," he said, in admiration. "What about tools like a saw, a couple 'a hammers, 'n some nails?"

"We can get 'em up at the house and stash 'em down here in the boat house between times," I said, with presumptuous authority.

A wooden foot bridge, perhaps 18 feet long and supported on log pilings driven into the stream bed, led to the island. We scampered over it, and searched about for the best location to begin construction. A few young maples near the island's center were positioned at the corners of a rough rectangle.

"Hey, look at this," I called. "We could use these trees as the corner posts and nail boards between them for the walls."

"Say that's a great idea," my friend replied.

"It'd be sturdy, better'n trying to hold up corner posts while we drive nails into 'em," I said. "Let's get started."

"Oh boy! Looks like it's going to be a swell cabin," he said, catching my enthusiasm.

We worked the remainder of the day, mostly sawing boards into shorter lengths, and carrying them across the bridge.

On ensuing weekends of a protracted Indian summer, Bob and I nailed our walls into place, remembering to leave openings for the door and windows. Soon, we had the beginnings of a structure that would give credit to any hobo jungle in the country. As more and more leaves fell from the trees, its crude outlines became clearly visible from the Balfour house.

One afternoon, after he had returned from a day's yard work in the country, John Tewes came into the garage to see my father. "Nels, I was down to the river today. Is somebody putting up some kind of shack out on the island?"

"No!" answered my father, surprised. "Who would do such a fool thing?"

John removed the corncob pipe from his mouth, cocked his head, looked at my father sideways from under the bill of his cap, and said, "Maybe Bob?"

John knew very well that we must have had some reason, other than the mere pleasure of his company, for repeatedly catching rides to the farm with him. But in his kindly bumbling way he did not wish to create strife between my father and myself.

Dad asked me at the dinner table that night. "Bob, what ware you doing out there on the island at the farm?"

"Bob Seaman and I are putting up a cabin for Scouting, a place where we can practice outdoor stuff when we can't go to Kamp Kahler." I explained.

"Well, you got to find some other place. You can't put it there! You yust take it down as soon as you can. You hare?"

"Yessir," I said.

We did not discuss the matter further. My father failed to explain that the river and its island were props in a planned rustic scene, designed to be viewed from the living room of the country house. He did not make plain that all elements of the home and the estate were strictly off limits to Twedt family usage, particularly to the young Twedts.

◆   ◆   ◆

The winter was unusually harsh that year, with many heavy snow-falls that blanketed the fields and made country roads impassable. With my school assignments, Boy Scout meetings, and home chores, I thought very little of the island cabin, and its snowy surroundings.

In March, there was a break in the weather, with warm sunny days. Streets in Rochester now flowed with slushy water and the road to the farm became passable. An inspection trip to the cabin seemed in order. I had quite forgotten my father's edict.

One Saturday Bob and I caught a ride with John Tewes. We were encased in heavy overcoats, decreed by cautious mothers, but decidedly excessive on this bright morning. Soon the heated truck cab, suffused with John's pipe smoke, and our perspiration, was stifling. John seemed not to notice. Mrs. Johnson, the farm operator's wife, was feed-ing chickens when we drove through the yard, and she waved to us. We lowered the window, mostly to get a breath of fresh air, and called back, "Hi, Mrs. Johnson." When we arrived at the circle drive fronting the Balfour house, Bob and I jumped down from the truck, gasping for breath.

"Thanks, John," we said, with relief.

"Now you boys be sure to get back to the house in time. I got to leave for town about three o'clock," he warned.

"Sure John, we'll be here."

We unbuttoned our overcoats, doffed hats and scarves, and set off for the river. Dirty snow, tarnished to dingy brass by the low-lying sun, still lay in the furrows. Bumptious rivulets of icy water snaked their way down the ruts in the sloping, gravel road. Avoiding these, we sloshed through the slush, turning occasionally to watch our tracks fill with water. The wind, blowing across the open fields, challenged the brave foolishness with which we had loosened our coats. We began to run, arms flapping to keep our balance, metal clasps on overshoes slapping noisily in rebellious bravado.

"Oh, gosh, look at the river!" I exclaimed, hurrying forward.

"The bridge is gone, but, the shack's still there," Bob shouted, over the noise of rushing water. The river now boiled around the nearly submerged island, thundering past the remnants of the earthen dam that appeared to be melting away as we watched.

"Do you see any damage?" I asked.

"I can't tell. There's still too much snow over there."

"Well, I'm going over and take a look!" I announced with empty-headed bluster. We looked about for something to replace the foot-bridge, found a log on the bank nearby, and lugged it to the approximate spot where the bridge had stood. With immense and noisy exertion, we upended the log on the near bank, tipped it toward the island, and stared in disbelief as it splashed into the stream, turned slowly in the current, and was whirled away.

"We'll just have to use a boat and row across," I said, looking at the green boathouse nearby. Its large double doors, held closed by a rusty hasp and bent nail, opened to reveal a canoe upturned on a rack along one wall. There was no other boat!

"Here, help me drag it out, will ya?"

"I'm not going over there in a canoe!" Bob announced without hesitation.

"Okay, fraidy cat, I'll go alone!" I said, the hero of the hour. "I'll need a paddle, and there isn't one anywhere in there. Maybe I could use a board."

"You're crazy! You can't paddle a canoe with a board! How will you steer?"

"Oh, for cripes sake!" I said with exasperation. "It's just a short distance over there. With a good shove off, and some healthy swipes with the board, I'll be there in a jiffy!"

We carried the canoe over to the bank. It was then that I noticed why this canoe was the only craft left inside the boathouse. It was a derelict, victim of age. Its painted canvas hull was cracked in several places, and there were holes where the cracks intersected.

"I'll have to stuff these with daub, like the pioneers filled the chinks between the logs of their cabins. Why don't we gather some leaves to mix with this mud and then we'll chink up all the leaks?"

Soon, we had filled each hole with a brown bolus, and the interior of the canoe resembled a child with the pox. We slid the patched craft into the stream where a submerged log formed a relatively quiet backwater, and I climbed in while Bob steadied the stern.

"Okay! Give me a shove off," I called, readying my paddleboard. I felt the canoe being sucked out of the eddy by the main current. It was only then that I saw, in shocked surprise, that the daubing had melted away like butter in a pan. The icy river water poured through each rent in lively geysers. It was obvious that the canoe would not stay afloat long enough to reach the island. I paddled wildly, first on one side, then the other, as the canoe twisted out of control. Bob followed on the bank, yelling and gesturing. I couldn't hear him, only the rushing water, splashing and crashing against the canoe that was now beginning to swamp.

"Gimme a hand, will ya?" I screamed. Panicking, I stood up, and plummeted into the rushing river as the craft capsized.

The freezing water left me numb with shock, too surprised to be frightened.

I stared at my own breath, bubbling away to the surface, and then kicked with all my strength trying to swim. Hampered by my overshoes and winter garments, now heavy as lead, I flailed my arms wildly and could barely kept my head above the surface. I knew that I could make no headway against the current that was now propelling me past what was left of the dam. Standing at the outermost end of its ruin, where the roiling river thrust through, Bob crouched, holding a long branch. His eyes were wide with fear.

"Grab hold of this," he yelled at me, and leaned as far out over the water as he dared. I felt the bark and held on with both hands, while the current turned me into the bank.

"Oh gosh! Thanks! Pheew! I thought I wasn't going to make it. Thanks, Bob," I said to my rescuer. I was completely exhausted and icy cold. My teeth chattered continually as we trudged up the road toward the house that appeared askew and blurred in the distance. Suddenly I realized that I'd lost my glasses, a sacrifice to the torrent! *Good gosh! Now I'm in for it. What'll Dad say?*

In the snug, windowless basement of the stone mansion stood a large oil-fired furnace, now mercifully running to keep the house above freezing in the owner's absence. With its reservoir of heated water, there was very little else in the cozy room. A worn leather sofa, a frayed Navaho blanket concealing the stuffing protruding from several wounds, sat against the wall, near the furnace. John's noontime napping place could be discerned in its depressions.

As soon as we had entered, I took off my wet garments, laying them on the furnace to dry. Emptying the galoshes over the floor drain, I upended them on a mop and a broom handle. In my BVDs, with the blanket around my shoulders, I sat on the couch to await John's arrival.

After a long interval of silence, I ventured an opinion. "I guess coming out here today wasn't such a good idea."

"Nope," said Bob, who, though a year younger than I, still knew a dumb thing when he saw it.

"Maybe a cabin on the island isn't very handy," I ventured the obvious.

"Nope!"

"Anyways, Kamp Kahler will be open pretty soon. We won't need an ole *shack* anymore," I concluded.

"Nope!"

Soon my wet things had dried enough that I could get dressed. John appeared in the truck, and we piled into the cab. He did not seem to notice my still soggy appearance, and so, suffering unpleasant odor and desultory conversation, we rode home.

◆   ◆   ◆

Meanwhile, the capsized canoe continued its erratic journey, observed in its passage by farm neighbors downstream, who recognized the craft and its source. Mrs. Johnson, concerned for my safety, called my mother with the news. Wild with fright, fearing the worst, Mother rushed downstairs to the garage.

"Oh my God! Nels, I know it's Bobby! I couldn't stand it, Nels, if anything happened to him. Oh! My only son, my own dear son! Nels, what can we do?" Beginning to cry, she covered her face with her apron, and fled back upstairs into the kitchen.

Following her upstairs, Dad tried to calm her. "Now, Stella, don't yump to conclusions! It's yust a boat they've seen. We don't know what happened. He is probably out at the farm right now. Maybe the boat yust fell into the water. The boathouse is on the bank. Maybe the water…" His drawn, white face betrayed his own anxiety.

"Please, Nels, go look for him. Hurry! He's in trouble, Nels! Go find him, now! Oh, God, what will I do?" She wrung her hands, weeping uncontrollably. Her hysteria was infectious.

Dad went into the living room, grabbed the telephone, and dialed the Johnsons at the farm. "Hello, Yon? This is Nels Twedt speaking. Yon, can you go down to the boathouse and see if that old green boat is still there? Maybe the boat your wife saw in the river was not that one. Yah, hurry up, can you? Call me right back. Yah, right away, Yon."

While Dad was talking, John Tewes stopped in the drive briefly, allowing his passengers to alight. I went through the garage and up the stairs into the kitchen.

Seeing me return unharmed, Mother cried out with unmixed relief, "Oh, thank God! Thank God! Where have you been? What happened to you? Oh, Bobby, we were so worried!" She leaned on the sink board for support and reached toward me.

Dad, who had recognized my footsteps while he was on the phone came in from the living room. "Vare is he?" he cried out, loudly. His held his right arm up as if he were still holding the receiver to his ear.

Surprised and shocked at their reaction to my return unharmed I said, "I went out to the farm to see how our cabin on the island…"

"I thought I told you not to put up a shack there," my father said, his voice strident, angry. "How did you think you ware going to get over there? The river is up, the bridge is gone!"

"Well, I was just going to take the canoe…"

"You ware going to what!" He was yelling now. Suddenly he comprehended the whole escapade in its foolishness, danger, and disobedience! His pallor changed to a fierce flush; he yelled with rage, and lunged for me. In confusion, and disbelief, I couldn't move.

My father struck me, repeatedly, with his fists, continually yelling erratic phrases, in English and Norwegian.

"Who do you think you are? Dum esel…how dare you…valen skalle…I show you who is boss!"

He knocked me to the kitchen floor, and kicked me with those awful, long narrow shoes! I screamed in fear, covered my head and face, drew up my legs to make as small a target as possible, and lay there feeling the pain of the blows and hating him! He kept on going around my prone form, shouting and hitting me. I thought he was going to kill me.

"Nels for God's sake stop! Stop Nels you're killing him!" cried my mother, trying in vain to pull him away. He merely pushed her aside and continued.

My sister, Nancy, hearing all the commotion, ran into the room, took in the scene in a flash. She hurled herself down on top of me to protect me from further abuse. "Oh, Daddy, stop! Please, stop!"

Suddenly, it was all over! Dad turned and walked out of the room and down the stairs, anger spent, drained, silent. No one mentioned these events again, neither my disobedience nor Dad's loss of control. I was relieved in a way, but remained wary of my father's temper ever after.

THE EASTER OUTFIT

In the spring of 1938, the Great Depression that had gnawed at the nation's vitals for nearly a decade, forever altering the lives of a generation, was sputtering to a halt. Better times resulted from numerous government make-work programs, and the ever-growing industrial demands created by European rearmament. The initial calamitous events in what became the Second World War were only six months away. I was nearly 14 years old.

My father, unlike many men at that time, had never been without a job. Dad began working for Dr. Balfour in 1911, and continued in that employment until 1950, when he retired at age 62. His wages were always modest, and our family's frugal life style remained largely unchanged. We were not poor during those years although, in my childhood, I thought we were.

My mother kept our modest apartment spotless, and always managed to prepare delicious meals from the limited Twedt family larder. She sent her children to school in clothes that were always clean and mended. Both of my parents regarded new clothing, particularly garments that were thought smart or trendy by my sister and me, as an extravagance. Gifts of good used children's apparel, on the other hand, were prized.

Fred and Elsa Young, close friends of my parents, lived but two blocks away in an unassuming frame bungalow. Fred worked for the Kahlers, owners of Rochester's finest hotel, The Kahler, located directly across First Avenue from the Clinic. His job was analogous to my father's, though Fred was not a mechanic and had no underlings. Fred, always impeccably dressed, balding, with a dour countenance and a condescending smile, was a man of few words. Elsa, thin, marcelled, and anxious, fluttered behind her rimless spectacles, chattering aimlessly. I was always uncomfortable in their presence.

Douglas, who had the unusual nickname, Jack, the eldest of their two sons, was only a year or so older than I. A lean, muscular, strikingly handsome youth with a thick head of wavy blonde hair, he resembled neither of his parents. Jack's outgrown but still serviceable garments often found a new home in my closet. When we were youngsters in elementary school, this arrangement seemed neither strange nor embarrassing to either of us.

By the time he had become a high school freshman, Jack Young had already acquired a manly seductiveness that propelled him easily into the heady world of grooming, girls, and giddy flirtations. He owned a dark navy serge suit in which he affected the role of a teenage Clark Gable, not only capturing feminine hearts, but also establishing cachet to enter the finer homes on Pill Hill. Heavy usage on the dance floor soon reduced the trousers to a frayed and thin shadow of their former insurgent elegance. But the suit coat that was so often thrown off in the heat of terpsichorean footwork retained its good quality, and eventually became mine.

My parents sought to recapture the suit's magic by purchasing a separate pair of trousers that exactly duplicated the coat, but this dream never materialized. The closest match they found were trousers made of a thin black cotton material with a faint gray plaid pattern. They wrinkled when stared at sideways and required pressing after each wearing. Brown sharkskin-toed shoes, a diminutive black bow tie, breast pocket handkerchief, and an imitation-felt fedora, made of starched, navy fabric completed the ensemble. My mother assured me that I looked very smart!

Nancy and I, Easter 1938

Smiling like a mentally defective funeral director in this mismatched outfit, I posed with Nancy for the obligatory Easter Sunday Kodak snap. I had a premonition of trouble to come, when she, with superior prescience in many matters, including that of sartorial correctness, frowned into the camera lens and assumed a grumpy silence.

At the Congregational Church a majority of the membership came from Clinic physicians' families. Their children would certainly not attend Sunday school in secondhand clothing, particularly on Easter. Not surprisingly, when I entered the junior boys' Sunday school classroom, my attire became the occasion of amused stares and harsh raillery.

"Hey, Bob, wake up. You've put on the wrong trousers. You better hustle on home and change before church."

"Yeah, Bob, and the same goes for the brown shoes."

"That's a fine topper you've got there, Bob. I hope it doesn't rain before you get home. It might melt!"

Surprised and shocked, I could only counter with the feeble reply, "Sticks and stones." I scurried for the rear and sat down to lick my wounds. My parents had done their best to provide the Easter ensemble, had assured me of its correctness, and even complimented me on my appearance. Now these boys had made fun of me. I was so bewildered, hurt, and embarrassed that I wished that I could vanish—be somewhere, anywhere else—where I couldn't hear their mocking.

The class turned its attention to the teacher and his lesson for the day. Taken from the gospel according to John, it was a thorough discussion, with inspiring class participation, of our Lord's new commandment to *love one another!*

The painful incident, with all its puerile pathos, was a watershed event. I began to appreciate the truth of the old adage however vain it might have seemed that *Clothes make the man.* No more secondhand clothing for me. From now on I determined that somehow I must choose my own attire.

TOO HOT

My only defense against the insecurities that assailed me during the two years of Junior High School was to withdraw from the company of the classmates whom I feared. Books had always been good companions; now they were my only sure friends. I read voraciously, without direction or purpose.

In conversations with his employer, Dad had always described his son's scholarship at Edison Elementary with pride and pleasure. The pronounced slump in my grades that followed my entry into Junior High profoundly troubled him, but he continued to say, "Oh yah, Bob always got his nose stuck in a book. We can't get him up out of the chair long enough to come to the table."

"Well, sounds like you've got a smart son, Nels. Head him in the right direction. See that he gets his education. Only worthwhile thing in life, work of the mind," Dr. Balfour boomed.

"We do that, Doctor. Always we tell him to study hard so's he can amount to something. But I worry sometimes with all this reading."

"Nothing to worry about, Nels. Nothing at all. When he runs out of reading material, send him over to the house and let him have a look in the library!"

"Why, thank you, Doctor."

And so I graduated from our family's meager holdings to the enormous, eclectic, and uncatalogued Balfour collection. Books crowded and overflowed from the walnut shelves that lined all four walls of a large room on the front corner of the Balfour residence. Padded window seats, piled with pillows, looked out on great trees, and invited the reader to spend the day. A huge sand colored Navaho rug, with a bright design woven in red, black, turquoise and yellow, relieved the otherwise overpowering darkness of the walnut woodwork. Scattered all about were artifacts from the pueblo peoples: tables, chairs, basketry and beadwork. Over the fireplace on the north wall hung a lighted Remington oil of horses and men, racing and fighting.

The Balfours, like their in-laws, Dr. Will and his wife, loved the southwest, and their bookshelves showed that affection. The non-fiction dealt largely with the cultural history of the indigenous peoples, but there was also much of the boisterous, dangerous, and exciting history of the prospectors, miners, and cattle barons. The works of fiction ranged from the cowboy tales of Zane Grey to Willa Cather's perceptive and articulate novel, *Death Comes to the Archbishop*. I treasured the open door to all this wonder that the Doctor's invitation had provided, and spent many wintry hours, coiled in a deep leather chair, flying far from Rochester on a magical printed carpet.

Across the vestibule from the door to the library there was a butler's coatroom with a half-bath. Here one day I found some discarded, or at least they seemed to be, golf clubs at the bottom of a coat cupboard. The wooden shaft on one was fractured, another quite splayed, and all had frazzled windings, and were caked with mud. I asked my Dad about them.

"Oh, they ware young Donald's and he yust left them. I suppose they aren't much good. They really ought to go to the dump," he said. The dump was an unknown place where all things my father considered useless, whether reparable or not, should go.

"Do you think I could have them, Dad? I think maybe they could be cleaned up and fixed. Could I, Dad?"

"I'll speak to the Doctor," he said.

◆   ◆   ◆

The golf club restoration project was therapeutic. Dad left me to my own devices, watching but never interfering, unless I asked for his advice. He showed me how to use his tools for grinding and polishing, and helped me repair the fractured shaft. I sanded the wooden shafts to perfection, repaired the worn leather grips, rewound each joint, using Dad's hidden knot method, and shellacked them. When finished I had five new golf clubs, four irons with names like niblick and mashie stamped on them and a number three wood. They would have been a credit to any professional golfer of the previous decade!

Ready for the Links

My parents were proud of my accomplishment, and pleased by this sign of an improved mental outlook. In honor of the perceived change in attitude, they bought me a new canvas golf bag from the Montgomery Ward catalog. Of a sturdy gray duck trimmed in brown leatherette, with a pocket for balls and tees, it was a triumph of frugality over vanity. I was also proud of my work, and pleased with the result. Duffer perhaps, but a member of a new fraternity, surely.

During summer vacation, the parks department sponsored a program of storytelling, reading, and games for younger children at each of the elementary schools. For those of high school age, tennis and golf were offered in the form of coupons to be redeemed at a public facility. These coupons were relatively scarce, and my friends and I had to show up Johnny-on-the-spot when the Edison School counselor opened up in the morning, for she was the *Coupon Queen.*

The spur of having my own golf clubs and playing a grownup game with my neighborhood pals, honed my skill and whetted my desire to improve my game. I played as often as I could, which was usually every weekday morning.

One hot day in July, 1938, I returned from the links and saw my father working at his bench. His coveralls were open to his chest, and he was wearing no shirt! A loud metallic banging and the smell of gasoline vapors filled the air.

"Dad, hey Dad," I cried to get his attention. "I broke 90 today, and I made par on number 9!" My earliest scores had been above 120.

He looked up from his work, peering over the steely rims of his spectacles and said, "Well, that's good. But, weren't you supposed to get better at it with each game?" My father was a minimalist when it came to praise. Too much and his progeny might *lay down on the yob.*

"Where's Mother? I'm starved."

"Vare do you think? Upstairs."

I opened the door to our apartment, stashed my clubs on the landing, and bounded up the stairs calling, "Hey, Mom, I broke 90 today. What are we having for lunch?"

Entering the kitchen, I saw freshly ironed shirts hanging from every available knob, and from the doorframe. My mother was fanning herself with her apron. It was very warm in the kitchen.

"Oh, Bobby, is it lunch time already? I'm afraid the time got away from me, dear. It's so warm today. Would you mind if we just had toasted cheese sandwiches and a glass of lemonade? I don't think I can do much more."

"Gee whiz, Mother. That'd be just fine. It's awfully warm in here!" I replied. I had not noticed the heat as much while traipsing about after a golf ball.

Nancy came into the kitchen from her room. She had been drawing horses. "Look, Bob. This is a western saddle horse. I'm going to ride one someday," she said matter-of-factly.

"It's beautiful, makes you want to reach out and touch him," I said.

"It's not a him! Her name is Starlight," she answered, proudly.

Dad came upstairs. He had removed his coveralls and had put on a shirt, but no tie. "Goss she's a hot one," he observed, laconically.

"Nels, we're having lemonade and a cheese sandwich for lunch. I've been ironing all morning. Fourteen shirts, count 'em, fourteen! I bet you didn't even notice. I'm simply exhausted, Nels!"

"Stella, I noticed. Why you got to iron today, anyways? Can't that yob wait?"

"You know very well you're out of shirts. Oh, it's so warm up here!"

"It's hot everywhere, Stella. What you want me to do about it?"

"That's what I thought you'd say. I wish you'd tell me why we have to live up over a garage, anyway? Why can't we have a house of our own, Nels?"

Nancy and I looked at each other and continued to eat our lunch in silence; we were having a *scene*!

"Bobby, take your sister, and the both of you go down to the pool." She meant the new Olympic size municipal pool in the park at Soldiers Field. "I'm going in and lie down!"

Nancy and I were both tired when we walked home late that afternoon. We had spent hours splashing and diving. Despite the sun, that had given each of us enviable tans, we felt cool deep down within ourselves. The breeze from the southwest was still warm, iron gates along the way hot to touch, but our bodies seemed impervious to nature's sting.

At home, there was a noticeable difference in the air. Mother was setting the table and humming softly to herself. Dad was dozing in his chair in the living room. The pages of the afternoon paper, lying over his face, rose and fell, gently.

"You kids go wash your hands, and come to the table. We're having tuna fish salad for supper."

"Oh, rats," said Nancy. "I don't like tuna fish!" she complained! Neither did I really, but didn't think it very smart to say so.

"I'll have none of that, now," Mother said. "We've got prune whip for dessert, and if you don't be quiet, you won't get any."

"You heard your mother," said my father, who had come to the table.

It was apparent from their conversation that he had promised my mother to do something about the heat. Just what that might be was not discussed, only that, *"I think I got an idea!"*

After supper, when the table had been cleared, and the few dishes washed, Dad said, "Well, you two peanuts, you want to go for a ride?" This was my parents' usual method for cooling off in the evening before going to bed.

"Yay! Yay! cried Nancy, happily. If you looked into her eyes you could see the reflection of the A&W Root Beer sign.

I was doing a quick calculation of the times of arrival and departure of the several trains that would stop in Rochester that evening. I restrained my hopes, merely voiced the thought, "Gee, maybe we'll see a train."

"Now, Bobby, we're going for a ride, to get some cool, fresh air," Mother admonished. "The rest of us don't wish to watch some hot, smelly locomotive!"

Why do they always make fun of my trains?

The sun was low on the horizon, fiery and ominous, when we pulled away. The cloudless sky echoed the sunset with an orange overcast.

"Looks like another scorcher tomorrow," Dad said, canting his head towards the west.

"I suppose so," Mother agreed, with a sigh.

Dad drove west on Second Street, SW into the setting sun, seemingly with no destination in mind. People were sitting on their front porches rocking and fanning themselves. We left the city limits and I began to see garish posters, shouting the presence of a small carnival that toured the Midwest, season after season. In various sizes, they were affixed to every bare spot on telephone poles, fence posts, barns, and silos. Under the face of a particularly ugly baby, tears streaming, mouth wide, oversize letters proclaimed I WANNA SEE CHRISTIE!, and on the following lines, Christie Obrecht Shows, Kasson, August 7-8-9!

"Who is Christie, Daddy? Can we go see him?" Nancy asked.

"Shush, Nancy!" Mother warned. "That's a filthy old carnival show. Tattooed people and drunks. Only someone who doesn't know any better would go to one. And I don't want to hear that either of my children would go to a carnival!"

My sister wasn't convinced, but without a countervailing argument, further discussion was useless. Nancy sat back in her seat and pouted.

"Nels, let's go see Alice and Sam," Mother said, brightly.

"Yah, Stella that ware a good idea.

Oh, rats! Cowpies and stink—and sitting around talking about corn. During the last few years, my attitude about the pleasures of rural living had changed considerably.Alice and Sam Nelson lived near Byron, ten miles west of Rochester, on a farm that had been homesteaded by my great aunt Nelsine Larsen and her husband Jens. My mother's cousin Alice and her husband had three children: a son Stanley, nearly eighteen years old, and two daughters, Ione, aged fifteen and Doris, ten. Alice's father had died, and her mother, Tante Sine, had left the farm and moved to Rochester.

Nearing Byron, Dad left the highway, turning north on a gravel road that soon crossed the Chicago and North Western line to Rapid City and the Black Hills, and after less than a mile turned into the Nelson farm. A two-story frame house, with a front stoop facing the road, and a large porch that housed a summer kitchen on the rear, sat among tall elm trees. It was screened from the prevailing northwesterly wind by a band of tall fir trees. There was a large red barn that had been erected by my great uncle Jens himself. Under the hayloft there was ample room for sheep, milk cows and the necessary bull. The farm buildings stood in the northwest corner of a quarter section of rolling farmland, now covered in verdant stands of corn, rye and wheat.

Stanley, who was palsied, was the first to see us when Dad drove into the farmyard. He ambled unsteadily toward us, down a slight rise, wearing bib overalls and no shirt, his bare arms waving, a crooked grin upon his face. He stammered a nearly incomprehensible welcome, and then turned to yell for his family to come out.

With a loud squawk, the screen door on the porch opened, and Sam appeared with Alice and the girls close behind.

"Well, isn't this a pleasant surprise," Alice said, and hugged my mother. They both laughed with great pleasure, and began almost at once to compare notes.

"Hello, Nels, hot enough for ya?" Sam asked.

"Oh, isn't that the truth! Tonight's Post Bulletin weather forecast calls for rain on the weekend, though. That should bring some relief," said Dad.

"Come in, Stel," said Alice, putting an end to all such preliminary exchanges. "You too, Nels. I baked a fresh apple pie this morning. And there's a pitcher of cool milk. My, I'm glad to see you folks!"

The adults went onto the porch. We children invented things to do. Stanley wanted us to come to the barn and see the bull. Neither Nancy nor I liked the idea but we went along anyway, the two girls trailing behind us and giggling. Inside, the evening light barely pierced the gloom. We navigated by touch, and bumped into Stanley, who was standing at the end of the aisle between stalls. A sound much like a steam engine came out of the darkness and hot, moist fetid air blew across my face. Without warning, a rumbling bellow that raised the hackles on my neck and left me absolutely frozen in place, followed. Pop-eyed, I came to my senses and ran for the door, literally dragging

Nancy with me. I could hear Stanley's loud guffaws following me. Doris and Ione, who had remained outside in order to magnify the effect of the bull's bellowing upon us city kids, laughed at our now embarrassed posture.

We all retraced our steps and perched on a water pipe that ran from the windmill toward the house. As the wan first quarter moon rose, we each tried to outdo each other with anecdotes. "That's nothin'. One time when we were…" Time passed quickly and then I heard my parents begin their good-byes.

"Well, thanks, you folks. It ware nice to see you, but it's time to go."

"Same here, Nels. You know, you better bring Stel out here more often," said Sam.

"Oh, Stel, do you have to go?" said Alice.

"Yes, I'm afraid so. Good-bye, Alice, and thank you for everything."

"Yah, Bob got to see a train," said Dad.

What does he mean? At which depot? I wondered as we all climbed in the car.

Everyone waved and called, "Good-bye, Good-bye!" Then they were lost in the darkness, and we could only see the gravel road ahead in the circle of light from our headlamps.

Dad retraced our route toward the highway. When the crisscross RAILROAD CROSSING sign came into view he slowed, turned onto the shoulder, and came to a stop. He turned off the headlamps and switched on the parking lights.

"Come on, you two," he said, and got out of the car. Nancy jumped out of the back seat and Dad took her by the hand.

"Wait for me," I called, excitedly.

"Nels, be careful," my mother warned. She remained seated in the car.

The three of us walked forward the few yards to the crossing by the pale light of the quarter moon. The world was completely silent.

"What are we waiting here for, Daddy?" Nancy asked.

"Shhh! Be quiet now. Listen!"

From afar off to the east came a wail, high and plaintive, long notes and short, the unforgettable sound of a steam locomotive whistle. The engineer was working a crossing, coming out of Rochester and heading west. I was so happy that I could have danced all around the crossing sign for joy.

"Now, you kids stand back hare," warned Dad. I came to his side, grateful that he had stopped here just for me. I looked up at him, and he was gazing into the distance, but smiling.

"Do you see her yet, Dad?"

"Not yet," he said. "But she is coming!"

The excitement was filling my chest; I thought it would burst!

"Hare she comes," yelled my father, and put his hand around my shoulder.

A headlight came into view, growing ever stronger, and bearing down upon us. A distinct, rapid drumming sound swelled, and you could detect the staccato blasting of steam and smoke. The noise, light, and heat rose to a crescendo, accompanied by the steady banging of steel wheels passing over rail joints. High up I glimpsed a gloved hand raised, a pair of goggles peering ahead, red hot coals, and then the cars came by, rat-a-tat rat-a-tat, baggage and mail, coaches and parlor. A distinguished looking man in a dark pinstripe, smoking a cigarette, diamonds flashing on his cuffs, held a newspaper, while a white-coated porter extended a tray and glass before him. The gaily-lit lounge car glided by in a hail of cinders, red lights and she was gone. I was weak in the knees and thought I would pee right there.

"Come on, now. Watch your step in the dark. Nancy, keep hold of me!" Dad took us back to the car where my mother was waiting.

"Bobby wasn't that exciting," she said.

"Oh, yes," I answered. It was more than exciting. I was delirious, filled with the extreme happiness of someone who has drunk until sated at the fountain of his desire.

On the return to Rochester I paid little attention to the buzz of conversation, simply sat like a turnip and dreamed of the train. I thought of myself, riding fast to the west, leaving for adventure, success, riches, and power. *Someday I'll be on the cars, too!*

We came to a stop and I sat up straight to find that we were not in the garage at home, but angled to the curb on Broadway in front of the Marigold Dairy store.

"Yay! Yay!" Nancy said, clapping her hands.

Dad opened the front door and then bent his head inside. "What you want, Stella?"

Mother looked up at him with just a hint of distress and said, "Oh, dear, I'm so full. Just get me a small scoop of vanilla ice cream in a cake cone."

Nancy and I joined my father on the curb, happy in the cool night air, freighted with a touch of sour sweetness that blew from the dairy store whenever the door was opened. The street lamps were encircled by pools of illumination that trailed off down the sidewalk like diminishing rosary beads. In a nearby tavern window the happy hum of a neon sign beckoned the thirsty. *Leinenkugel's* in pale blue neon glowed above the words **CHIPPEWA PRIDE BEER**, painted in bold white letters. To seal this message, medallions depicting a feathered Indian, and a mighty waterfall appeared at each corner.

We entered the dairy store, walked across a largely empty room that had once sold feed and seed. The ceiling still wore the ornate tin tiles of its previous owner, but all was now painted in shiny white. Only the linoleum flooring, chipped and dirty, displayed the weariness of its history.

At the rear counter, Dad gave the aproned clerk his order, "Two vanilla cones, one cake and the other one of those newfangled waffle cones you got. And what do you two peanuts want?" He bent to look at Nancy.

"I want a colored one," she said. Besides vanilla and chocolate ice cream, sherbets had recently been added, both lemon and lime. "I want a yellow one."

I asked for lime sherbet. The scoops at Marigold were elongated ovals, to more efficiently deliver the ice cream into the cone. I was convinced that the result gave more to lick. We wrapped our cones, especially Mother's, in the tiny napkins that were crammed in the nickled holders and returned to the car. On the ride home, only satisfied, but delicate, slurping could be heard.

"Darn it, the house is still warm, Nels. You've got to do something."

"Stella, I told you I think I can do something tomorrow! But I can't do a thing tonight. Why don't you give them a cool bath?"

We were sent to bed still dripping, and I dozed off almost at once. Wonderful dream landscapes glided past my parlor car window as I relaxed in a huge, overstuffed chair on a luxurious "Limited" speeding west.

♦   · ♦   ♦

After breakfast the next morning, I retrieved my clubs from the stairwell where I had laid them, shouldered the strap, and stepped into the garage. Through a north window I was startled to see what appeared to be a green snake slithering upwards, and I recognized the sound of a garden hose being pulled past the eaves. Out of doors, under a brilliant, cloudless azure sky, I shaded my eyes and peered at the carriage house roof. I could see my father making some repairs.

Good gosh, he's got a lawn sprinkler up there. A green and brass, double-armed lawn sprinkler stood on a wooden platform attached to the highest point on our roof, and a hose ran off down the north side. My father was no longer visible.

A swooshing sound of arching water, and the slap of the streams hitting the roof unevenly as the sprinkler turned, could be heard. I stood, gaping in disbelief at the sight. *Has he gone crazy? I hope that's not his idea! Ours will be the only house anywhere with a lawn sprinkler on its roof. What will people think? They'll think we're all loony, that's what! How awful, how simply awful!*

I hurried off as fast as I could, so that I wouldn't have to answer his query, *"Well, Bob, how you like that?"* On the way to the schoolyard, I looked surreptitiously into the yards as I passed. I didn't want anyone to whisper, *"There he goes; that's one of those crazy Twedts."*

I stayed away all day, what with golf and then going to the pool. When I returned for supper, the sprinkler was still running. I snuck upstairs without saying anything. Through the kitchen door I could hear Mother's voice.

"Oh, Nels! You dear, sweet man! It's been so cool in here today, really very comfortable. I can't thank you enough, dear."

"Well, Stella, when you let the kids go to bed wet last night to cool them off, I thought 'why wouldn't the same thing work up there'?" And then I heard only silence.

Opening the kitchen door quietly, I saw my parents kissing each other, and she was crying.

THE NEW SUIT

I t was nearly impossible to influence my parents' choices where my clothes were concerned, since the inevitable determinant was price. I knew that I could not hope to persuade them to my way of thinking unless I could somehow contribute the major portion of the cost. I had deposited the small gifts of money that I had received on past birthdays and holidays in a cast iron *Liberty Bell* bank. The coins made a curious clinking sound that bore slight relation to the value of the hoard and absolutely none to its availability. It was obvious that I would need far greater sums than these occasional gifts and my weekly allowance would provide. I needed a job!

Heretofore, I had received nickels and dimes for running errands. I began to actively solicit odd jobs that paid larger amounts. Then, by the proverbial stroke of fate, I was handed the chance to deliver a daily newspaper. *The St. Paul Pioneer Press*, oldest of the Twin Cities dailies, was trucked to Rochester for delivery before breakfast. It had a decidedly conservative stamp and was much prized by Rochester's elite. My 60 subscribers lived all across Pill Hill, so bicycle delivery was a real trial of strength, particularly when the heavy Sunday edition pancaked my front tire. The weekly profit from my joint venture with the publisher approached $3.00, not counting the chiselers. I was astonished at the huge pile of coins that was accumulating from this effort. By allowing The First National Bank to become its caretaker, I was left free to savor the growth of my small fortune in a green savings booklet, now an object of my parent's respect.

One Saturday morning in the early fall of 1939, I modeled the hated Jack Young suit coat for my mother, who was in the kitchen peeling potatoes.

"Mother, this coat is much too small! My wrists stick out like a scarecrow! I need a new suit. I've saved up almost thirteen dollars from my paper route and that ought to buy a swell looking one, even a tie, maybe shoes…" I trailed off, not wanting to get in too deep.

She wiped a lock of thick hair from her perspiring face, and looked at me quizzically, without answering.

"Can we at least go to Hanny's and see?" I persisted. I had already seen the suit that I wanted.

My argument must have been compelling, for later that day we went shopping. My father's agreement being crucial, Mother had asked him to come with us to Hanny's Men's Wear.

Marvin Hanenberger, called Hanny by his many friends, taught the senior boys' Sunday school class with gifted understanding of the adolescent male psyche. He had recently graduated, with a degree in business, from Rochester Junior College, where he had excelled in individual sports, avoiding the unkempt appearance and physical pain associated with team conflict. He was respected and admired by the boys, who believed that he was the worthy embodiment of collegiate sophistication.

On Sundays, after church, Hanny invited a few of the boys, including myself, to accompany him the short distance to the Weber and Judd Drugstore soda fountain. There, in the green and gold refinements of an Art Deco interior, we lounged stylishly on wire-back chairs at round marble-top tables. He treated each of us to a G and G, a tingling mixture of ginger ale and grape juice, served with a barkeep's aplomb. I luxuriated in these moments, feeling deliciously decadent.

When he opened his clothing store next to the Kahler Hotel on First Avenue, it was only a matter of time until it became a Mecca for Rochester's worldly-wise, young adults, including me. Hanny taught us to discriminate that which was merely faddish from clothes that had style, chic.

"Looking for a something snazzy, Bob?" Hanny smiled, sensing that, of the three, I would be the most susceptible to his sales efforts.

"I've got some really fine new designs, just in from New York." Briskly, he strode to a wall rack, and selected several suits in various styles and prices.

"Marvin, the boy really needs a new suit," Mother declared, while I busied myself with trying on the suit coats and posing before the full-length mirror. "But, he still hasn't reached his full height." She was introducing the need to economize on apparel that she was certain would soon be outgrown.

"Well, maybe, Stella," he replied, half agreeing with her. They stood appraising me, as if I were a racehorse at auction. "But I think he's probably gotten as tall as he's going to. And I'll bet it'll be a good long time yet before he fills out. Look at his father. There's not a man in Rochester that's as trim as Nels is."

"You've carried the same weight as long as I've known you, Nels," he said, turning toward my father, who had thus far said nothing,

"Yah, you ware right, Marvin. I got a pair of pants that I bought in Norway yust before I come hare, and I can still get in them!" Dad rocked back on his heels, hands in pockets, and grinned with pride. He did not realize that by the flattery, Marvin had already won his favor in the coming negotiations.

But Mother fully understood what had happened and interrupted her husband with an exasperated smile. "Nels, hush! Marvin doesn't want to hear about your waist size. We're talking about Bob!"

"Golly, feel how soft this is, Mother."

"That's an imported English flannel, Bob," Hanny said with some pride. The price tag on the coat sleeve was an astonishing $29.95, as much as for a good quality man's suit! All three of us gasped, to no surprise of Hanny, who now steered us to a lower-priced gabardine that I had already admired on a previous visit. It was spring green.

"Now that is a good choice," Hanny enthused. "This is real 100% gabardine. It will outwear that soft flannel but never get shiny. And, it's wrinkle resistant. Look at this hand." He caught up a piece of the sleeve, clenched it in his hand, and then let it fall free to immediately resume its original, smooth appearance. Though only $15.95, it would still exceed my savings. But with Hanny contributing the alterations at no cost and with an "advance" on my future paper route earnings from my parents, the purchase was made.

I had won—actually gotten what I wanted. I was in control of my own affairs—the awful obsolescence of my parent's opinions had been overturned and all because of my own money. I savored the power but could not see the responsibility that went with it.

THE NO-FAIL DANCE METHOD

When, at last, I had become a high school upperclassman, I was astonished to discover how very pleasant and attractive girls had become. They smiled in such a beguiling way, and their eyes spoke invitation. I devised ways to meet them and talk with them. Very often the subject was dancing, a social art that was a complete mystery to me. I needed to overcome this character blight.

Shortly after school resumed in the fall of 1939, I bought a pamphlet at Kling's Music Store entitled *Learn to Dance in the Privacy of Your Own Home—Fox-trot, Waltz, Tango, Rhumba—The Bernie Hazlett No Fail Method–Twenty Five Cents*. After purchasing the Hazlett instructions, I hurried home in mounting excitement, and unfolded the diagram of the fox trot on my bedroom floor. The first shoe pattern was in black; the rest were in outline and contained a number. I stepped my way through the numbered sequence, following the dotted lines. After that, whenever my parents left the house to visit friends or attend a movie, I would search the radio dial for music to hone my dancing skills.

"And now, direct from the Cafe Rouge, high atop the Hotel Pennsylvania in the heart of Manhattan, the NBC Blue Network brings you the delectable, toe-tapping music of Glenn Miller and his Orchestra," came the indolent, syrupy voice of the announcer. "What delightful ballad do you have for your eager fans, tonight, Glenn?"

"The boys and I are going to lead off with a new tune by Jerry Gray, Sid," was the reply. "Carl Sigman wrote the lyrics. I think it's a good danceable number. It's called 'Pennsylvania 6-5000.' All right boys, one, two, and three..."

As the bouncy swing music poured out of the speaker, oozing around my ankles, I stumbled about on the fox-trot diagram, bending over to see the numbers. Ultimately, I memorized each dance sequence until I could learn no more from Hazlett. But I still sensed his terpsichorean inadequacy, acutely and accurately. I closed my eyes, held my pillow in my arms, and imagined myself dancing in movie sequences that I had seen. I was riven with doubt. Nevertheless, I was determined to launch my new skills at the Homecoming Dance to be held in the high school gym after the Rochester—New Ulm football game, still several weeks away.

But first there was the matter of permission, since the dance was not scheduled to end until the unheard of hour of 11 P.M.! When I broached the subject with Mother one day after school, she exclaimed in apparent surprise, "Bobby, I didn't know you could dance."

"Golly, Mother," I dissembled, examining my shoe closely, "the gym coaches teach dancing at all the sock hops."

This was true as far as it went. Dance instruction was available at these shoeless, evil-smelling affairs held in the late afternoon, after pep rallies. Conceived as a support for the football team, they were a poor forum for lessons in the ballroom art. Those benighted males, who constituted the ranks of the rhythmically disadvantaged, were understandably shy of revealing their clumsiness, particularly before members of the opposite sex.

"Well," she said, "we'll have to see what your father has to say. Did you invite someone to go with you?" She gave *someone* a coy emphasis!

"No, I thought I'd probably meet people there that I could dance with." I used the word people so as to neutralize the subject.

"I had better iron your white shirt," she said, speculatively. Her musing was a clue that she would give permission for me to attend, and that my father, who usually followed her lead, would also assent. I was elated!

"Are you going to wear your fine suit with those clodhoppers you have on now?" Dad asked me later. He peered over his paper at the scuffed pair of Buster Brown sharkskin-toed shoes that I wore to school.

"Yes, I guess so." *What a question! He knows I've exhausted my savings on the new green gabardine suit.*

"We better go see Art," he said, smiling at Mother.

Nachreiner's Boot Shop, established in the first decade of the century, had always been located in the Masonic Temple Building, where it shared the ground floor with Weber and Judd Drug Store. When the old building was destroyed by fire in 1916, Arthur Nachreiner moved into the new Temple erected on the same site. As Rochester's acknowledged purveyor of Fine Boots & Shoes, he refused to demean himself by advertising in the public press. Conservative in politics, prudent with money, he relied upon gracious, personal service and a full inventory of quality merchandise to attract and hold his customers. In 1939, Nachreiner's continued to be the shoe store preferred by Rochester's most-discriminating residents

"Good morning, Nels," beamed Art, warmly. "And Stella too! What a pleasure to see you both! Isn't this a wonderful sunny day? What can I do for you fine folks this morning?"

Art's portly figure was neatly framed in his shop's doorway, like a lord at the portcullis gate waiting to greet honored guests. He was attired in a brown pinstripe linen suit, ecru silk vest from which a gold fob dangled. Gold pince-nez perched on his ruddy cherubic nose. From the light brown toupee to the ecru spats on brown kid shoes, his appearance confirmed his expertise in the artifices of gentlemanly grooming.

"Morning, Art," said Dad. Art Nachreiner and Nels Twedt were both 32nd degree Masons and they had spent the previous evening playing whist together amidst the cigar smoke and brown leather ambiance of the Lodge Hall. Art had won handily, Nels being an indifferent player. But each had enjoyed the convivial conversation immensely.

"Well, Art, my boy has got it into his head that he ware a dancer now. He ware over to Marvin Hanenberger to buy himself a fine new suit. Now I guess he needs new shoes to complete the picture." He breathed the sigh of the oppressed parent!

"Well, you've come to the right place, folks. I am sure you know that. Yes, indeed!" exclaimed Art, proudly.

While my parents continued the required introductory conversation, I wandered about the store examining the footwear on display. I tried to imagine myself wearing each of the different styles, without much success. Then I spotted the most beautiful pair of shoes I'd ever seen in a case against the wall. They were very expensive, costing $4.25.

"Aren't those beauties, my boy?" said Mr. Nachreiner, who had observed my browsing, even while conversing with my parents. "You would be mighty attractive to the ladies with those on your feet. Here, let me show them to you." He placed one of shoes in my hands. Made of pigskin, the shoe had a large, square toe, exaggerated moccasin-like stitching, leather soles and heels. It was mustard-yellow!

Judging from their deafening silence, my parents certainly did not agree with Art's aesthetic opinion.

"Bobby, dear, I think you need something more reserved to go with your new suit." Mother glanced knowingly at Art Nachreiner, who assented easily to perceived higher authority.

"Sit down, Bob. Let me take your shoe size."

I sat, removed my right shoe and disclosed a narrow, bony foot that was doing its level best to burst the bonds of a much-darned sock. My mother blushed but remained silent. Art completed his measurements, plunged into his stockroom, and returned with a half-dozen different pairs of shoes. He shoehorned each in turn upon my socked foot, all the while making noncommittal comments. During the process of "letting the customer sell himself," several of the styles met with my mother's enthusiastic approval and my father's less involved concurrence. But to me they were all dull as dishwater. I coveted the square-toed yellow shoes!

After purchasing the green suit, I was bankrupt. My only remaining weapon in the hoped-for acquisition of the yellow shoes was time. With considerable skill, I examined all the alternative styles that Art brought out, careful not to slow the process so much that I would anger my parents. Art was helpful, making inconclusive observations about each shoe style. I could see that Dad was becoming restless. He looked at his wristwatch, and wandered aimlessly among the display tables, handling shoes without seeing them. Under the influence of his restlessness, Mother became anxious and signaled the need to conclude.

"Pick the ones you like, Bobby," she said, looking down at the various unwanted styles, not realizing that this comment would open the floodgates.

"I like these best, Mother," I replied, indicating the yellow shoes with exquisite nonchalance so as not to betray my elation.

"That is a good choice, son," declared Art, easily. "Take them back to Knute and he'll wrap them for you." Then, with finesse, he turned to my father and opined, "These are well-made shoes, Nels, and easily worth the slightly higher price. I know he will get a lot of good wear out of them." And to my mother, "Your son has an eye for style Stella, he must get that from you." Mother smiled, ruefully.

I took the yellow shoes to the cramped cubicle at the rear of the store where Knute Amundson sat cross-legged, atop his work bench, awash in the aroma of burnt machine oil, newly tanned leather, stitching cord, and shoe polish. He was hunched over a pair of wing-tip oxfords and had removed his artificial leg, letting his stump project jauntily over the edge to let it breathe! In his early manhood, soon after arriving in America, he had been gravely injured in a Wisconsin sawmill. Unable to work as a lumberman any longer, he had been taken in by Art, who let him sleep in the small room in the rear of the store. He rarely left it now but lived a hermit's life, content within his memories. I loved the chance to talk with Knute and listen to his tales about the old country. As the fractured English circled about me, I imagined days long ago when Viking warriors ventured as far as Constantinople, Greenland, and even America, extending their trade and authority.

"Hi, Knute. Will you wrap these shoes for me?"

"Dot is a luffly shoe!" said Knute. "Where you going in those pretty ones. You got girl friend? I'll bet you got girl friend. She luffs you in dose, you bet!"

"They are pretty neat," I said, evading the question. "They're to go with my new suit. I'm going to wear them to a dance next Friday."

"Ja, you be *pen prins* at dot dans," smiled Knute at his young friend.

◆   ◆   ◆

With the approach of Homecoming, my confidence began to erode, and my nervousness became obvious to my sister. One evening, when we were doing the dinner dishes she rejected one of my plates with, "There's soap on this one. Rinse it off, please."

I examined the offender and could detect no telltale foam. "No there isn't. You need glasses!" I handed it back to her.

The scenario was repeated a few minutes later over a saucer. "What's the matter, Bob, your mind's not on your work," she teased.

"You just mind your Ps and Qs," I replied. "Those dishes are rinsed."

"Are not!"

"Are too."

"I'll tell Dad," she said!

"Hare, hare, what you doing there," my father's loud voice came from the depths of his favorite easy chair. "You kids be quiet now and do those dishes or your mother will be mad."

There was only silence from the kitchen. Both of us knew that our real concern was our father's anger, not our mother's. I bent myself to the dishpan, paying close attention to the rinsing.

On the evening of the dance, I stayed for an inordinate amount of time in the bathroom, "Come on, are you going to spend all night in there," Nancy teased, banging on the door.

"Just a minute, willya? Keep your shirt on. I'm almost done." I emerged amid an overpowering aura of Brilliantine and Bay Rum, and raced past my sister, bare legs flying beneath a freshly pressed white shirt. Closing the door to my room, I finished dressing and gave my thick, black hair one more fillip before returning to be surveyed by my admiring audience. Attired in the new green gabardine suit, mustard-yellow shoes, white shirt, and green and yellow plaid tie I resembled a topsy-turvy forsythia in blossom.

Trailed by oohs and aahs I started for the door.

"You be home hare by eleven o'clock, you hare," Dad said, emphasizing the hour.

"Yessir," I said, not wanting ruffle his feathers.

The Rochester High School gymnasium had been transformed into a smallish version of a Busby-Berkely set. Twisted crepe-paper streamers plunged and looped the school colors about, nearly obliterating the basketball backboards and gallery seats in a dimly lit fantasy of red and black. Pete Parker and His Polka Pals blew mediocre renditions of swing favorites from a raised platform beneath the home basket. A background buzz of conversation enveloped the waxed dance floor upon which couples circled in a faintly discernible aroma of perspiration and Evening in Paris perfume. Joining the first rank of singles, hemming the sidelines, I felt awash in anticipation and anxiety, desire and dread. Bernie Hazlett's No-Fail Method had deserted me. Yet I clung to the unlikely hope that I would find an attractive dance partner—someone who might rekindle my home-taught dancing skills, to the astonishment of all those in attendance, and Pete Parker as well.

While I scrutinized the ranks of idle sideliners with increasing hopelessness, Martin Adson and his date, Dorothy Eusterman, disengaged themselves from the syncopating mass of indistinguishable couples on the dance floor, and glided smoothly towards me. Marty had just spurred the Rochester Rockets on to a heart stopping 13 to 12 football victory over the New Ulm Unicorns before hundreds of enthusiastic parents. Fresh from the showers, his countenance wore the laurel of victory and the plaudits of his classmates with ebullient ease. When he had come close enough to take in my attire from head to toe, Marty smiled broadly, and turned Dorothy so that they both faced me in an open dance step. "Hey, Bob, did you forget your shoes. Looks like you put on the boxes by mistake," he jeered, loudly.

I was struck dumb with astonishment. Why was my stylistic judgment, so dearly acquired, and with so much thought and planning, an object of derision? My deep scarlet blush was mercifully hidden from view by the dim lighting. I beat a hurried retreat from imagined stares of contempt and went out to the comforting loneliness of the cold night air. Walking slowly home in bitter confusion, I raged at that crazy old Mr. Art Nachreiner who had encouraged my choice of the yellow shoes.

My mother was still in the kitchen when I returned home around nine o'clock. "Bobby, why are you home so early," she asked in surprise. "We thought the dance lasted until eleven. What's the matter, dear? Are you all right?"

"Yes, Mother. There just wasn't anyone there that I wanted to dance with," I said, crestfallen.

"What brings you home now, eh? We thought you would be out late," came my father's voice from the living room. And then, more strident, "Did something happen?" There were rustling sounds from his newspaper, as if he were preparing to enter the kitchen.

My mother, who sensed immediately that my hurt was emotional, not physical, called, "Sit still, Nels. Nothing is wrong. The boy just didn't enjoy the dance and came home early, that's all." Silence from the living room.

I went to my room and hid the offending shoes on a closet shelf in a box of my childhood toys. My parents never mentioned them again.

GONE WITH THE WIND

The embarrassing events at the Homecoming Dance had exposed the folly of depending upon Bernie Hazlett to teach the art, much less the artifices, of ballroom dancing. My humiliation had been so complete that I sought refuge in social isolation, at least as far as the opposite sex was concerned. With reluctance I determined on a manly, celibate life. As fall turned into winter, I made no further sallies into Rochester's teen-age social whirl, but spent my idle hours reading. My father took little note of this momentous change in my destiny, but Mother, who was far more cognizant of her children's moods, divined that something was troubling her eldest. One Saturday afternoon she came into my room to investigate.

"Bobby, dear, don't you have anything else to do?" she said, her voice casual, controlled. "You can't spend all your time buried in a book. Why don't you go over and see one of your friends?"

"But, Mother, I like to read! I learn all kinds of stuff. Anyway, you and Dad are always telling me that education is the key to success!" I said in defense.

"I know, dear, but there is more to life than what you can read in books! I thought surely you would be going to parties, and having fun with your classmates. Don't you know any girls?"

There it is—girls! Lots of guys got along just fine without girls! What about Prince Valiant…Lindberg and his plane…Charles Darwin…and Buffalo Bill…Geez, all kinds of famous guys!

"Good gosh, Mom, all they ever do at those parties is put records on the Victrola and dance, and…I'm no good at dancing!" *What would an ole girl want to dance with me for? I'd prob'ly step all over her!*

"I thought you told me that you had learned to dance at school, at the sock hops," she said with surprise.

"Noooo, I just didn't seem to get the hang of it. But that's okay," I said, playing the martyr.

"Well, we'll just see about that," she replied, and left the room.

Now what is she going to do. Tell Dad? Gosh, why can't they leave me alone?

My mother made inquiries among her friends and acquaintances, the ladies of the Eastern Star and of the Ladies Aid Society. She learned that a new dancing instructor had come to town, and was already highly regarded among the parents of her growing number of pupils. She taught the entrechat and pas de deux to budding ballerinas, polka and schottische to the elderly, jitterbug to young adults, and ballroom dancing to highschoolers with two left feet. Mothers of socially inhibited and ungainly youngsters reported that this teacher had, "done wonders for our William!" Mother was pleased with these reports, and convinced my father that an investment in terpsichorean tutoring would be good for me. He apparently saw the prospect of my getting out more as an aid to domestic peace and quiet.

Mother broke the news after dinner one evening. Dad sat in his chair, hidden behind his newspaper, but by his presence gave assent to her message.

"Bobby, some of the mothers tell me that a wonderful new dancing teacher has come to Rochester. A lot of their kids are taking lessons from her and they really like her. A new class is starting tomorrow after school, and your father and I think you should attend."

"Aw, Mom, not dancing lessons! I don't need dancing lessons. Only sissies take dancing for gosh sake!"

"Mrs. Dallman told me that her son was going to take lessons. I don't think you would call your friend Jack Dallman a sissy!" Jack Dallman was a friendly extrovert, loved camping and the outdoors. He was an athlete, on the track squad and gym team. We had been good friends from our first meeting at Sunday school. Jack had integrity and courage—was certainly anything but a sissy!

"Well, no. But golly, Mom! Do I have to?"

"You be quiet! Listen to your Mother and do what she tells you!" This came from behind the newspaper.

"Yessir," I said in defeat.

"Dear, it's not a question of have to, it's a question of knowing how to behave and carry yourself on the dance floor. It's part of being a gentleman!"

The discussion was over.

◆   ◆   ◆

Miss Adele Hughes, the driving force behind the Hughes School of Dance, was a vivacious, petite woman in her late thirties. Her black hair, worn shoulder length, set off the whiteness of her complexion, giving her the appearance of a china doll. Her pale blue eyes, twinkling beneath high-arched brows, seemed to encourage her smile, which was wide and confident. She commanded respect from her pupils, who were won over instantly by her sprightly, positive attitude, that encouraged even the most backward and clumsy boy in the class. I loved her at once.

The ballroom class, held each Thursday for an hour after school, met in rented rooms in the Mayo Civic Auditorium. Dedicated earlier in 1939 to the memory of Dr. W. W. Mayo, the father of the famous physicians, the building was a multi-use, T-shaped structure housing a sports arena, a theater, the American Legion clubrooms and the School of Dance. The latter met in an oversize meeting room that was decorated in the speedy, Spartan, Art Deco style in which the Auditorium had been erected. Light was admitted through glass blocks on the south side, chairs ringed the walls. There was a long mirror and ballet bar on the north wall, but the most important fixtures in the room were a studio piano and a record player.

Miss Hughes' lessons began with motivation, preceded with encouragement, and always ended with reassurance. When the basic steps for each dance lesson had been demonstrated in slow time, she would repeat them with each member, leading or following as required. Those students who had caught on were encouraged to dance as couples. And so we learned to waltz, fox trot, tango and conga, always varying the orchestra and music to avoid the pitfalls of memorization.

"Bob, you have a natural sense of rhythm!" Miss Hughes said, as we whirled about the floor to the strains of the Blue Danube one afternoon. It was difficult for me to concentrate when holding her tantalizing body. Her breast pressed softly into my right side, her back swayed gently beneath my hand, and her perfume swirled past my nostrils. It was difficult to formulate any but the most passionate thoughts. Her voice awakened me, "Now class, and listen while I play for you the music in next week's lesson..."

The only student who was shorter than Miss Hughes, over whom she actually towered, was my high school classmate, Betsy Faber. Betsy was a lively brunette, with wavy auburn hair that fell below her shoulders, wide-set brown eyes, dimples, and a starlet's inviting smile. She was as warm and gay as a rainbow in spring, a good dancer, and the object of an older student's affection. He had that air of callow suavity that high school seniors everywhere affect, and though Betsy adored his attentiveness, her pursuer had a serious fault. He was a mediocre dancer.

Perhaps sensing the need to dampen my inappropriately upwelling ardor, Miss Hughes paired me with Betsy in an exhibition of light-footed talent. The introduction was inspired. Betsy and I, shaped by egotism and attraction working in tandem, became a twosome, excelling in every dance form for the sheer delight of it. Our appreciation of one another soon overflowed the confines of the Dancing School and became a recognized dating phenomenon among our classmates. I was especially pleased with myself, for this was the first time that a relationship based on ardor for a member of the opposite sex had been success-ful.

In November, Betsy introduced me to the illicit passions of Margaret Mitchell's heroine, the tortured Scarlet O'Hara. One day, in Latin class, she leaned across the aisle and directed me to place *Gone with the Wind* within the pages of my upturned copy of Virgil. Her note said that all her friends were reading the book, that it really expressed her own feelings so well—about what I didn't know. And thus, buoyed by the heady mix of war, destruction, and rapine I plodded through the entirety of the novel.

Just after Christmas, the movie version of Mitchell's novel, shot in glorious Technicolor, and so lengthy that it required an intermission, premiered to enthusiastic crowds in Atlanta, the central city in its action. Release to local cinematic houses followed, and in Rochester the film was scheduled to open at the Chateau-Dodge in early February.

The Chateau was Rochester's best motion picture theater. It showed only first-run films, favored by my mother and her friend Elsie Young, and dismissed by Nancy and me as kissie movies. Jeannette Mac-Donald and Nelson Eddy, Fred Astaire and Ginger Rogers, Myrna Loy and Bill Powell made frequent appearances on its silver screen. The Chateau was glorious in the palace tradition, being designed to mimic the courtyard of an Italian-baroque village. It had a plethora of columns, porches, balconies, tapestries, stuffed doves and, best of all, a ceiling painted to resemble the evening sky, replete with twinkling stars.

I asked Betsy for a date to attend the opening of the Mitchell epic amidst the ornate splendors of the Chateau, and she accepted, with apparent delight. Because of its length, the film was shown only once each evening; there was a matinee performance on weekends. I purchased assigned seats for the next Saturday performance, and because I had never had access to the family car, we walked to the theater. Totally engrossed from the time the lights dimmed until the final credits, I sensed Betsy's alternating emotions by the varying pressures of her small, moist hand in mine.

Afterwards, we discussed the movie's faithfulness to the novel's characters and plot over double-chocolate sodas in the off-lobby Sweet Shoppe.

"Boy, that was the best picture I've ever seen," I said, for openers.

"Oh, I thought it was simply wonderful," Betsy gushed. "Bob, do you think that Rhett will ever come back to her?" she asked, with undisguised hopefulness.

"I don't think so, Betsy. When he walked out on her with that 'I don't give a damn' speech, I think it was for good."

"But don't you think she had changed, finally knew that Rhett was the only man who had loved her, totally...and completely!"

"Well, probably, but it was too late. She'd spent so many years mooning over that wishy-washy Ashley, that Rhett just got fed up and cussed at her. He musta been real sore about all the nasty treatment Scarlett gave him to have done that. Real men don't ordinarily cuss a woman," I said, self-righteously.

"Oh, I wish that I could write like Margaret Mitchell. I'd start a sequel right away," she said.

"I wouldn't hold my breath!"

We discussed the film for days afterward, divined multiple endings for the "don't give a damn" speech of Mr. Gable. It was apparent that I had made a great coup by taking her to see the film.

My dancing lessons continued into the spring. Miss Hughes divided her students into basic and advanced sections, meeting at different times. Betsy and I were members of the latter. Our group focused on more complex steps that give flair and finesse to the dance routines we had learned earlier. Betsy and I became very adept ballroom dancers, complementing and supporting each other, admired on the dance floor. I was delighted and proud. From wallflower and butt of my classmates contempt to suave ballroom sophisticate in a matter of months! It was a heady transformation.

◆   ◆   ◆

The Junior-Senior Prom was always held in May of each year, sufficiently early so that the excitement it always generated would dissipate before final exam week. Everyone even remotely aware of the rituals of teen age socializing had procured a date for the dance. Couples, like Betsy and I, that dated regularly were off limits to singles that were prowling about in the social pond.

As Prom night approached, the various working committees charged with responsibility for hiring the band, arranging for an intermission entertainment, decorating the gym, printing posters and prom programs, and conducting the grand march worked with increasing frenzy. Girls spent hours in confidential discussions about their formals, those who made their own worrying that their dresses would appear tawdry when compared with the gowns of those whose parents could afford to buy them. Very few of the boys owned or rented formal wear, and would simply wear a suit and tie.

Betsy hinted that her gown, made by her mother, would be something spectacular, truly unique. It was apparent even to a dimwit that she was dying to reveal its secrets, but I told her that I would rather be surprised, and to wait until I called for her the evening of the prom. I did ask, of course, what was the predominant color, in order to purchase a becoming corsage.

"Welllll," she said. "If you must know, it will be mainly a bright red, with touches of white. I guess you would call it scarlet!" she said with a mysterious smile.

"Golly, I can hardly wait to see you in it," I replied, thinking already that such a gown would need one of the newfangled wrist corsages in red and pink sweetheart rosebuds mixed with baby's breath. I hurried off to place the order at Fiksdal Flowers.

"What'll it be, Bob?" Mr. Fiksdal asked. "I'll bet you're looking for a corsage for Friday night. Who's the lucky woman?"

I described the situation; he nodded in agreement with my suggestion for a wrist corsage.

"Listen, Mr. Fiksdal. Betsy Faber is a small girl and she's got really small wrists. Can you make me something really stylish—on a small bracelet?"

"Don't worry, Bob. This will be the most beautiful presentation at the Prom. Leave it entirely to me! Where shall we deliver it?" And he wrote down Betsy's address.

On Friday, Prom night, I had dressed early in my green gabardine suit, and my school Oxfords, that I had brought to dazzling brilliance by zealous polishing. Consumed with nervous anticipation, I barely touched my dinner.

"Bobby, you haven't eaten a bite! Aren't you feeling well, dear?" queried my mother.

"I'm fine, Mother. Just not hungry, I guess."

"Bob's going out with a midget!" teased Nancy.

"Oh, shut up! She's just petite!"

"Bobby! Is that any way to talk to your sister?"

"Oh! I'm sorry," I said without conviction.

I was not yet permitted to drive the family car, but my father had volunteered as chauffeur. At last Dad folded his newspaper and said, with some amusement, "Well, Bob, come on, we go get your sweetie!"

"Now Bobby, you behave yourself! Mrs. Faber is a friend of mine!" admonished Mother, though what her friendship for Betsy's mother had to do with anything was beyond me.

"Yes, Mother," I said, with a sigh.

It was not far to the Faber residence. In fact, Betsy and I had always walked on other occasions. But tonight the girls were in formals and it would not do for an assured gentleman like me to walk to the dance. I was secretly pleased, and looked forward to snuggling with Betsy in the back seat!

Mrs. Faber, who opened the front door, was a jolly, good-natured woman, with a sunny smile, a rosy complexion, and was diminutive like her daughter. She invited Dad and me to come in, but he preferred to wait in the car. "Betsy will be down in a moment, Bob," she said. "Won't you be seated in the living room?"

"Betsy, dear. Bob Twedt is here," she called up the stairwell.

Betsy appeared on the upper landing and stepped slowly down the stairs, for dramatic effect.

I rose from my chair, thunderstruck, agape in wordless dismay! Betsy was dressed like a diminutive Scarlet O'Hara. Her dress was flaming red, as was the wide-brimmed hat that hid her lovely wavy hair. She wore white pantaloons, trimmed in lace, and black patent leather slippers. The skirt flared on wire hoops—wider than she was tall!

"Isn't she lovely, Bob," prompted Mrs. Faber.

"Yeyees," I stammered, "just lovely."

"Have a good time now, you two," Mrs. Faber said, and opened the door.

Good time! Oh, my gosh! How can she ever dance in that get-up? I'll have to bend over double just to reach her! We're going to look absolutely foolish. Everyone will laugh at me. My chances for being the best dancer in the whole school are gone—absolutely gone!

My father got out of the car when he saw us coming and opened the rear door for Betsy, trying valiantly not to laugh. When she sat down, the hoops flew up in front of her face, blocking her vision. With legs encased in the heavily starched pantaloons, her feet would not touch the floor, and her skirt took up the whole rear seat!

Dad closed the door quickly and said, "I don't believe there ware room for you in the back, Bob. You'd better sit up in front with me!"

Despite my misgivings, Betsy and I had a good time at the prom. Of course, we could not dance cheek-to-cheek, but we had learned from long experience to anticipate each other's dance movements, and didn't miss a beat, even at arms length!

DOWN UNDER

My sister and I believed that our father could do anything, and do it far better than any other man. We accepted his unparalleled skill as a driver even before we were invited to ride in his automobile. In my early childhood, when I saw him at his bench, using his shiny steel tools, I was awestruck. I very much wanted to be initiated into the mysteries of their use, but he discouraged all my approaches.

"Hare! Hare! What you doing there!" he would cry out in exasperation when I examined one of his tools. "Stop playing with things on the bench. Get away from there, before you get your clothes greasy. Mother will have a fit if that happens!"

He treated me kindly, but with anxious strictness, and before long I discovered that the bonds of love and affection between us did not extend to the world of machines and their workings.

With the exception of game-bird hunting, my father showed little interest in sports. He had never tossed a ball, or played games with me, leaving such activities entirely to my peers. As a result, I never learned the ways of competition and confrontation in a secure arena where mistakes were not greeted with contempt.

Nevertheless, he was proud of my quick wit and as a result, I strove always to excel in my schoolwork. My reward for that effort was the keen pleasure of hearing him praise his son to other men, often in my presence.

"Yah, Calvin, that boy of mine is smart as a whip," my father would boast to the pharmacist at Weber and Judd's Drugstore. "Yust yesterday he came home with a 95 in arithmetic. What you think of that?"

"It was 98, Dad."

"You hare, Calvin—98!"

Dad at his Bench

"That is fine, Nels. Mighty fine. You will see him in the White House one day, I bet," Calvin Berg replied. It was an innocent time when such an achievement was seen as a verification of intellect, perseverance and honesty!

And then, a new boy, Johnny Berkman's age, moved into the neighborhood. Bayard Horton's family was from Virginia. His father, a thin-faced, quiet man with courtly manners and an aristocratic demeanor, was a neurologist at the Mayo Clinic. Mrs. Horton's gracious charm and obvious, sincere kindliness won my heart at once. There were two well-behaved younger children. Bayard was like neither of these. He was shorter than Johnny, and had a slight, wiry frame, surprising strength and agility. His thin black hair could not hide a high, domed forehead, wide-set merry eyes, and two jug ears. A gum-chewing, wise-cracking prankster, he had a brilliant mind and loved machinery, especially the shiny green Harley Davidson motorcycle that his father had not the stomach to deny him.

Johnny loved Bayard's bizarre sense of fantasy and humor. Their friendship seemed to eclipse the relationship that Johnny and I had enjoyed for as long as either of us could remember.

My father recognized that Bayard had an unusually keen understanding of engines and mechanics. They developed a strong liking for one another. Dad spoke to him of the machinery that he so loved and Bayard enjoyed the role of equal. It was difficult to conceal my jealous, inner rage. I was simply devastated that Bayard now enjoyed the relationship with my father that I had always longed for. Bayard, in turn, sensed my dislike, an attitude that he had often encountered with other boys, and he treated me with condescending raillery.

A fortuitous event brought Johnny, Bayard and my father together in a joint endeavor. It began in the spring of 1939, when Dr. Berkman purchased a new outboard motor for the trolling boat that he kept at the family cottage at Cedar Beach on Lake Zumbro, a few miles north of Rochester. Johnny acquired the old motor. It was loud, cumbersome, and heavy, with a single cylinder that produced but two and one-half horsepower. Even so, Johnny and Bayard hoped that it might be capable of propelling a light, step-bottom boat at much improved speed. They consulted my father.

To my dismay, Dad welcomed their questions and soon the three had torn the motor down to its constituent parts for overhaul. My father was enthusiastic, helping them understand both the motor's workings, and how its power could be improved. At his suggestion, they replaced the head gasket with a single sheet of copper, hammered thin, to increase compression. I watched them, pretending interest and excitement, hoping they would fail, yet knowing that success would follow inevitably from Dad's tutelage.

During the previous winter months, Bayard and Johnny had constructed a one-man hydroplane in Horton's basement, where Bayard had a well-equipped woodworking shop. The frame was made from lightweight pine, the prow, stern, and step from thin plywood. For the rest of the hull and deck they applied a veneer of balsa wood. The boat was so light that one person could lift it with ease. Their major concern was whether they had properly calculated the hull's displacement, and whether the loaded craft could be trimmed.

The two boat-builders planned to test both propositions on the waters of the lake that had formed behind a dam thrown across the Zumbro River to generate power for an early-day Rochester. As the reputation of the Mayo Clinic and Rochester's population grew simultaneously, the generating plant's capacity was soon outstripped. After that, it was relegated to providing lake dwellers with meager illumination. The summer cottagers were attracted to the lake primarily for the fishing, water recreation, and cool forested surroundings.

The light green leaves of spring gossiped softly, and the warm sun flashed off the mirrored surface of the lake on a warm, calm day in May. Slipping repeatedly on the dew-wet grass of the sloping lawn in front of Berkman's cottage, Johnny and Bayard struggled to carry both boat and motor down to the boat dock. Johnny waded into the still, cold lake to steady the motor; Bayard clamped it to the stern. When

Johnny squeezed into the cockpit, the boat trimmed nicely, its stern well down, but not shipping water.

A single snap of the starter rope and the motor came to life, shrouding boat and driver with clouds of oily, blue exhaust. Johnny gingerly advanced the accelerator, and the motor's muffled staccato became a steady drone. He guided the boat out into the lake, increased the accelerator sharply, and the boat leapt forward, rising nicely up on its step. It turned in a wide arc and returned to the dock.

"Wow, you looked really keen out there," cried Bayard, running forward to catch the prow.

"She rose up on the step just like we thought she would. I can't wait to cut her loose," Johnny said.

"Take her up easy," cautioned Bayard, "and don't cut her too sharp, or she'll ship water on you!"

"Okay, gotcha!" Johnny turned back to the business at hand.

Bayard ran up the lawn toward the front of the cottage, where he had a good view of the lake to the north toward the dam.

Johnny was out of sight to the south. Then Bayard heard the motor roar. Shading his eyes against the reflected brilliance of the morning sun, he peered in the direction of the sound.

Johnny, hunched forward behind the windscreen, gripped the steering wheel in both hands. The boat had risen well up on its step, and was just skimming the surface. It was a grand and beautiful sight, a wonderful reward for all the hours of hard work that had gone into its construction. Roaring past Bayard's vantage point, trailing spray and exhaust fumes, Johnny could neither see him excitedly waving nor hear his wild yells.

Suddenly, the hydroplane's forward motion ceased and it foundered. The bow pointed skyward, the stern submerged, silencing the motor. Johnny swam free and the craft sank from view. He was a good swimmer and made rapidly for the bank.

Johnny had hit a small floating branch, and it had torn a gash below the water line for the entire length of the balsa wood hull, just missing him. It had all happened in an instant, the boat filling and sinking quickly by the stern. He was crushed over the failure of their grand conception and by the abrupt loss of the motor that he and Bayard had so lovingly overhauled.

When I heard their story later, I expressed relief because Johnny was safe, but laughed inwardly with sweet revenge because their creation had suffered such an ignominious catastrophe. Angry over the perceived loss of my father's affection, I thought, *it serves them right!*

Johnny spent hours that summer diving at the site of the sinking, but recovered nothing. The water was too muddy and too deep for an unaided swimmer. Bayard rode out to the cottage on his motorcycle to offer encouragement, including the proposal that he and Johnny build a bigger and better boat—one that was submersible! When I heard the idea, I couldn't believe my ears. I felt like hooting in derision, but checked myself.

Shortly after resuming high school in the fall, Bayard and Johnny laid the submarine's keel in the Horton's basement. The boat would measure 15 ft. in length, with a 4-ft. beam. Both keel and deck, topped by a 2-ft. conning tower, would be flat. The sides, made of tongue and groove flooring would be tapered to a prow at stem and stern. Rectangular pieces of window glass were installed in each of four faces of the diamond shaped conning tower. With generous rope and tar caulking, they believed the joints would be watertight.

As the winter wore on and the boat began to assume its final shape, I became as excited as the two boat builders did. Even though not privileged to take part in its construction, I paid frequent visits to the basement dry dock and pestered the other two with questions. I sensed that Bayard's sarcastic answers were laced with hyperbole, but that merely served to spur further queries.

"How's it going to submerge?" I asked, peering at the galvanized diving planes, permanently fixed at a downward angle.

"Are ya blind? Can't ya see those planes there, kid? We're gonna go down as smooth as down yer kiddy slide," he said, referring to the now unused childhood playthings in my yard.

"No you're not. Where's the motor? They have electric motors in real submarines because gasoline engines need air." I knew this was true from reading my encyclopedia.

"Don't worry about that. We're goin' to get air down there with this here hose." With that he produced a garden hose to which a galvanized funnel, surrounded by a ring of cork, had been attached.

"You expect to get air for an engine with that!"

"You betcher life we will. Only *we're* goin' to be the power plant! See this propeller shaft. See that crank on the other end. Well, one of us is gonna turn that crank and send her forward while the other peers and steers. Peers and steers! Yuck! Yuck! The hose is to get air down there for us!"

"You're crazy," I said. "You guys will pass out from your own stink."

"Mind yer beeswax, kid. It's gonna work. You'll see."

In April of 1940, the boat was completed. Bayard adjusted its displacement with cast-iron sash weights so that the conning tower would project just six inches above the surface of the water.

On the day of its christening, the builders assembled neighborhood boys to help them maneuver the submarine from the basement. After much huffing and puffing, skinning of knuckles, and even some forbidden epithets, it was plain to all that the boat's dimensions prevented its passage through the door.

"Criminy, how could we be so dumb?" complained Johnny, angry and embarrassed at the same time.

"Now, don't get yer water hot, Johnny me boy," Bayard replied, hopefully. "There's more 'n one way to skin a cat! If we can't get her out the door, let's try the window!"

While the volunteers stood by, they removed the sashes from a bay window, but found that they were still an inch shy of their goal. On the sidelines, some embarrassed giggling, and a few derisive catcalls arose.

"Better get a horse!"

"Why 'n' cha flood the basement!"

"Try a shoe horn!"

"Shut up, you wiseacres," snorted Bayard. "We got one more trick up our sleeves."

With dexterous nail pulling, the window casement went the way of the sashes, and the hostage set free. Everyone cheered and Bayard hurried about supervising, beaming, and bantering about the future accomplishments of their marvelous creation.

During all the alterations, Mrs. Horton remained smilingly calm, confident in her clever son's ultimate resolution of the launching dilemmas. In fact, when the boat was finally placed upon blocks in the yard, she covered its deck with a luncheon cloth, and set out milk and cookies for all the volunteers. Dr. Horton was equally calm, his pressing medical duties preventing his appearance at the boat's resurrection.

The next day, the two boat builders loaded the submarine on a trailer and towed it to the cottage. Struggling, they dragged their creation onto a rusting child's wagon, poised at the top of a ramp of discarded boards leading down the sloping lawn to the water's edge. Retaining ropes secured the wagon and its precious load to convenient elms.

"Johnny, take hold of your rope and let her down easy when I give the signal," directed Bayard.

"Okay, tell me when you're ready. Count it out!"

Neither had foreseen that the submarine's accelerating velocity would multiply its apparent weight. Skidding, sliding, and then running beside the rumbling vehicle as it moved ever faster down the slope the two friends shouted at each other in vain, "Hold her! Hold her!"

They lost all control, and could only watch with mute anxiety as the boat plunged into the water, floated ponderously out into the center of the lake, and submerged steadily and irretrievably beneath the surface!

ON THE ROAD TO SALEM CORNERS

My father drove the big green Oldsmobile home from Detroit in late December of 1935. When he entered the garage and sounded the horn, his wife and children rushed downstairs with eager anticipation.

Mother clasped her hands to her breast, and cried, "Oh, it's just beautiful, Nels."

Nancy danced around it waving her arms and singing, "We've got a new car! We've got a new car!"

Mother, Nancy, and I with the Olds

I could hardly believe my eyes; it was so gorgeous, sitting there amongst the inevitably black Balfour sedans. The magnificent conveyance was a completely unexpected Christmas gift for my mother from Uncle Leo Madsen. Showing disdain for the depression styling that had enshrouded all the Detroit products, our new car was a gorgeous creation with smooth streamlining, a split windshield, and great tear-drop headlights. Much more than mere mudguards, the fenders draped the wheels artfully, revealing nary a hint of the practical chassis beneath. At the rear of the car, the trunk was actually a part of the body, and not simply an attachment strapped to a bumper rack. An Art Deco hood ornament, thrust proudly forward, proclaimed the power beneath, and promised great speed.

By careful economizing, my parents, had managed to purchase a cheap, used car, but they gladly adjusted to this much grander automobile. Though it was hers, my mother never learned to drive the new car, but simply accepted my father's driving experience as unspoken license to chauffeur her about. On those rare occasions that she overindulged this privilege, Dad would sigh, slump his shoulders and complain, "Stella, you think I got nothing else to do but take you everyvare?"

I longed to drive the Oldsmobile, and yearned for the day when I could "casually" offer my buddies a ride. Meanwhile, I determined to ingratiate myself with my parents by preserving the car's shiny newness. In a curious twist, I became the self-appointed lackey to the machine. I applied a dust cloth after it had been driven, vacuumed and washed it weekly, and frequently waxed it, a tiresome, daylong process requiring two paste applications, and hand buffing. When finished, my arms were limp as cold spaghetti but I could see my own reflection in the doors!

Mother was pleased by my zealous diligence. "Bobby, dear, the car looks lovely. Doesn't it, Nels?"

"Yah, it ware a good yob, Bob," he replied, without elaboration, making plain that my efforts were something he expected me to do anyway.

"I think you work too hard, dear," Mother said. "I don't want you to overdo." She had a concerned maternal expression, a mix of love and worry.

"I guess I can keep our car clean, all right," I replied, proudly. "I sure wouldn't want anyone to see her muddy." *Nosirree, this car is going to stay brand new 'til I get my hands on the wheel!*

I began to observe my father's driving actions much more closely and to question him about the principles and art of driving a car. I memorized his motions during the gear-shifting operation, and mimicked the sequence while seated alone in my room. However, without ever having a chance to actually put them into practice, I learned little in the way of practical steps, but much of the lore of the automobilist.

"Bob," he admonished, "never turn left into a filling station. You got to cross traffic twice, once to go in and once to go out. You're yust asking for trouble!"

"Steering is the most important thing. Without brakes, even without lights, you still can steer out of danger. Without steering you got nothing!"

"When you clean your windshield in a filling station, use the wet rag to wipe your headlights. If your lamps are not bright, a clear windshield won't help you!"

"Don't yam on your brakes to stop quick, especially in winter. You pump your brakes so the car won't skid!"

"Put your hands on the steering wheel at 10 o'clock and 4 o'clock. You can turn quick each way and your right hand is close to the gear shift!"

It was plain that Dad's first interest was in anticipating and avoiding problems that could threaten his command of the machine.

But these conversations and my efforts to be his eager helper did nothing to hasten the day when I should be seated behind the wheel of the Olds. Meanwhile, like my mother and sister, I continued to be a passenger.

◆   ◆   ◆

In 1940 the requirements for obtaining a motor vehicle operator's license in the State of Minnesota were quite minimal. I had long committed them to memory by the eve of my sixteenth birthday, Independence Day. Putting them into action was another matter. My father seemed content with my non-driving status and made no mention of applying for a driver's license. Taking matters into my own hands, I posted the brief application form, proof of my age, and the required fee of thirty-five cents, to the Department of State. Then I waited, strategically placed by our post box each morning at 11 o'clock, when our mailman, Otto Dahlgren, regularly made his appearance.

"Good Morning, Mr. Dahlgren," I said. "Sure is a swell day today, isn't it?

"Yah, Bobby, and a fine morning it is. But still no mail for you!"

How does he know I'm looking for a letter?

One morning several weeks later he smiled at me and said, "Bobby, you got lucky." He handed me a beige post card with the printed signature of Mike Holm, Secretary of State. It said that Mr. Robert Madsen Twedt was legally entitled to operate a non-commercial passenger vehicle on all the state's public roads and highways. *Yippee, now all I've got to do is show this to Dad; if the State of Minnesota says I can drive, he should too!* But the time for asking never seemed to come around.

I continued to ponder the problem of permission. Wandering down the driveway one morning, hands in pockets, absentmindedly scuffing the occasional stone, I heard Johnny Berkman yell from across the street.

"Hey, Bob, wanna go for a drive." He was sitting behind the wheel of his father's new Pontiac coupe. It was a deep navy blue in color—suitable for making house calls.

"You bet! Wait up," I replied, ran across the street, jumped the low barberry hedge around his lawn, and opened the passenger door.

Johnny was not alone. Billy Furlow, four years younger than his idol, occupied the narrow rear seat. Billy lived in the corner house formerly occupied by the Hansen brothers, Leck and Mike. His father, an attorney, had purchased the home when Helga and the boys had gone south—to sunny Iowa.

"Where'll we go? How 'bout Mayowood?" Johnny queried. The estate of Dr. Charles H. Mayo was about four miles from town. A large tract, it was replete with fenced exotica: buffalo, diminutive Japanese deer, peacocks, and ostriches. However, from the vantage point of the county road that sliced through the grounds we would be lucky to catch even a glimpse of these creatures.

"Why not drive out to Balfour's farm?" I said. "I know how to get in the main house. There's a keen billiard table in the game room!"

"Okay, swell. We'll take the Salem road out past Baihly's farm," Johnny agreed.

He accelerated sedately out of his driveway, left past the Furlow house, then south toward the country. We passed all the familiar landmarks: Doc Prendergast's, Bobby Faust's, the By-Low Grocery, and Edison School. A few more blocks and we had reached the city limits, marked unofficially by the Plummer House with its curious round tower, perched on the crown of Pill Hill.

At the edge of town, the residential street became a narrow, gravel township road that meandered along the course of the South Fork of the Zumbro River. The Scandinavian immigrants, who had settled the fertile river valley in the mid-nineteenth century, had lined their fields with stone walls, now ruinous where huge elms had grown through them. Sunlight poured through their waving branches, glittering and shimmering on the roadway ahead in ever-changing kaleidoscopic patterns.

After three miles, the road forked at the Township School. The right fork led west toward the village of Salem Corners, a long straight stretch that passed the entrance to the Balfour's country estate.

"Do you want to take her the rest of the way, Bob?" asked Johnny with a smile.

"Gosh yes! May I?" *I don't believe it! Is he really going to let me drive his dad's car?*

"Sure thing. Do you think you can handle her?"

"Course I can. I've got my license right here." I showed Johnny the postcard from Mike Holm.

"Okay." Johnny brought the car to a stop. We quickly changed places.

The wonder of it left me giddy. Behind the wheel on my own! I was going to drive—actually take charge of the accelerator, brakes, and steering, without my father continually telling me what to do! I was so excited I peed my pants! Fortunately, it wasn't much, and didn't show through.

With the precision of a student of music theory who had yet to play a first note on his instrument, I placed my hands in the approved 10-4 position, depressed the clutch, shifted into first gear, and lurched forward with a fearsome clash and squeal.

"Take it easy, for gosh sakes," cried Johnny in alarm. "I thought you said you knew how to drive!"

"Sorry. My foot slipped. I'm okay now," I lied, hoping to calm my own nervousness as well as Johnny's real concern.

We shot down the road, gravel flying, with the motor roaring.

"Take her out of first, Bob!" Johnny yelled in exasperation, probably regretting his foolish offer to let me drive.

I shifted clumsily into second, and then third and we continued to accelerate. I was elated. This was really something! All the miles I had ridden with my Dad driving were nothing like the feeling of power, control, and manliness that swept through me now. The tall cornstalks to the left and right of the road, waving in the wind, seemed to be cheering me on! A light blue sky, buttoned with cottony puffs, smiled benignly. The road ahead seduced me. Faster, faster! Now I knew how Barney Oldfield felt in 1903 when the world screamed past his goggles at sixty miles an hour! The wind tore through the window, whirling away all further conversation. Zooming along, it was only minutes before we came within sight of a farm road that led off at a sharp angle to the left. Lightly graveled, with a dirt base, it crossed a culvert before heading southwest toward the Balfour estate.

"Slow down, Bob! Slow down!" I was deaf to Johnny's cry. I blithely swung the wheel into the narrow farm road.

The awful realization that I had lost control came when the car skidded to the right, the rear end swerving wildly, as if to overtake the front. I gasped for air, and hung onto the wheel in terror. The front wheels struck the culvert abutment. The noise of the crash filled my entire being—tearing, grinding, crackling and roaring! As the car careened over on its side, billowing dust clouds blotted out the sunshine. For a moment there was utter silence, and then Billy began to whimper in pain from somewhere to the rear. The car lay in the ditch, its wheels still revolving. My hands, clamped around the steering wheel, would not let go, and I hung suspended above Johnny, whose mute, astonished expression rang with accusation and fear! Waves of nausea, self-loathing, and fear of all the consequences to come washed over me.

After the dust had settled we extricated ourselves from the wreck through the driver's window.

"Oh my God. Look what you've done. I thought you said you could drive," Johnny cried. Then, with growing realization of his own negligence, he said mostly to himself, "What will my Dad say?"

Billy sat on the ditch bank, holding his arm and wailing repeatedly, "My arm! Oh, my arm!"

I ran around the car, taking in the full impact of the crash. I knew that it was my entire fault. I had lied to my best friend about being able to drive. I had caused serious injury to Billy, and great damage to Dr. Berkman's automobile. Johnny would have to face the consequences of allowing an incompetent kid to drive his Dad's car. *What on earth was I thinking of? What will my parents do when they find out?* I was filled with fear, shame and remorse. "I'm sorry, I'm so sorry," I cried, the tears running down my face. "I musta been going too fast. I shouldn't have been driving." No one was listening.

None of us saw the vehicle approaching on the farm road. It was the Balfour's yard truck, driven by John Tewes. It came abreast of the wreck and John looked at us with astonishment, at first not completely able to accept all he saw.

"What happened? You go too fast? Who was driving?" he cried, the words tumbling out all at once.

"Bob was. I guess I'm to blame," Johnny said, looking down. "I shouldn't have let him!"

"You boys sure got yourselves in some trouble!" John said, shaking his head as he spoke. "Well, get in, I take you home."

We climbed into the truck bed and sat without speaking during the ride back to town. Billy, looking white as a sheet, gripped his arm tightly, and moaned wordlessly. The giddy anticipation that I had experienced behind the wheel had given way to dreadful misery, and fearful anticipation of the reception I could expect from my father. As we jounced along my thoughts became ever more morbid. Remembering my father's rage and the fearful thrashing I had received after the canoe business, I was terrified that I should receive worse this time. I trembled visibly, could not hold my hands steady, mouth dry as newspaper. I tried to clear my throat but could only croak feebly. I wished I was dead—and for all I knew maybe I'd get my wish.

When we reached town, John stopped the truck in front of the Berkman house. Johnny helped Billy climb down and walk the short distance to his house. I watched them go. No one spoke. Then John drove into the Balfour driveway and parked the truck in its usual spot in the garage.

My father's legs protruded from beneath an automobile raised on jacks. He lay on a glider, peering up into the car's vitals.

"Well, John, how did it go today?" he asked, routinely.

"All right 'til I started home," John replied. "I brought the boys with me. They had an accident."

The heels dug into the floor and the glider raced out from under the car. "What?! What accident? Vare?" My father looked at me for the first time, puzzled, his face pale with anxiety.

"Out on the road to Salem Corners. They tried to make the turn into the farm. Going too fast. Ran off the culvert. She's on her side in the ditch." Then, as if in afterthought, "They're lucky to be alive."

John continued to talk, and I had started to skulk past them toward the door to our living quarters upstairs. "Smashed pretty bad. Billy broke his arm. Looks like Bob was driving," he said.

"You ware driving!" Dad hollered at me, his voice rising in pitch with each word until he was yelling. "Who said you could drive a car?"

I turned and held the beige post card before me like a shield. "I have a driver's license," I said, idiotically. "I sent away for it—to St. Paul—a long time ago. See?"

He leapt toward me, tore the license out of my hands, grabbed me by arm in a grip that sent bolts of pain clear to my shoulder, and began shouting questions I couldn't have answered even had they been spoken calmly.

"Do you ever think before you do stupid things? You could have been killed! Who you think is going to pay for this? Is it you? No, you didn't think of that, did you!" His face, twisted with shock, dread, and anger, was flushed, and the blood vessels in his temples throbbed visibly.

In disgust he shoved me away from him. I stumbled backwards, catching myself against a car, and ran toward the door. He outdistanced me easily, and yanked it open. "Get upstairs!" he spat out, emphasizing the command with a kick to my retreating backside. "You haven't heard the last of this yet!"

The injury to Billy's arm, though painful, was not as severe as had first been thought. Johnny received a severe tongue-lashing from Dr. Berkman, who held him entirely responsible for giving an incompetent permission to drive his automobile. But, because I was not listed as a recognized operator of Stella J. Twedt's Oldsmobile sedan, or of any other for that matter, my parents were liable for the repairs to Dr. Berkman's coupe. The total came to $175.00, more than a fourth the cost of the vehicle. It was a grievous economic blow that my parents simply could not afford. With a shamefulness that was painful to him, Dad had to turn to the Doctor for a loan against his future salary.

"Bobby, how could you do such a thing?" my mother asked me repeatedly over the next few days.

Riddled with guilt, ashamed, despising myself, I could not answer her except with a feeble, "I'm sorry Mother, and I'll never do it again."

Even she could not stomach such a silly reply. "I'll say you won't," she said with a no-nonsense flip of the dishtowel.

I was convinced then that as long as I lived under their roof I would never drive the Oldsmobile.

THE NEW COAT

E very autumn, the first hint of chill in the air prompted my mother to resurrect our family's winter garments from a wardrobe in the basement. A flimsy, cardboard affair, the wardrobe had a vertical sliding door that was never raised in summer except to add more mothballs. These it consumed voraciously.

The previous winter my father had bought me a full-length winter overcoat. Cheap and practical, it was made of heavy, brown, cotton-twill, lined in sheepskin, with a dyed sheepskin collar. Identical coats were worn by my friends, and probably most of the adult male population in farming communities of the upper Midwest. With collars turned up to muffle the cold, my schoolmates resembled plodding columns of Russian peasants. Observed in silhouette against the evening snow, vesper hymns descending from the Clinic carillon, the effect was haunting.

"Nels, take the kids' winter coats out and put them on the line to air," Mother asked my father one day in late fall. This "airing out" of a stored winter garment was necessary in order to avoid the telltale, filling-station odor of naphthalene that trailed the owner upon first seasonal wearing.

Before he could reply the telephone rang, and I answered. A familiar, deep voice commanded, "Tell your father that I'm ready now."

"Yessir," I said, replacing the receiver. "It was Dr. Balfour. He's ready to go back to the Clinic."

"When are we ever going to sit down to a meal when that man doesn't telephone? Just once! Just once, I'd like to eat a meal in peace!" objected my mother.

I had heard her complaint many times and while I sympathized with my father, as I did now, there lay within me the recognition that she was justified. I hated the nagging thought that perhaps he was too passive, that he should stand up to his employer!

"Oh Stella, be quiet!" he exclaimed. "It's my work! What you want me to do about it?" He rose from the luncheon table with a wave of his hand, indicating his bewilderment and exasperation. Nonetheless, that afternoon the coats were swaying easily on the clothesline.

"Nels, look at this!" Mother cried out in surprise the next day. "Bobby's coat is all to pieces. He can't wear it like this, and I certainly don't know how to fix it."

"What you mean, all to pieces? Let me see!" He took the coat from her and could easily see that its sheepskin lining was in tatters. In such inexpensive coats the linings were made by stitching together innumerable cuttings, often no larger than a postage stamp, obtained during the preparation of more expensive garments. In my coat many of these same pieces had dried and separated from one another.

"You're right, Stella," he cried in astonishment. "The lining is rotten! And Bob has worn that coat only one winter. Why they ought to be ashamed selling a sheep thing like this, and for good money, too. I'm going down there with this thing, you bet your life."

"Well, I certainly think they owe you an explanation. But, Nels, don't you make a scene," warned Mother.

"We'll see why they sell poor coats for good money," was his answer. "Come on, Bob," he called, peremptorily.

My heart was not in this quest. After all, the coat was not new. I had worn it for an entire winter and had rather intimate knowledge of all the harsh occasions that the coat had suffered. It had gotten wet, muddied, and bruised in more than one snowball fight, and now Dad was objecting because it was not in perfect condition! Besides, since I had spent all my savings on a new suit, I could not afford a more stylish coat. I hoped in some unformulated way that my parents might buy me a new coat.

We drove in silence to the town's mercantile hub where we parked in front of the J. C. Penney Store on the corner of First Street and South Broadway. My father stepped out of the car, removed the offending garment from the rear seat and strode with great long steps into the store; Leif Erickson in size 13 triple A shoes, a flapping black suit with shiny knees, and a pre-Bogart fedora!

Ignoring startled customers and obsequious salesmen with their papier-mâché smiles and bogus platitudes, he made for the rear of the store. "Hare, what you think of this, Clarence?" he demanded while still halfway down the center aisle, thrusting the coat forth with his left hand while pointing an accusatory finger at the lining with his right.

Clarence Fogelson emerged from his glass-enclosed office. A man of slight build, he wore a brown pinstripe vest and trousers, gartered sleeves, paper cuffs and a green eye-shade. He had been going over his books. His round tortoise-shell-rimmed glasses teetered on the end of his nose. "What seems to be the trouble, Nels? Is that one of our coats?" said Clarence with reserve. He leaned slightly backward on worn heels as though trying to avoid his customer.

"You know it is, Clarence. You sold it to me last year. Now look hare at the sheep thing. The lining is rotten. It is poor quality and I paid good money for it! I want you fellows to make it good!"

There it was, the ridiculous idea was out in the open and my father had just said it for all Rochester to hear. I glanced around and, sure enough, everyone in the store was looking at us. I wanted to die, drop through the floor, and disappear—just die!

"Well now, Nels, you've had the coat for a whole season. The boy has worn it. I can't hope to sell it now. I'm sorry but there's really nothing I can do for you." His commiseration was transparent.

"Clarence, you got your money, but I got nothing. That ware not honest," Dad said evenly. "All I can do now is to tell others how I been treated hare. I am going to hang this coat on the lamppost in front of your store, and I am going to stand there and tell everyone who goes by how I paid good money for shoddy. Clarence, you know I mean it."

"Come on, Bob," he said, turned about and headed for the door. There was only silence in the store.

"Now Nels, hold on, there is no need for that," Clarence called frantically after him. "Come back to my office, Nels, I think there is a solution here. Your coat will undoubtedly qualify as a manufacturer's defect. This year's style is priced somewhat higher, but we'll overlook the difference."

My father turned without a word and accompanied Clarence into his office. I remained in the store, where the buzz of sales conversations once again filled the air. It seemed to me that all the customers were smiling.

We left the store in silence, my father calmly serene, with me carrying the new coat. When we reached the car, I put my hand on his shoulder and said, "Thanks for getting the new coat for me, Dad. I think I'll wear it to church this Sunday with my green gabardine suit and the new yellow shoes!"

THE GREAT COMMUNIST
SPY INCIDENT

The map of Rochester, like that of most Midwestern towns founded after the passage of the Homestead Act, resembled a waffle. The two intersecting main streets were named Broadway and Center. Broadway, Rochester's widest street, was the original site of commercial activity in the town, and during my youth was still the address of storekeepers who supplied the needs of farmers from the surrounding rural areas. When the first Mayo Clinic and St. Mary's Hospital were built on land to the west of downtown, the more enterprising businessmen began moving west with them. During my high school years newly erected or remodeled buildings located on the streets to the west of Broadway were decorated in Moderne or Art Deco style, while the older, nineteenth century storefronts on Broadway slumbered on into obsolescence. Elbowing each other in ragged irregularity, they were mostly of brick, and had impressive ornamentation, sometimes in stone or cast brick, more often of cast iron or pressed sheet metal. The name of the original owner, his business, and the date of construction were proudly displayed on diminutive pediments or on the cornice beneath.

For Johnny Berkman and me, Broadway held many attractions, not the least of which were Montgomery and Ward's catalog store, Hansen's Hardware, and the F. W. Woolworth Company, its red and gold sign trumpeting Five and Ten Cent Store. Innumerable trips to Broadway over the years had given us easy familiarity with every decorative detail of all the structural landmarks there.

One sunny Saturday in the spring of 1941 we went shopping for phonograph records featuring the great jazz cornetist Bix Beiderbeck, at Kling's Music Store on Broadway. When he was not within earshot, we dubbed its gregarious owner, Vincent Kling the King of Swing,

"Bob, can you think of any old building in Rochester that doesn't have the date, or something, printed across the top, like these?" Johnny posed the question with a mischievous smile.

"Noooo!" I answered slowly, feeling that I ought to know the answer, but was really not certain.

"Look, every one of them has somebody's name up there at the top."

"That's the pediment," I said, recovering. "The guys that built these stores were copying the decorations on ancient Greek temples."

"Okay, smart guy, if you know so much, answer my question!"

"I don't know, really. At least I can't think of a building with a blank pediment."

"It's our old school!" exclaimed Johnny. "Edison has that goofy shield up above the front entrance and there's nothing on it. What's it there for anyway?"

Later that afternoon Bayard Horton rode up on his motorcycle and Johnny put to him the same architectural query that had stumped me. He couldn't think of the blank pediment on Edison either, but when the answer was given him cried out with glee, "Guys, we need to remedy that situation! Whadaya say we head down old Edison way and put an end to all that nakedness!"

Johnny was eager to complete Edison's adornment. Bayard took up the challenge and said, matter-of-factly, "We'll sneak in tonight and paint something up there that nobody will understand." Perceiving the look of shocked incredulity that crossed my face, and cognizant of the tight parental reins under which I operated since I had wrecked Dr. Berkman's car, neither friend spoke of my accompanying them on this latest feat of nefarious derring-do.

Edison Elementary School

"Wow, that's great, Bayard! What should it be? Lemme see now," said Johnny. Eagerly and with increasing good humor they proposed various words and phrases, finally contriving to compose a nonsense word of one syllable. The word was "glebe."

After dark the two friends met in the alley behind the Berkman house, and walked silently to Edison School. Bayard carried a can of red enamel paint and a brush.

"How are we going to get in?" Johnny queried.

"Sssssh! Cut the chatter for criminy sake. Ya want the whole world to know?" Bayard responded

When they reached the rear of the school building, the pressing silence and murky dark laid firm hands on Johnny's resolve. "Hey, I don't think this is such a good idea. This is breaking and entering. We could go to jail!"

"Oh for cat's sake, Johnny! No one will be in the place at night. Who's to find out?"

In the ceiling of the main stair well, they located a trap door that gave access to the roof. However, it could only be reached by a long, heavy ladder that they dragged from the basement. When it was fully extended and leaning out over the stairwell it barely reached the trap door.

"Holy cow, Bayard!" whispered Johnny, considerably shaken. "We've got to shinny out over a two story stairwell in the dark!"

"Never fear, Johnny, old boy. Just keep looking up at my butt, and don't look down.

"Aw come on. I can't see my hand in front of my face. How am I gonna see your butt?"

"Well, keep touching my heels then. All set?"

"Okay," said Johnny.

"Remember! Don't look down fer anything! Just follow my dancing feet. Yuck! Yuck!"

The boys climbed steadily, the ladder swaying gently, and Bayard pushed the trap door open. Once on the roof, they could see that the building's outer walls rose nearly three feet higher than the roof's surface, making observation from the street nearly impossible. In a low crouch, they trotted quickly to the front of the building on the still-warm, gravelly tar. Bracing themselves against the lip of the wall, they leaned out and painted GLEBE in large capital letters on the face of the sheet metal pediment. Then they retraced their steps, failing to replace the ladder, and emerged, slapping hands, laughing, and shushing each other.

Later that night, I lay in bed, wondering if Bayard and Johnny had carried out the planned escapade. Shivering with anxiety, I had trouble going to sleep.

After school the next day, Bayard and Johnny drove slowly past Edison and were pleased to see a crowd of children gawking and pointing up at the school's new embellishment. But there was also a knot of curious adults that included several men in Humphrey Bogart rain-coats and fedoras taking notes, while Miss Leonard and the ever-faith-ful Fred Klampe gesticulated in the background. Bayard and Johnny drove off immediately, swearing each other to secrecy.

When I reached home that evening, my father was seated in his favorite chair, reading the *Rochester Post-Bulletin*. He whispered each sentence slowly to himself while following the English words with his forefinger. The lead article read, "Communist Sign Painted on School," and the subhead continued, "Spies gain entrance to Edison School. Deface building in Russian language. Police and Federal Bureau of Investigation called in." I couldn't believe my eyes. Looking over Dad's shoulder, scanning the whole article, I discovered that the five letters *g l e b e* formed a Russian word that described a parcel of land.

At the dinner table that evening, I asked to be excused before Nancy and my parents had finished.

"You got homework to do. No going out tonight," said my father.

"Gee whiz, Dad! I've got to talk to Johnny Berkman about school work," I lied. "Please, just for a little while. I've almost finished all my assignments, anyway."

"Well, all right. You better get back here in ten minutes or you'll wish you had," he replied...

Nancy looked at me, quizzically. Though she was four years my jun-ior, she maintained that she could read me like a book! She recognized the unusual note of insistence in my voice.

I found Johnny and Bayard sitting on the curb in front of the Berk-man residence. "Geez, what are you going to do?" I said to them both in a low whisper. "You haven't got a chance if the FBI's been called in."

"Aw, don't get excited, Bob!" exclaimed Bayard. "The FBI's got more to do than hunt down sign painters in a dinky town in the Mid-west."

"Yeah, but you're forgetting that Russia has signed a peace treaty with the Germans, which makes them just as bad as the Nazis. The FBI is looking for you 'cause they think you're spies for Hitler 'n Stalin! Cripes, that isn't just a game of cops and robbers!"

"Nothin's goin' to happen if we just lay low and keep our mouths shut," 'hissed Bayard. "Nobody knows who went up on the roof last night. Even if they get fingerprints, we've never had ours taken and they don't have 'em on file. If we clam up, we're in the clear!"

"Let's all three swear never to tell," said Johnny.

"We haven't got a Bible to lay our hand on," I countered.

"Oh for gosh sakes," said an exasperated Bayard, "do it when you get home!"

Each of us held our right fist forward, placed one atop another, and chorused, "I swear not to tell and be struck dead if I do!"

In a remarkably short period of time the great Communist spy incident faded from public concern. No culprits having been arrested, the event became just another dusty unsolved entry on the Rochester police blotter.

Both Johnny and Bayard had left home that fall to enroll in the College of Engineering at the University of Minnesota in Minneapolis. It was a wise choice, considering their inquisitive natures and mechanical talents.

After the shock of Pearl Harbor in December of 1941, with Uncle Sam's beckoning finger steadily approaching, the two friends chose separate paths. For his sophomore year Johnny stayed at the U of M, planning to enlist in the Navy. Bayard transferred to Carleton College, a prestigious liberal arts institution in Northfield, but appeared to have no clearly formulated academic objective. In addition, without his Harley-Davidson, because student-owned transportation was not permitted on campus, a compensating social life was severely curtailed. Even hitchhiking to and from engagements became almost impossible under the severe restrictions of total, civilian gasoline rationing. As the summer of 1942 stretched into fall, gossip from Carleton described a rambunctious Bayard, and associated him with unsolved and unusual culpable acts that had crossed the fine line between prank and felony.

The Jolly Viking Tavern, a boisterous watering hole in Northfield, was a favored destination for Carleton students in a festive mood. On a mild evening in early autumn Ivar Sorensen, a Steele County farmer driving a load of hogs, paused at the Viking to quench his thirst. The saloon was midway between his farm just west of Owatonna and the St. Paul Stockyard. Intending to reach the stockyard when it opened the following morning, Sorensen was in no hurry, and no pain. Emerging from the Viking at closing, he was disoriented and dismayed because his truck and its load were not where he had left them. In fact, both had long since made the journey to St. Paul where they were later located by police. No arrest was ever made and no culprit was indicted.

Even official vehicles were not safe from the stealthy hand of the "Northfield Houdini," as the unknown thief came to be known. A squad car was stolen from its official parking space in front of the Northfield Police Station and later recovered in a well-to-do St. Paul residential neighborhood. A zealous and thorough examination of the purloined cruiser yielded meager clues—a few smudged fingerprints, and a partial footprint. Chief Karl Magnuson swore a great oath that promised difficulties for the perpetrator, were he ever to be apprehended.

Later, a similar daring theft occurred in the city of Rochester. At 6:30 a.m. on a bitterly cold Friday morning, a full hour before his usual run to the Twin Cities was scheduled, Vern Hauge, a driver for Northland Greyhound Lines, reached the Ford garage, where the bus company stored its machines. Being the first to arrive, he pulled a key ring from his trouser pocket, blew noisily on his hands to warm them, and unlocked the front door.

Vern knocked the snow from his boots, and entered the now bare showroom at Universal Motors. With wartime conversion from manufacturing automobiles to producing armaments, it contained only a cardboard cutout of a Ford car and a V for Victory message. At first the dealership was pleased to have the added rental income from storing buses, but as their size increased, had begun to worry about possible property damage. Greyhound had acquired a new, 33-passenger Scenicruiser only a month previously, before wartime restrictions had gone in force. It was a very tricky job maneuvering the oversized monster around support columns and between parked cars. Vern wanted plenty of time to accomplish this task, and also to allow the interior of the new bus to warm up. Skinny, with wispy gray hair, he claimed that he was cold natured and declared that he really should leave Minnesota and buy a retirement home in Fort Lauderdale.

Selma Hauge, who was definitely more warm-natured than her husband, bitterly opposed the contemplated move away from her family, friends, and her snug little home. To the girls at Alma Severud's beauty salon Selma sniffed that her husband's fires had been banked for many years, and that his cold nature affected other activities besides his bus driving!

Vern walked through the garage, repeatedly slapping his thin arms with his hands to stimulate circulation. He stopped abruptly, slack-jawed with astonishment, when he saw the very empty, bus-sized, parking space against the rear wall. Telltale tire tracks on the dusty floor led to the front door, but were lost outside in the snow-covered street. Whoever had taken Greyhound's newest vehicle from its narrow confines in the darkened garage had done so with expert knowledge of its operation, and without hitting anything!

Vern panicked. What if the bus company were to conclude that he, Vern, had something to do with this? He thought that he ought to call his boss right away and deflect suspicion from himself. In a crisis Vern had never acted without advice from higher up, and today was no exception. He grabbed the phone and called Selma.

"Call the boss, my foot," she said. "You ninny, call the police. The bus has been stolen! You slept like a log all night and didn't get up once. I can certainly vouch for that." The ambiguity, but not the logic, of her harangue was lost to him. He called the police.

The team of police officers and detectives that arrived shortly, swarmed over the garage, asking pointed questions, and poking everywhere for evidence. They dusted every begrimed surface within and around Universal Motors in a luckless, ultimately failed effort to find the thief's fingerprints. They posted an all points bulletin for the missing vehicle.

A temporary lull in the search occurred when Chief Bernard Lunde had exhausted his stock of ideas. Then, about mid-morning the telephone in the Union Bus Depot rang, bringing a much-needed break in the case. The caller, Hjalmar Swenson, was a tank-truck driver for the Zumbrota Cooperative Creamery, and was making his morning raw-milk collections.

"Say, did you fellows misplace one of your buses?" Hjalmar said, chortling into the mouthpiece. Among his fellow drivers, who called him "Swede," he was considered a natural-borne comedian. "Pretty careless of you guys, I'd say."

Getting the gist of the conversation, Arne Paulson, Greyhound's District Manager, seized the telephone from his ticket agent. "Who are you? Where are you calling from? Where did you see our bus?" he exclaimed, with runaway anxiety.

"She's plumb off the road a little south of Oronoco where I'm callin' from, mebbe five miles north of Rochester on Highway 52," replied Hjalmar, identifying himself. "She's layin' on her side, straddling the ditch."

Alerted by the conversation that he could hear, Chief Lunde picked up an extension. "Did anyone see what happened?" he asked.

"Heck, no, most guys ain't finished their milkin' yet," was the reply. "Its been snowin' all night, and folks in town ain't even begun to stir."

"Don't touch anything! Ya hear?" said the Chief.

"Whadaya mean? I got no time to mush through snow up to my waist. I got milk to deliver!" And before he hung up he offered, "Mebbe the driver skidded on a snow-covered patch of ice. The ditch is completely drifted over and maybe he thought he could ride her out."

Hjalmar said this out of sympathy for the dumb cluck that chucked the bus in the ditch and now probably would lose his job.

With sirens wailing, Chief Lunde and his men, along with Arne Paulsen, were soon careening toward Pine Island. "Watch it, Bernie," worried Arne aloud, "or we'll end up out there in the snowdrifts with the bus." The Chief didn't reply but did decrease his speed slightly.

At the crash site there was more poking and fingerprinting. This time the detectives got lucky. The thief had left a trail of footprints in the snow, all the way to the highway, where they disappeared. They resembled the tracks around the broken skylight on the roof of the Universal Motors garage. Casts of the footprints were promptly made and taken back to Rochester where their image was shared, by wire, with area law enforcement agencies.

That was what stirred the memory of Chief Magnuson, in Northfield the next day. Reading his daily reports, the Chief instantly recognized a footprint that he'd spent hours scrutinizing with intensity driven by exquisite hatred. "Tillie, get me the file on that goddamn Houdini," he roared to the prim spinster. Mathilde Vaag had served five Chiefs during her 40-year career with the department and was surprised at nothing.

"You needn't shout. I've kept it ready on top of my desk. And that's no way to speak to a lady," she reprimanded him.

"Aaaah, I'm sorry, Tillie," replied the abashed Magnuson with contrition, "but you know how much I want to nab the sonofabitch."

"Well I should say," she sniffed, turned stiffly, and returned to her cubicle.

The Chief placed the images received from the Rochester police beside footprints attributed to the notorious local heister. Tell tale cuts and worn spots were identical.

"Hot damn, it's him all right! Half-ass Houdini hasn't even changed his shoes! Sweet Jesus just let me get my hands on him! Then we'll see who's Houdini and who isn't!" An audible sigh came from the direction of Tillie's cubicle. After that it was only a matter of time before the roof fell in on Bayard Horton. It didn't take a genius to associate the Northfield thefts with a college student and from that to narrow the suspects to students from Rochester. Chief Magnuson, himself, rapped on the door of Bayard's dormitory room several days later.

"Hi there, Houdini," the Chief grinned, and he snapped the cuffs on Bayard's wrists.

An indictment by the Rice County Attorney followed quickly, but the defense, citing the need for documents and testimony necessary to their case, requested a change of venue to Olmsted County. To Magnuson's disgust, the request was allowed.

The case was heard in the court of District Judge Vernon P. Gates. On a windy April morning the bailiff called the court to order in a barely intelligible staccato, "Allrise. CourtHonabulVernpeegatesnowinseshun." The sun angled in dusty beams through the tall narrow windows of the courtroom on the second floor of the Olmsted County Courthouse. Judge Gates gaveled the courtroom into silence.

The case for the prosecution was presented ably and swiftly by the Olmsted County prosecutor, who called upon technical witnesses, including detectives assigned to the investigations in Northfield and in Rochester. Their testimony, for the most part uncontested, related to the details of time and circumstance as well as the conformity of the damning footprints. The shoes were found without difficulty in Bayard's dormitory closet at Carleton College. The defense attorney questioned the accuracy of statements by witnesses who had seen Bayard in the Jolly Viking the night of the pignapping. Though reminding each of the dangers of perjury, he could uncover neither errors nor contradictions. The same result was forthcoming when he questioned dormitory residents who could verify Bayard's comings and goings. Both Chief Magnuson of Northfield and Chief Lunde of Rochester were smiling broadly at what appeared to be the defense's discomfiture.

Then the attorney for the defense called his witnesses to testify as to Bayard's character, and to point out the contributions that he could make to the life of a nation now at war, if he were not incarcerated. As one, they spoke of Bayard's brilliant mind, mechanical skills and acquired engineering knowledge—painting a picture of an Einstein who loved high jinks.

Dr. Horton, suave, dignified and soft voiced, spoke of his son with affection, saying, "I am the one who, because of the inexorable demands of the medical profession, has neglected my son, Bayard. I should be in this dock, Your Honor."

Mrs. Horton, demur and charming, would not so condemn her husband, but pled with the judge to give her son a chance to correct his life. "I am as sure that Bayard has learned his lesson and will turn to a life of good works, as I am that there is a merciful God, Who knows all, and forgives all," she said with a lovely smile.

Johnny Berkman and I were each called to the stand and spoke glowingly of Bayard's honesty and fairness in all of our past relationships. But the one who made the deepest impression on the Court was my father.

"Do you, Nels Twedt, swear to tell the truth, the whole truth and nothing but the truth, so help you God," intoned the clerk.

With his hand on the Bible and looking directly at the flag of his adopted country, Dad replied, "Before God, my family, and my countrymen I do swear." He sat down, turned to the Judge and began to speak.

"Your Honor, I know this boy. He is a very smart boy, like my own son, Bob. He has come to me many times for help with repairs to engines. I have worked with him like I would with a man. Your Honor, this boy understands how machines work yust by looking at them, like a doctor who looks at your body."

Judge Gates listened to Dad intently because it was clear that he spoke from his heart.

"I know this boy has a good mind. He will invent new machines; watch them take shape in his hands. Your Honor, I think these things he has done are to him like yokes. He did not think they hurt anyone.

But I know that he understands now, and is sorry. I ask you, please, Your Honor, help Bayard, and help my America. Let him show that he is sorry in some useful way." With that Dad took his seat and looked straight ahead of him with moistened eyes.

. There was a short recess, after which Judge Gates called for quiet and addressed the plaintiff who stood before the bench. "Young man, you are accused of felonious acts that are, by their very nature, harmful to property. More importantly, your deeds have caused injury and worry to the owners of that property though, by the Grace of God, no harm has come to any living person. Your acts have crossed the line separating prank from crime. I have no other recourse than to find you guilty and to sentence you to serve five years in the State Reformatory at St. Cloud."

There was a restrained gasp from Mrs. Horton. The Judge then looked at Dr. Horton intently, and asked him to stand beside his son, before the bench.

"Sir, I am persuaded by your remarks and by my own experience, that your son has suffered neglect and loss of parental companionship, in consequence of the nature of your profession and its demands on your time. I am convinced as well that you recognize your partial responsibility for the felonious acts that your son has committed. Furthermore, I have carefully considered the testimony of those witnesses who have spoken highly of your son's talents and ability. I gave particular merit to the very moving testimony of Mr. Nels Twedt, who is a man of unquestionable integrity and honesty. In the light of these compelling testimonies it is my opinion that no benefit to the community would accrue by incarcerating your son. Therefore, it is the Order of this Court that Mr. Bayard Horton's sentence will be commuted to voluntary enlistment in the Armed Forces of the United States for the duration of the present war against fascism. Furthermore, I warn you, Mr. Horton, that should I see an army tank parked in front of your parents' home, you will be remanded immediately into the custody of the warden at the State Reformatory, to serve your full sentence." This last remark produced the barest trace of a smile on Judge Gate's face. "This Court is now adjourned." He banged his gavel.

"All rise," called the bailiff. After that his family and supporters gathered about Bayard, whose relief was very evident, to wish him well. In the rear of the room a noisy ruckus arose.

"My men do all the work, we arrest the bastard, turn him over to you and you lose him," shouted Chief Magnuson between clenched fists.

"You'd still be lookin' for 'im if we hadn't given you the clincher," hissed Chief Lunde. "You're outa your jurisdiction here, Magnuson. Go home and cool off."

"Clear the Court," ordered the flustered bailiff and with a few more muttered imprecations, all parties to the quarrel dispersed.

Rochester City Hall and First Ave., SW

When Rochester's Police Chief climbed the stairs to his second floor office in the City Hall, his resentment of Karl Magnuson's remarks had enlarged to include the entire Case of the Purloined Bus. He threw the box of evidence his men had collected on his surprised assistant's desk and commanded, angrily, "File this damn stuff so far away and so deep that I'll never have to see it again, Cartwright. And do it now!"

"Yes sir, Chief," replied Joe Cartwright, tiptoeing around his superior's anger.

That evening Joe worked late. He carried the casts, made from the footprints in the snow, to drawers where similar material, filed over the years, laid gathering dust. He looked idly at the casts of Bayard's footprints, when a peculiar pattern of sole cuts and abrasions caught his attention. He had seen that footprint pattern before, but when and where? Was it two years ago? He rummaged further and then found what he was looking for. It was a cast of a footprint from the roof of Edison School, made at the time of the communist spy break-in! Shouldn't he tell Chief Lunde? Remembering the Chief's recent peremptory order and his dire mood while issuing it, Cartwright imagined what would happen if he learned that the Northfield Houdini and the GLEBE painter were one and the same.

The sound of green plaster of Paris fracturing into hundreds of unrecognizable pieces on shiny terrazzo echoed eerily through the empty Rochester Police Headquarters.

LEAVING HUMDRUM BEHIND

I was ecstatic. The day that I had anticipated for so long, with ill-concealed eagerness, had finally arrived. And just as it had been in my daydreams, this was the most brilliant, most perfect day of my life. The hazy azure sky was choked with great cumulus clouds that sailed before a mild wind, their yards sheeted with billowing whiteness. My heart ached with the joy of being alive this morning and I felt a thrilling tightness binding my ribs. I inhaled deeply so that I could catch and savor each breath for a moment. I had completed my junior year in high school and here I was—leaving Rochester's boring people and humdrum confines forever! Instead of returning in the fall for my senior year in high school, I would enter the renowned California Institute of Technology. I believed without question that this would lead to an illustrious scientific career; the possibilities were endless and wonderful! I leaned slightly forward, searching the horizon, beyond which lay the sun-drenched gateway to my destiny.

The tires of the heavy car emitted a hypnotic thrumming on the fresh macadam. We had come straight south from the town where I had been born and spent all of my growing-up. A steady breeze, inadequately deflected by small tilt-out front windows, tousled my hair, and filled the car's interior with the dusty, pungent odors of rural Iowa. The Owner's Manual that lay in the glove compartment, termed this minor squall No-Draft Ventilation. The windy concept had earned my father's understandable disdain. "Bob, those enyineers, they don't know nothing," was his only comment to a yearly succession of similar gimmicky model changes.

The green Oldsmobile sedan in which we rode was the same one that had been given to Mother six years before by my Uncle Leo, who lived in California. The apparently lavish gift was actually a long delayed repayment of money that she had lent him for medical school.

We had left Rochester early that morning. My mother had packed a luncheon and a thermos of coffee. I was reluctant to leave home with picnic food in a basket, deeming it plebeian. Mother cried when I kissed her goodbye. She wrapped me in a possessive embrace that we had not used since my infancy. I felt embarrassed by her unrestrained maternal love, ashamed of myself for having such feelings, and assuaged my guilt by imaging the brilliant success that awaited me beyond Rochester. When I was famous and returned home to visit I would make my mother and father proud!

"You behave yourself out there, now, you hare," Dad's sermonizing broke into my reverie. His voice showed great concern for my welfare but his words never told me how to behave! "Out there" was Uncle Leo's southern California ranch, where I was to spend the summer vacation before enrolling in Cal Tech. My uncle had offered to support my college education, in part because of my demonstrated scholarship, but also as another grandiloquent demonstration of his own success in medical practice.

"Yessir, you bet," I replied with a smile. I certainly did not intend to make some mistake in social behavior that would jeopardize my rosy prospects.

Assuming my smile to be one of anticipation and excitement, he said, "We are making good time today. I bet you we will beat him there."

"Him" was Dr. Fred Gruber, a medical associate of my Uncle Leo. Dr. Gruber was driving a brand new car home from Detroit, and would take me to California and my uncle's home. When Dad and I arrived at the prearranged meeting place, a junction with US 30 between Cedar Rapids and Ames, Iowa, there was a huge grin on his face. "What did I tell you, we got hare first!" he chortled with decided satisfaction in his own automotive performance.

We turned our attention to the luncheon that my mother had thoughtfully sent with us. My hunger, fueled by my excitement, banished my Epicurean principles without compunction, and I wolfed the picnic food with relish!

Inside of a half-hour, Dr. Fred Gruber drove up in a blue, two-door business coupe that he had accepted at the Pontiac assembly plant in Michigan. Dr. Gruber and Dad introduced themselves. The physician was a darkly angular man of average build and sturdy confidence. Dad, a full head taller than he, bent forward while shaking hands, not out of obsequiousness but rather to better address him face to face. The two of them exchanged opinions about the weather, the best route to travel, and prospects for a fast trip west—one free of mechanical troubles. I paid little attention to these verbal exchanges, wishing only that they would cease and my adventure begin.

Dad turned to me, with a mixture of pride, hope, and anxious hesitation, and said, "Well, Doctor, this is my son, Bob."

"Hello there, Bob," said Dr. Gruber. "Glad to meet you."

"How do you do, Sir," I said, and took his extended hand. He had a firm grip, not hard, and I liked him at once.

"Bob is a good boy and a smart boy, Doctor. He's always done his schoolwork and now Leo says that he will help him to get a college education. His mother and I are grateful for that but we know that it is up to Bob to study hard and make a success of himself."

"Bob is lucky to have parents like you and your wife, Nels," the physician said.

Turning to me he observed, "Not many boys have been given the opportunity that Leo is offering. I am sure Bob understands how much you have done for him and will do his best at Cal Tech."

Then Dad put his hand on my shoulder and, looking out, wistfully, over the corn tassels toward the western horizon said, "I wish that I had been given such a chance. You be a good boy, Bob, and make Mother and I proud of you. Now don't you forget to write to your Mother."

"I won't, Dad," I said. "I sure won't." Then we shook hands.

"Doctor, you make him mind."

"He'll be fine, Nels," said Dr. Gruber. "Don't worry."

"Goodbye, Bob."

"Goodbye, Dad."

"Goodbye."

The automobiles churned into motion and set off in opposite directions. Soon I could no longer see the green of the Olds or my father behind the wheel. I turned to face the shimmering highway, whose two lanes seemed an enormous avenue trailing off westward toward the future. Despite my earlier elation, a curious sense of melancholy intruded upon my sunshiny optimism. Tears dimmed my gaze, and I turned to look out the right side window, away from the driver.

TOWARD A BRIGHT NEW LIFE

Fred G. Gruber, MD, the youngest partner in the Madsen Medical Group, and himself only a few years removed from erratic adolescent emotionalism, turned and spoke to me with kindly understanding. "Can you drive a car, Bob?"

"Oh yessir. I've got my driver's license right here in my wallet." I replied. I made no mention of how it had been acquired and the subsequent unfortunate consequences.

"I'm sure you do, and that's what I hoped for," the physician said. "I have to be in the office Monday morning. The other doctors, especially your uncle, have covered for me while I've been at a medical meeting. If I fail to report on time they might not extend the courtesy in future. You understand, don't you?"

"Oh sure," I replied, worriedly calculating the extent of the task that he was setting for us. It was almost noon, and this was Friday. I had traced our proposed route to Los Angeles on the map at home many times. It was almost 2000 miles from Ames to Uncle Leo's home in Santa Monica. If we drove steadily with only the briefest stops, we should need eight more hours today, and twelve hours on Saturday and Sunday. *Good gosh, that works out to better'n 55 miles an hour!* I shivered with mixed excitement and dread.

My reinstatement behind the wheel had begun with brief excursions under my father's supervision. All were within the confines of Rochester, and all at a cautious 30 miles an hour—or less. On those occasions, my hectoring parent teetered on the edge of his seat, white-knuckled. Mindful of the unease that the driving instructions caused both Dad

163

and me, Mother had begged my father to allow her brother, Norman, to assume the role of tutor.

Uncle Norman, ten years younger than my mother, was the young-est of the four Madsen brothers. A rotund, round-faced, unassuming man, he had been the sedate driver of a rest home shuttle bus for many years. This distressed my mother, who read it as a sign of limited ambi-tion. But Nancy and I enjoyed his gentle, generous, and fun-loving nature; he was our favorite uncle. The rest home vehicles were invari-ably the latest cast-off Balfour limousine, and were the basis for a close and friendly relationship between Norman and my father.

With Uncle Norman in the instructor's role, I had made rapid progress in the art of the automobilist, even venturing onto highways outside of town. Now, suddenly, I was going to drive another man's new car at high speed for long distances, without any further instruc-tion!

I sat in uneasy silence as we rode west on US 30. Dr. Gruber, sens-ing my nervousness, plied me with questions about Rochester, my fam-ily's history, and my future plans and ambitions. The conversational diversion had its desired effect and I grew more confident, less tense. I liked this doctor who spoke to me as no other adult ever had—as an equal!

Answering simply at first, I became gradually more expansive, at last revealing grandiloquent dreams that fanned a burgeoning ambition. Chattering on, I was quite unaware of the passage of time and miles.

"We'll soon be in Carroll, Bob. I'm going to stop for gasoline and then you can take the wheel," I heard Dr. Gruber saying. "It will be best if we exchange driving every hour from now on. I'd like to reach North Platte before nightfall. The Hotel Ak-sar-ben is small, but clean, and they have a coffee shop that opens at 6:30 in the morning. We want to get started early tomorrow, before seven if possible. That sound all right with you?"

Yanked from the circuitous flight of my rambling autobiography, I surfaced, sputtering, and gasped out, "Oh sure, Fred." We were on a first name basis by then. "That suits me fine. I'll relieve you, soon's you tell me." Actually, I had been hoping that my new friend would forget about the driving stuff and just bask in the unfolding sonorous saga of a Norskie boy's life.

After filling the Pontiac's tank with Mobil Premium at the Sign of the Flying Red Horse, I moved into the driver's seat, adjusted the rear view mirror like Uncle Norman had taught me, and eased the Pontiac out into the street. Carroll, Iowa, appeared to be even smaller and less exciting than Rochester. Happily, this being the noon hour its streets were deserted. Most of its citizens were indoors, enjoying dinner, the main meal of the day in rural America. I shifted gears smoothly, and accelerated slowly, watching the speedometer needle advance through its arc to an astonishing 50 mile per hour! *Boy this car is smooth, and has such power!* All I had learned flooded back, and I felt quite masterful. The car rolled steadily onward, impatient under my cautious control, eager to race for California.

"Bob, if we keep on like this it will take us a week to reach Santa Monica. Give her the gas, she won't bite!" There was a sense of urgency in Fred's voice.

"Okay, you're the doctor," I replied with banal humor, and gingerly accelerated, holding the wheel in a firm 10 o'clock—4 o'clock grip, as did my father. With little effort the car reached 60 and then 65 miles an hour. "How's this?" I asked, my voice shrill and unsteady.

"Just fine, Bob. Keep it up. You're a good driver, just need some experience under your belt."

Unaware of the passage of time, I became confident in the car's operation, learned to judge distances, and how to pass safely without panicking. When it became Fred's turn to drive, I gave up the wheel with reluctance. After crossing the Missouri River, we began to follow the valley of the Platte River westward. We passed a seemingly endless sequence of small Nebraska towns that sprouted on the horizon, shimmered for a time in the distance and were gone. Originally construction camps that had sprouted along the tracks when the transcontinental railroad was being nailed down in the 1860's, the highway that had followed the same route connected them now.

In Kearney, where the river made a great bend southward, Fred suggested we stop to eat. The Hook-Um-Cow Coffee Shop had high-backed wooden booths, green oilcloth seat covers, a nickel-plated coffee urn, and the wonderful aroma of "home cooking." Smothered steak and mashed potatoes slathered in brown gravy tasted delicious after a long day behind the wheel. During dinner I listened, mesmerized, as Fred described life in Santa Monica on the coast, Hollywood and Beverly Hills where the film stars lived, and Pasadena where I would begin a bright new life at Cal Tech!

A huge orange sun glared low in the sky when we resumed the last hundred miles to North Platte and a bed. Concentrating on the road ahead, and the occasional oncoming car, I was unprepared for the exquisite display of colors, rose blending to peach that painted the cloud masses after the sun dipped below the lip of the prairie ahead.

Suddenly, I heard a familiar syncopated drumming, very rapid but still faint. In the rear view mirror, I saw a single amber eye peering out of the blue-blackness. I knew by the insistent rhythmic panting that it was a steam locomotive. It was going to pass us on the Union Pacific Railroad line paralleling the highway—and we were traveling at a spine tingling 67 miles per hour! The locomotive came abreast, the long black boiler, the ravening din, the steam and oily smoke, filling my consciousness. As the engine steadily swam past, its rods and valve gear thrashing wildly, I looked into the cab, lit by dim, yellow, electric bulbs. The engineer leaned over his windowsill, peering ahead. He turned, looked directly at me, grinned hugely, and raised his gloved hand. A deep booming steamboat whistle filled the night. My hair prickled—I was absolutely awestruck!

Later, lying in my hotel room, exhausted by the day's events, I found it difficult to fall asleep. I heard the insistent hoot of switchers shuffling their apathetic charges into orderly lines in the nearby yards.

On Saturday, Fred and I resumed our driving, after downing a solid breakfast with more cups of coffee than I had ever been granted at home. West of Ogallala, Nebraska, the railroad and parallel highway left the broad valley of the Platte to follow the Lodgepole River into Wyoming. I knew that the eastbound *City of Los Angeles* streamliner was due in Cheyenne at 8:45 AM, and stared at the tracks in the distance for the telltale glint of its headlight. Even so, I was not prepared for its passing. The striking yellow and silver locomotive screamed past, followed by an anxious thrum-ba-ba-bum, as each of the luxurious Pullman cars hurtled behind. A billowing, brownish cloud of ballast-dust chased the rounded observation car.

My excitement was so great that I had overlooked urgent distress signals caused by the morning's excessive coffee. "Fred, do you think we could stop along the roadside for a moment," I pleaded. "I don't think I can make it to the next town."

"Sure, Bob. That baby sure does tear across this part of the country, doesn't she! I thought I was going to wet my pants." He gave me a kindly wink.

I had assumed that we were passing through the prairies, a vast, table-flat land given over to cattle, cowboys and Indians. When I returned to the car I began to see that we were actually making a gradual assent. The horizon visible in my rear view mirror was more distant then the one to the front, and far below my line of vision. We were gaining altitude, and probably had been ever since crossing the Missouri!

In Rawlins, we ate luncheon on stools in the Divide Diner and then left US 30 within sight of the palisades that marked the crossing of the Green River for the pioneers wending west on the Oregon Trail. We drove south to Vernal, through rich farmlands along the Duchesne River, and climbed the Wasatch Range to enter the valley of the Great Salt Lake near Provo.

Fred had been born and raised in the village of Goshen, on the southern tip of Utah Lake about 30 miles south of Provo. We spent the night with his parents in a small white-clapboard bungalow that was as shiny and neat as the tiny, bird-like, white-haired woman who hugged each of us. Her husband, wearing the bib overalls and blue denim shirt that marked the farmer, welcomed us with a warm smile.

Otto and Hettie Gruber had met, become engaged, and married in the Church of Latter Day Saints in Goshen. Hettie had borne Otto seven children and the couple had raised their five sons and two daughters in the same faith that had drawn their German parents to the State of Deseret in the last century. All of their sons, with the exception of Fred, the lone professional man among them, were farmers, tilling the valley that Brigham Young had told his followers to settle and make fruitful. They resembled their father, who was tall, diffident, and silent. Like Otto, they deferred to their mother, whom they loved with a fierce, no-nonsense loyalty. Fred, his mother's son, possessed her confident, exuberant, sunny disposition. When her friends spoke to Hettie of her son's medical prospects, they confided that he had a wonderful bedside manner! The Grubers were delighted that their youngest son had come home to visit, if only for an evening. Fred had telephoned from Chicago, telling them when he would arrive and that he would be bringing the young nephew of his employer. I was treated as if I were one of the family and, in the glow of their unqualified attention, babbled on about Norwegians, Rochester, and my future plans.

Finally, with a half-concealed yawn, Fred was forced to call a halt. "Well folks, this has been a wonderful evening, but I'm tired, and we've still a long day ahead of us tomorrow. Come on Bob, time to hit the hay!"

"Oh dear! Fred, the time just flew by. I wish we could talk longer, but you boys do need your rest. We are so thankful that you both came to visit us." And with those words Hettie, Otto and their son bowed their heads and Hettie began to offer thanks to God for the fellowship that they had enjoyed that evening, and to ask His blessing upon the two travelers.

I was confused and embarrassed. In the Twedt household, prayer was accepted as a private conversation between each individual and the Almighty that, as far as I could tell, dealt with weighty matters such as pain, shame, and desired eventualities. With the exception of Thanksgiving and Christmas dinners, when my father intoned grace in Norwegian, more as a ceremonial than an invocation, our family ordinarily confined public petitions to their Maker to the confines of His House. Hettie's easy dialogue with Him about mundane matters like gratitude for friendship and safe travel seemed presumptuous, almost flip.

I bowed my head and searched through slitted eyes for some clue as to my expected behavior. Then Hettie took my hand in hers, and in tones both sincere and sweet asked the Father to give me the wisdom to recognize the right road in my life and the courage to follow it.

In the morning, I washed and dressed hurriedly, determined not to keep Fred waiting. I entered the small kitchen, filled with wondrous aromas, and beheld a breakfast table heaped with more food than the Twedts would consume in a week of breakfasts. *Darn it! He beat me again!* Fred was already seated.

Otto was dressed for church in a neatly pressed, starched white shirt, and navy bow tie. The sleeves of his ready-made seersucker suit could not compensate for his long arms, giving him a curiously raw-boned appearance.

"Good morning, my boy," he chimed. "Did you sleep well?"

"Oh, yessir," I replied. Actually, I had not moved a muscle after my head hit the feather pillow in the tiny guest bedroom that Hettie had shown me. "Like a log, yessir."

"Well, good. You boys have a heavy drive ahead of you. Dig into breakfast now and eat enough to hold you for a while!" Otto's relative loquaciousness surprised me. The previous evening he simply nodded bib-overalled assent to Hettie's comments. Perhaps it was the suit that gave him the stature to assert himself in front of his wife.

Hettie stepped from the stove with a plateful of eggs, sunny-side-up, sausage, biscuits, and flapjacks smothered in honey. There was fruit on the table and cool apple juice in a tall glass pitcher. It was tantalizing fare to a hungry teen-ager. But there was no coffee! Before I could request a cup, Hettie brought me a tall glass of fresh milk. She gave me a motherly smile and bowed her head to offer Grace.

When we had finished what was certainly the most extensive and lavish breakfast that I had ever experienced, the Grubers and I stepped out onto the drive beside the pristine little house. There were affectionate good-byes, accompanied by some tears. Fred gathered his little mother in his arms and told her that he loved her and that he would see her again soon. I was astonished when Fred and his father hugged one another, like two tender grizzlies. I could not remember my own father ever embracing me in such an unabashed public display of love, and I was not a little envious.

Fred and I eased slowly away from the Gruber residence, waving until his parents were but dim specks on the rear view mirror. We faced a bright and cloudless azure sky spreading to the far horizon. This third and last day of the drive promised to be hot, long and dusty.

Fred spoke first, "Bob, there's a garage up the road in Eureka; it's run by a crotchety old guy I've known all my life. Einer Haugen was never one to let the Mormon saints tell him that his cherished coffee was a 'sinful stimulant.' He'll have a pot on the stove and be glad to share it. And I'll tell you frankly, I can't imagine starting across that desert out there without my morning coffee! Can you?"

"Gosh no, Fred," I replied, my curiosity peaked by his description of Einer, a Scandinavian who was not a Lutheran, and who wore his association with the saintly brethren like a hair shirt. Fred was a high school student in Goshen when he met Einer for the first time. Fred's first automobile, a hand-me-down jalopy that had served his grandfather and his parents before hosting each of his brothers in sequence, proved the catalyst of their friendship. By the time of Fred's ownership, the car's consumptive performance had become decidedly unreliable. Transporting the Goshen baseball team to a match with Eureka, the car had the prescience to erupt in final catarrhal collapse within hailing distance of Einer Haugen's place of business. After that, the rebuilding of the wreck and the growing admiration with which each viewed the other served to bind them in a lifelong friendship.

The hand-lettered sign on the half-open front door of the All Right Garage, read CLOSED ON SUNDAY. The sound of hammering came from the dusty interior. Inside, a lean man, whose iron-gray hair was shorn in a flat-topped, burr cut, stooped over the innards of an eviscerated Ford. Einer Haugen stood to greet us, greasy coveralls flapping about his skinny frame like a tattered tent on a pole. When he recognized Fred, he grinned from ear to ear, eyes sparkling, and his weathered, unshaven face shattered into uncountable wrinkles. He and Fred greeted each other like long-lost buddies, with roars and backslapping, much handshaking and arm punching. Einer invited us into his office, where the pungent smell of fresh-brewed Columbian assailed our nostrils.

"Bob, this is my old friend, Einer Haugen. We've opened a lot of hoods together."

"I'm pleased to meet you, Mr. Haugen." The hand was gnarled and wiry, but his grip was strong.

"Aw, call me Einer, son. Everybody around here calls me that."

There was much stirring, joking, clinking, and slurping to certify our contentment. While the two older men refurbished cherished old tales with the glue of their long-established friendship, I sat quietly amidst the hummocks of a huge, worn leather couch, and listened to their pleasant raillery. Suddenly, I remembered drifting off to sleep in my room at home, and overhearing my father regale guests, who had dropped in for coffee and conversation, with tales of his automobile adventures in the west. I felt quite homesick and sad.

"Well, Einer thanks for the coffee. It's been wonderful seeing you again," said Fred, rising. "But, all good things come to an end and we've got to get going. There's a long drive ahead of us!" There was a hint of anxiety in his voice. With grins, good-byes and handshakes all around, Fred and I set out on the final leg of our journey.

Driving west on US 6 across the arid desert of southwest Utah, signs of human habitation were sparse. Fantastic color changes mobilized the sand in sheets of challenge. We threaded our way between distant purple mountain ranges with sinister names: Confusion and Snake, and came at last to Tonopah, Nevada, center of what had been a thriving and populous gold mining region, the Comstock!

Garlanded about the hills and canyons of this dusty, lusty Eldorado, a now-vanished network of narrow-gauge railroad tracks once squealed with the passing of diminutive trains hauling ore from the mines to stamp mills. Where they had not been obliterated by ever-lengthening auto roads, Fred pointed out the remains of roadbed, between abandoned piles of ore-tailings that were all that remained of the brawling mining towns. His descriptions fixed themselves in my vivid imagination. I fancied faint wisps of smoke just over each horizon.

Soon after entering California, we turned south into the narrow, empty Owenyo valley. In the spreading orange tint of the late afternoon sun, the valley floor resembled a Halloween sheet cake. Purple shadows crept ominously towards us from the deep lavender fangs of the distant Sierra Nevada Mountains. To the east, the Inyo Mountains dozed in faded yellow

Darkness fell shortly after we passed through the town of Mohave. Exhausted, I dozed on the passenger seat and dreamed of piloting the little trains around the thriving Comstock. Taking pity on his young passenger, Fred drove the remainder of the way around the head of the San Gabriel Mountains, down through the Hollywood hills, and into Santa Monica.

"Wake up, young man. We're here." Fred was gently shaking me by the shoulder.

Sleepily, I sat up, and recognized Uncle Leo's latest house from photographs that were pasted in Mother's album. It was a rambling, multi-gabled structure, with extremely wide eaves that barred the sun from direct entrance into its solarium. A millionaire's mansion masquerading as a bungalow, a flowering forest of semi-tropical shrubbery surrounded it. The house exuded electric warmth from its floor length windows, but there seemed to be no one about.

Retrieving my luggage from the trunk, I followed Fred to the door. After several rings, we heard footsteps and a woman's voice calling, "Coming, I'm coming." We were bathed in amber light from within as the heavy, Spanish oak door opened to reveal a short, lithe, and astonishingly lovely woman in evening dress. She waved a welcoming gesture with an impressively long cigarette holder held in her right hand, like a baton. In her left she had a partially empty goblet.

"Fred, darling," she gushed. "You look marvelous. And little Bobby. So good of you to come all this way, dear. Do come in, both of you. You must be absolutely exhausted!" This last, though true, was said without conviction.

"I'll take a rain check, Car. I'm really bushed after three-four days on the road, and need to get a good night's rest before going in to the office tomorrow. By the way, where is Leo? His car is not in the drive. Out on a case?"

Golly yes, where is Uncle Leo? I thought he'd be here to greet me on the first day of my new life. I felt as empty and betrayed as a jilted bridegroom!

"Oh yes, damn it, Fred. Whenever we've something planned Lee gets called out to hold some neurotic actress' hand while she makes goo-goo eyes at him from her couch."

"Part of the game, Car. Part of the game," rejoined the physician as he took his seat behind the wheel and waved goodbye.

"Thank you, Dr. Gruber. Thanks for everything," I said as he drove off.

"Now Bobby," said my aunt, moving indifferently toward the library. "Come sit down beside me and tell me all about your trip.

She looked absently at her diamond bracelet and patted a spot next to her on a leather divan.

"Yes'm," I yawned, and promptly fell asleep.

WELCOME TO
CALIFORNY, SONNY

"**W**ell, here comes the weary traveler now! Good afternoon, my boy!" The thinly veiled criticism in Uncle Leo's booming voice drifted around the doorway like clammy ground fog.

Uncle Leo and I in 1942

He had already finished his luncheon, and was enjoying a final cup of coffee, when I entered the sunny, plant-filled breakfast room. "Sit down ,and join me, Bob. Sorry I missed you last night. You were already sawing logs when I came in. Did you sleep well?"

"Oh, yessir," I foundered, searching for safer ground. "That sure is a keen bed. I think I must have fallen asleep as soon as I climbed into it. Leastwise, I don't really remember how I managed it."

"You don't remember because you fell asleep in the library when I asked you to tell me about your trip," said Aunt Carmen, coming from the kitchen with my breakfast: a plate of soft-boiled eggs, Danish bacon and blueberry muffins that she set in front of me.

"Dr. Gruber told me that you were a great help to him on the way out; that you were a very good driver," Uncle Leo said. "Nels appears to have trained you well."

"Yessir. Dad taught me all the basics, but it was Uncle Norman who went on practice drives with me."

"Norman, was it? Well, I suppose Normie would have accumulated a great deal of experience after all those years behind the wheel of the Samaritan Hotel bus! It's a cinch that's all he's acquired, if I know that sanctimonious, penny-pinching bunch of hypocrites at the Samaritan!" He smiled, condescendingly. It was clear he didn't much approve of his youngest brother.

"You know, Bob, it won't be long before every high school will offer a course in driver's training. Every family will own a car and our country will have a modern highway network, like the one Hitler is building in Germany. There's no speed limit on 'em, divided roadways, banked curves. We saw what the Germans were building in '36, when I took Car and the kids over there. It was obvious, even then, that they were preparing for war."

"Yes, and one of those terrible Hitler youths yelled '*Amerikana gehe nach hause!*' and spit at Lee through the driver's window of our Olds. It was frightening! We left for the good old USA the very next day, I'll tell you!" echoed my aunt.

"War with the Axis is inevitable!" my uncle declared.

He turned toward my aunt, "Car, I've got to run. Patients waiting." He strode rapidly from the room, his pace belying his bulk, and in a few moments I heard the low throaty rumble of his Cadillac convertible backing out of the driveway. Aunt Carmen waved to the disappearing auto.

Alone in the cheerful room, I gave free rein to the latent hedonism, that my straight-laced upbringing in the provincial environs of Rochester had denied me. *This is the life, all right. Breakfast at noon, the rest of the day free to read and loaf—no chores! People of quality like Uncle Leo and Aunt Carmen certainly don't saddle their children with nasty tasks like taking out the garbage and burning the trash! Why are my parents so old-fashioned?*

"Bob," my aunt's voice intruded on these reveries. "This morning your Uncle Leo asked me if I would take you with me when I drove down to the ranch on Saturday. He is so busy these days, Bob. Between the hospital, his office and emergency calls, I swear the man has no time left for his family! Do you mind very much?"

"Gosh no, Aunt Carmen, I don't mind at all," I said without conviction. *My gosh! I won't even have a week until I have to start the ranch hand stuff.* I was a little miffed.

"I usually take Grandpa his groceries and supplies once a week," Aunt Carmen said. "My father has been living at the ranch ever since my mother died two years ago. It's a good place for him. He watches over the house, not that anything could happen. He feels useful, thank goodness, and has his privacy. But, you have almost a week to rest and enjoy yourself. What would you like to do?"

"Read, I s'pose," I faltered. I had never before been asked how I should like to utilize time. In Rochester my life had been apportioned between school and chores by my parents, who always knew best!

"Oh grand! Perhaps you'd like to read a wonderful novel that I've just finished." She stepped into the library and retrieved a copy of "Vanity Fair" lying on an end table.

"Gosh thanks, Aunt Carmen," I said, accepting the thick novel without much enthusiasm. "This looks—ah—very interesting." I opened the front cover tentatively and perused the title page with the naive inattention of the schoolboy-pedant. *William Makepeace Thackeray first printed in 1848! Gee whiz, Miss Knight never mentioned him.* Miss Iris Knight taught English to Rochester High School college-bound juniors. Demanding and beloved, she managed to instill an appreciation of the thrill and beauty in poetry and prose.

I'd never heard of Thackeray, except as one of the face cards in the game of *Authors* that I'd played out of sheer summertime boredom with Bill Knapp and his aunt on her front porch. Bill Knapp's aunt was a big-chested soprano who pompously belted out special music for Sunday morning worship services in the Rochester Congregational Church. During the whole card game the Knapps perspired and gossiped. I always felt queasily damp when I departed.

"Boy, that Thackeray sure wrote a long time ago, didn't he?"

"Yes, he was one of the Eminent Victorians," said my aunt. "But this is a new edition, just published by Heritage Press and was the April choice of the Book-of-the-Month Club!"

"Well, thanks. I'll just keep it handy on the night table in my room," I said, and promptly confined Becky Sharp to oblivion, without a pang of remorse.

"I know, boys your age are "dating," aren't they. Even in Rochester! I'm sure Lee and I could introduce you to some nice girl of your own age."

"You bet. I've gone out with a whole lot of girls," I boasted. "Dinner and a show, or dancing with late supper." Using hackneyed Hollywood phraseology I was describing going to the movies, or sock hops in the high school gymnasium, with a soda afterwards.

My aunt struggled to contain her amusement, and managed a restrained smile. "You know, I've got someone in mind even now. Esther Williams is a lovely young woman and an aspiring actress. She's had small parts in some films and I believe she'll become a star before very long. How would you like to take her to dinner at the Coconut Grove with dancing afterwards? Your uncle and I will foot the bill."

There was a thunderous silence while I digested what had just occurred. I had exaggerated my popularity with the opposite sex, enhanced my social life, and invented a cosmopolitan personality; all were now to be measured against reality. *Esther Williams for cripes sake!* Of course I had seen her in pictures. She was an excellent swimmer and appeared in water ballet numbers. Her astonishing figure, revealed in a tight fitting maillot, sent the hackles on my neck rippling with excitement. The possibilities loomed maddeningly before me. *Dancing at the Coconut Grove to Horace Heidt and His Musical Knights, with Esther Williams in my arms!*

"What do you think of the idea, Bob?" The bubble of my fantasy burst with the harsh intrusion of my aunt's question. I saw myself, the rube from Rochester, not yet ready for the big time! If my ignorance of haute cuisine and the art of fine dining failed to expose my lack of suave urbanity, my provincial ballroom style would.

"No, Aunt Carmen, I better not," I gloomed. "I've got a steady girl back home. We're engaged to be engaged!" I lied, grinning idiotically.

"I'm sorry," she replied, with but the hint of a smile, perhaps in sympathy for my callow lack of social assurance. She strode to the library table, took a cigarette from an elaborately engraved, cedar-lined, silver box, and lighting it, exhaled smoothly with long practice. "Perhaps we can think of something else. Oh, by the way, Bob. When the children come in with Nana, will you take my car and return some chickens to the butcher for me?"

"Sure I will," I agreed, glad to be on safe conversational ground once more.

A short time later, my cousins, Loralou, eleven, and Leo John, Jr., twelve years old, came breathlessly into the house. The governess had purposely kept the noisy children occupied with a roller-skating outing in the nearby park so that the tired traveler could recover. They greeted me with huge hugs and squeals of happiness. Young John was particularly delighted with the prospect of accompanying me across the city to the butcher.

The chickens were not at all the pallid, plucked, and lifeless creatures that I had carried home many times from Mr. Fritz Hagen's butcher shop in Rochester. These chickens were alive—but just barely. I was certainly familiar with healthy chickens, having seen them at Mrs. Johnson's on the Balfour farm, and at Alice and Sam Nelson's farm near Byron, but these were quite something else. I had never seen a sorrier bunch of birds. Confined to a cage in the small open space reserved for trashcans, between the garage and the alley, these birds appeared to have been chewed upon. Largely defeathered about the head, some without eyes, they drooped and cringed miserably.

"They're sick," remarked John laconically. In point of fact, these sad creatures were the finale to my uncle's mythologizing those simpler times when he was a child, tending his own father's chickens in Rochester. My uncle had purchased the pullets in order to have plenty of fresh eggs for breakfast. Of course, the notoriously successful medical practitioner had no time to practice the farming fantasy, and had left poultry management to the careless mercies of his children. The well-recognized tendency of the white Leghorn to exhibit peck-order and cannibalism had accomplished the rest. And so, at Aunt Carmen's insistence, the plentiful-egg experiment was terminated. The tatterdemalion flock would be returned to the poultry purveyor from whence they originated.

John, who was overjoyed to be relieved of his debilitated charges, and I gave careful study to the problem of transportation. The cages were too large to be placed into the trunk of my aunt's LaSalle. But what if the dozen survivors were crammed into a single cage, the trunk lid propped open, and the cage secured with some scraps of clothesline rope, found in the garage? The cage and its contents soon swayed gently across the bumper. I backed the long, dark-blue, four-door sedan out into the alley with exquisite care. I certainly did not intend to damage her automobile, and irrevocably confirm the disappointment I had seen in my aunt's eyes after the Esther Williams fiasco.

"Let's go, John," I said, motioning for him to get in the car. "You be navigator. Just give me sufficient warning when you want me to turn, okay?"

"Okay," he replied, and leaned forward, intent upon his task.

We swerved out into the boulevard and picked up speed. I paid close attention to the operation of an unfamiliar vehicle. John was a capable guide, smartly calling out directions by landmark. "Turn left at the next street; follow the red sedan." *This will be a cinch*. As we plunged deeper into the city, the traffic noise mounted. Horns blared imperiously, stop signals clanged as they changed, and streetcars clamored incessantly for attention.

Neither of us had the presence of mind to anticipate what effect this din was having upon the frightened passengers, who were now pecking one another and the frayed rope holding the cage door closed. Suddenly, I was startled to see a feathery explosion in the rear view mirror. Chickens, having severed the feeble closures, were jumping ship, at least those with sufficient strength to perform the necessary athletics. Trapped in the streaming traffic, there was little that I could do to recover the fugitives that were flapping off to see Los Angeles. Finally I was able to turn into a quieter residential side street, bring the LaSalle to the curb, and stop. John and I ran around to the rear to resecure the teetering cage and diminished number of occupants. Only six of the most enfeebled tenants still remained.

My cousin and I readily agreed not to mention our untimely detour, and continued our trip to the poulterer, who expressed dismay at the condition of the remaining birds, but did not otherwise comment. To my surprise, neither did my aunt and uncle. Aunt Carmen had never concerned herself with the details of Uncle Leo's egg-producing experiment and had no idea how many chickens were kept behind the garage. Only my uncle addressed the issue.

"We should have had more room for them to roam," he said. "Continual confinement must have weakened them. They weren't good layers and they certainly must have been in poor condition to bring such a small price. At home Mama had a wonderful back yard for her chickens. She had the fattest flock of cacklers you've ever seen." To my great relief he had begun to reminisce and never mentioned the chickens again.

The rest of the week passed uneventfully. My aunt, who had taken the measure of my immaturity, spoke no more about dates with starlets, consigning her nephew to a lesser, more puerile rung on the ladder of social development. I continued to sleep late, lounge about, and occasionally play with my younger cousins.

On Saturday morning I was busy loading the car for the trip to the ranch. Mostly, it was groceries for Aunt Carmen's father, who had telephoned his needs earlier in the week. William Edgar Schwerer did his own cooking; had done so for years, having been the owner of a Minneapolis diner until his wife's death. The staples of his diet were meat and potatoes, the frying pan his main utensil. In addition to the groceries there was my cardboard suitcase, whose original contents had been mostly cotton shorts and shirts, neatly pressed and packed by my mother. These things my aunt had replaced with jeans and blue denim shirts that were far more practical for ranch work. My feet, shod in unaccustomed leather boots, seemed unbearably heavy.

My aunt drove the big LaSalle. I sat in the front seat with her. My cousins squeezed into the back surrounded by the stacked grocery bags. We took busy Wilshire Boulevard into Los Angeles following much the same route I had traversed earlier with the sick chickens, then eastward on Whittier and the less-trafficked Yorba Linda, around the northern tip of the Santa Ana Mountains to reach Corona and the road to the southeast. Another fifty miles of narrow, crumbling, and sun-bleached macadam that looked to be losing the battle for existence to the creeping sand, and we reached Temecula, a place trying bravely to pass for a farming community. Beyond Temecula the road was only a gravel track that snaked around hills, under bluffs, across arroyos, many with small fordable rivulets. Veils of feathery seeds drifted like an early snowfall from the giant Eucalyptus trees that lined their banks. Occasionally, in a grove, we saw a small home surrounded by children and dogs.

The Madsen ranch, a thousand acres of beige-colored semi-desert, lay in the Pala Valley, more than a hundred miles south of Santa Monica. Rimmed by low, mesquite-covered hills, the valley was home to the Pala Nation. Its people had been uprooted from their buffalo-laden, prairie homeland in the central plains and herded into a reservation on these inhospitable, arid environs in the previous century. The Madsen spread lay six miles due south of a reservation hamlet bearing the tribal name. Other than its huge size, the ranch had one principal advantage not readily available to its neighbors—plenty of water. A branch of the Santa Margarita River coursed lazily through it and thus, by the simple expedient of drilling a shallow well almost anywhere in the sandy soil, that vital commodity could be found in abundance.

Late in the afternoon Aunt Carmen piloted the dust-covered LaSalle beneath the arched gateway to Rancho Palomar, past the ranch buildings, and turned west up a dirt road to the main house. The home was difficult to detect, perched on the side of a ridge incised by gloomy canyons and now blindingly haloed by the setting sun. As we drew nearer I could see that it was a long, single story structure, actually two buildings joined by a breezeway. It was built in a style termed "Mission," common in the southwest at the time, and had arched windows, white-painted stucco walls, a low veranda, and a Spanish-tile roof. Where cracks had appeared, they were simply painted over so that the house would appear to be of adobe.

On the breezeway an elderly man dozed on a wood-frame lounger that had fearfully splayed wooden wheels. Its defeated mattress lay on a frazzled rope network that threatened imminent collapse. Aunt Carmen pulled to a stop in front of the house, calling briskly to her father from the driver's window. The old man stood to greet his visitors and immediately became the adored object of his grandchildren's boisterous attentions. He wore a shapeless fisherman's hat, brim pulled low over his eyes, and his gold-rimmed spectacles had round lenses in the style of the previous century. This being Saturday, he had bathed and shaved. He had donned a clean, long-sleeved, reddish-plaid shirt and a much-laundered pair of overalls, from whose bib-pocket protruded a gold watch chain, and a wadded red bandanna handkerchief. His dress code never varied. At age 73, a sunken, flabby chest and paunchy midriff had replaced the short stocky muscular frame of his youth, so that he appeared to be pear-shaped when standing upright.

"Vell, vell, here you iss, at last. Took you long enough, heh," said Bill Schwerer, looking petulantly toward his daughter.

"Oh, Dad, stop! We got a late start, having to load all that stuff for you, and that's the end of it," she replied, in a loud voice.

The old man had curled a cupped hand behind his right ear, in a futile attempt to overcome his advancing deafness.

"I'm tired and there's still dinner to prepare," she continued. "I've brought T-bones for you to grill, Dad." He grinned with anticipation as she handed him the package.

Speaking to my cousins and me, she ordered, "Now, you kids make yourself useful, and bring the rest of the stuff into the kitchen." With that everyone grabbed a bag and began to unload the car.

Bill started a mesquite fire in an outdoor brick grill built into the side of the house. The tantalizing smell of mesquite wood smoke soon filled the breezeway. Under Bill's practiced hands, steaks, hash-brown potatoes, pork and beans and cornbread were soon ready. My aunt made a fresh green salad for everyone except her father. Bill never touched rabbit food! We ate on the breezeway, and though it became much cooler after the sun had set, no one noticed. The moon rose casting a fairy light across the small valley and the faint occasional lowing of range cattle could be heard. In that magical moment I half-expected the *Sons of the Pioneers* to appear and serenade us from horseback. When we had finished eating and cleared the table, Bill washed the dishes while his daughter dried. My cousins and I sat on the porch looking out across the valley at the gathering velvety night. No one spoke and no one objected when my aunt directed us all to our beds.

Early Sunday morning, I was jerked into consciousness by the tell-tale aroma of freshly brewed coffee. Dressing quickly, I followed my nose to the kitchen. Aunt Carmen and her father were both dressed and preparing Sunday breakfast. My aunt, warned of a scorching-hot day to come, wanted to start back to the city as soon as they had eaten. Bacon, eggs, and Bill's baking powder biscuits with honey helped to create the illusion of a culinary bond between the old man and myself.

After breakfast, the good-byes were said, my aunt promising to return at least biweekly, and the big LaSalle rolled rapidly down hill, carrying her and my cousins back to Santa Monica.

I turned toward the house to see Bill enter the guesthouse that was his domain, shut his door, and disappear. I was left alone. I set about to unpack my few belongings, arranging them in a chest of drawers in my bedroom.

A half-hour later I returned to the veranda seeking a breeze that would bring relief from the increasing heat. I was surprised to find Bill lying on the sway back lounger, mouth agape, snoring like a suffocating dinosaur. Leaving the old man to his siesta, I set out to explore the site of my summer's employment, to commence officially tomorrow.

I walked down the hill toward the ranch buildings. The dirt road lay between range lands defined by strands of barbed wire. I could see no cattle, but their droppings lay everywhere. It was a long while before I neared the ranch yard that had appeared so near when I began. By now I really began to feel the sun, oppressive at midday. *Gosh, I wish that I had worn a hat!* There were straw hats aplenty back at the house, but I had not taken one for fear it would spoil my well-combed look.

No one appeared from the ranch foreman's house; the yard was as silent as a movie set before a gunfight. I had a nebulous sense that hidden eyes were watching and left the yard in the direction of the arched entrance gate. It, too, was much farther along the track to Pala than I had remembered while riding in the car. *Boy, I'm kinda tired!*

In time I came to a short timber trestle straddling the creek that flowed through the ranch. Eucalyptus trees growing on the banks, the little islands, and actually in the streambed, gave the only shade available on Rancho Palomar. Stepping onto the trestle's wooden deck, I walked the few steps to its midpoint, and leaned against one of its guardrails. It was made of roughly trimmed eucalyptus limbs, had a decidedly rickety appearance, but seemed sound enough. At first glance it was difficult to determine in which direction the shallow water, mumbling gently in the shadows a few feet below, was flowing. The Zumbro River, back home in Rochester was insignificant as rivers go, but it was certainly a more respectable stream than this. Thinking then of Rochester, I wondered what my parents and sister were doing now? I guessed that they must be out for a drive in the car.

Both Nancy and I had arrived at that stage in a young person's development when the Sunday afternoon drive had become a total embarrassment, a living nightmare. We had rebelled after years of hearing our father command, "Get in the car, you two, we go for a ride." Our repeated objections to the hateful Sunday obligation, had finally gained us a measure of freedom. But now, I wished that I were with them!

I looked north up the road toward Pala, eyes moist with homesickness, and saw an enlarging cloud of ochre dust coming nearer. From its center, a gray Chevrolet business coupe of recent vintage emerged. The car stopped on the bridge, that continued to undulate gently, and an unshaven, snaggletooth man, who appeared ancient to me, but was probably about fifty, leaned out the window.

"You lost, young feller?" he grinned.

"No sir, I'm staying here at the ranch for the summer," I replied. And then, for effect, "I'm going to college in the fall—Cal Tech in Pomona." I beamed at the stranger with fatuous pride.

"Well, by jingoes, you must be Uncle Doc's nephew from the East. We've been hearing about you from Mrs. Doc and Old Gramps," said the grinning man, extricating himself from behind the wheel of the car. He left the Chevy idling indifferently in the center of the span, posing no hazard to the non-existent traffic, while he loped over to me with outstretched hand.

"Welcome to Californy, sonny. I belong to the place too. Name's Hillebø—Lars Hillebø. Out here, most people just call me Pop." He was a startlingly tall, gaunt figure dressed in a faded, worn, blue denim shirt. A metallic watch fob with the numerals 40 & 8 hung on a greasy braided-leather cord from the pocket of his frayed overalls, whose knees had worn completely through.

"I'm pleased to meet you, Mr. Hillebø," I said, pronouncing the name correctly. "My name is Bob Twedt, and I'd be happy to call you Pop. That is if you don't object." We shook hands vigorously, arms extended.

"Of course I don't mind, Bob. Didn't I say so? You must be a Nor-skie boy with a handle like Twedt. Where you hail from, Bob? Must be someplace like Wisconsin or Dakota, eh?"

I began to expound about Rochester and my family while Pop drew a small sack of Bull Durham tobacco from his breast pocket and rolled a cigarette. The complex and delicate process was accomplished with a casual dexterity that held me completely spellbound. At its completion, when Pop had returned the Bull Durham sack, which he had cinched with his teeth, to his pocket and set the wooden match ablaze with a flinty thumb nail, I had become completely silent, transfixed in awed admiration!

Breaking the silence that he had come to expect after one of his dis-plays, Pop said, "You look kind of tuckered out, Bob. Been walkin' long?"

"Yeah, I sure have! After my aunt and my cousins left for the city around noon, I got kinda bored, I guess, so I started out from the ranch house. I just wanted to look around, but I've not met a living soul, that is until I met you, Pop. I guess I am sorta winded. Gosh, it's farther than it looks!"

"Get in, Bob, I'll drive you home," invited Pop, understandingly. And then, to avoid the appearance of condescension, "I have some mail here that I was taking up to Old Gramps anyway."

"Thanks, I believe I will," I replied with relief. And, with a triplicate acceleration through the gears, we headed off in the direction of the setting sun in a repeat of yesterday. Pop stopped in front of the house where Bill, who had just awakened, stood to greet us.

"Got some mail for ya,' Gramps," yelled Pop. He handed the old man a bundle tied with twine. "An' I brought yer boy here. He was headed this way when I met him on the road," he lied. Turning to his passenger he whispered, "Ya gotta talk loud to Old Gramps, Bob, he's deef as a post."

I climbed out of the car and, with a reassuring wave; Pop drove down the hill.

"I been lookin' for ya, boy," said Bill. "Time fer me to cook supper and I never wait fer latecomers. I'm tellin' ya now, just so's we understand each other." Bill turned and headed into the kitchen. The supper was a mediocre collage of last night's leftovers, but after my explorations I was ravenous.

"That was a great supper, Mr. Schwerer," I said, overloud and with undisguised enthusiasm, at the conclusion of the meal.

"Call me Bill, boy. You don't have to yell. Yessiree, I got the chef's touch, ain't I? Comes from many years of practice, boy. Let's clean up. You wash and I'll put 'em away. They ain't many."

We cleared the table, washed and dried the dishes, working in silence. When we had finished, Bill returned to his quarters saying, "Well, I guess I'll have a look at my mail and turn in." I was once again left alone.

After thumbing through various dog-eared magazines that had, without justification, been saved from the Santa Monica trash bin, I sighed and went to my room, undressed, washed my face, brushed my teeth, and went to bed. I lay in the darkened room, under the dim light of a young moon, reviewing memories of Rochester and home. Among the occasional creature sounds I could discern the lonely cry of a coyote, and felt quite sorry for myself.

THE GOPHER WARS

Monday dawned, and the insistent sunlight clamored over my pillow, warm on my cheek. This, I remembered with considerable reluctance, was to be my first day as a ranch hand. I expected to be given some important responsibility that I would not know the faintest thing about. At best I would be clumsy, at worst I would probably fail. I dreaded the day. I put on my new denim shirt and trousers, pulled on my work boots, and headed for the kitchen. The smell of coffee and bacon declared that Bill was practicing his fry-cookery.

"Look sharp, boy. Breakfast's ready. A mite more an' I'd be washin' up," Bill said with the compassionate understanding of a stick.

"I'm sorry, sir, er Bill. I'll be on time after this," I promised.

"See that you do, and we'll have no trouble," countered the curmudgeon.

Without saying grace, we ate in silence. Afterwards, with proud humility, Bill volunteered to wash up.

"Well, I'll be going then," I said.

"Better take this, boy." It was a battered straw hat. I put it on with distaste even though I remembered how much I had wished for such haberdashery on the previous day.

"Thanks," I said.

I retraced my steps of Sunday, and arrived at the ranch yard and the surrounding complex of buildings sooner than I wanted to. A crowd of expectant men was lounging about. A number of them were on horseback, the reins slack, and the animals waiting patiently, nostrils flared in anticipation. Though their dress had not betrayed them, I could see that most of the hands were not white men. I searched in vain among the few who were for my newfound friend, Pop.

191

Suddenly, the screen door that hung precariously on the rear of the ranch foreman's home opened with a tormented wail. A sandy-haired man in his 40s came out upon the back stoop, letting the flailing screen slap closed. The man stretched his muscular arms above his head, clasped both hands and yawned loudly. Bushy hair appeared through ragged rents in the armpits of his soiled tee shirt. He looked with undisguised contempt at the assembled ranch hands, who had obviously observed this loutish show many times before. The man's puffy face was red, but not from the sun. A distinct ring of fat at his midriff anticipated a paunch.

The screen door shrieked once more and a thin, slatternly woman in a nondescript, gray housedress appeared, holding a dishpan against one hip with wash-reddened, bony arms. She tossed the greasy contents of the pan into the ranch yard, narrowly missing the man.

"Watch what yer doin', woman. Damn near slopped it all over me," he yelled at her.

The woman stared at her husband through unseeing, washed-out blue eyes, but did not respond. She turned to reenter the house, shoulders slumped with resignation, as a shouting group of urchins tumbled out past her into the yard, cuffing and cursing each other.

"Where the hell is Pop? The old fucker must be sleepin' one off," the sandy-haired man said, to the rapt indifference of his audience.

"Hold yer hosses, Gid," said a voice I recognized. It was Pop, who had entered the yard from the tool shed, carrying a shovel. "I suspicioned you'd want to do some waterin' this mornin' and so I went to get my equipment," he continued laconically.

"Goddammit, Pop. I'm the foreman of this ranch and I'll decide when we irrigate and whose gonna do it, understand?" said the sandy-haired man.

"Okay, okay, I ain't telling' you your business, Gid. You just fire away." Pop leaned expectantly on his shovel.

◆   ◆   ◆

Gideon Rufus Simpson came with the ranch. He had been the fore-man for the previous absentee owner, a Los Angeles legal firm, and agents in foreclosure. It had not been his first job, but simply the latest in a series, each remarkable in its brevity, tracing his westward drift from Clay County, West Virginia.

Over time, in bits and pieces from various sources, I learned Gid's history. He had been born and raised in a decaying shack that squatted dejectedly on the banks of the Lilly Fork of the Elk River. He was the hapless son of a hard-coal miner, who had been killed in a mine acci-dent when Gid was a still a toddler. The mine's owners had at first resisted making any restitution, maintaining that drink had been the cause. Perceiving the injustice in such parsimony, his fellow workers, who had liked the man, raised a hue and cry that threatened to become ugly. As a result the widow was placated with a pittance that she was too fearfully destitute to refuse.

Each of the Simpson children was expected to contribute to the sup-port of the family. Gid, the youngest, was no exception, and had worked odd jobs for as long as he could remember. Sparked by lazy creativity, he learned to augment the fuel supply by hurling insults at the men aboard the Buffalo Creek and Gauley Railroad coal trains that ground slowly up the line along Lilly Fork. Such taunts, particularly if calling the crew's ancestry into question, would invariably result in good-sized lumps of coal being hurled in his direction. The days and years passed sooty gray in all seasons. The lumbering locomotives panted invitingly, "Come-with-me-Come-with-me." He finished high school and, unable to bear the guilty sight of his mother's futile drudg-ery or the bleak prospects of life along the Fork, Gid clambered aboard a slow-moving coal train headed for the outside world, and left home for good.

Gid obtained work as a hired hand, drifting with the seasons until he arrived in Morgantown, where his employer encouraged him to get an education and better his prospects. He enrolled in the University of West Virginia and graduated with a degree in Animal Husbandry.

His first job was managing a dairy farm for an elderly couple who had retired from farming and moved to Morgantown. The Ag School faculty, impressed that he had maintained a respectable academic record despite having to support a wife as well as himself, had recommended him. But after only one season, Gid, his wife, and an infant baby daughter had left the place—some said they had been asked to leave. They began to drift west.

This same pattern was repeated many times thereafter. The Simpsons never seemed to stay in one place for more than a season and their departures were always fraught with mutual dissatisfaction. Gid always prevaricated when a new employer asked for his references, offering some curiously inspired if none too plausible hard luck story to cover the years since his graduation. He and his wife lost confidence in the present, hope in the future and interest in each other so that the increasing numbers of their progeny was a paradox rather than a comfort. When Dr. Leo Madsen accepted his credentials and continued his employment without too much inquiry, Gid's tenure as foreman at Rancho Palomar became the longest he had ever held.

◆   ◆   ◆

"Pop, take the big Cat down to the lower alfalfa field and do some waterin'," said Gid, at last. "I noticed yesterday that it was getting mighty dry over there," he continued, relating what Pop had suggested as though it were his own idea. "Take whoever you want with ya, but get her soaked down today, ya hear?"

"Okay, Gid, yer right," replied the older man. "I'll take Sundance, Pablo, and Coyote," he said, shortening the Pala's given names for easier usage. "And Paco better come, too. That's a lot of pipe to string along the east line."

Pop and his men assembled their tools, and entered the machine shed where the large caterpillar tractor was parked. Sounds of spasmodic coughing, gasping, and backfiring accompanied by clouds of unburned exhaust, filled the yard. At last, when these metallic protests had settled to a steady rumble, the tractor crawled into view, with Pop in the driver's seat. Paco backed a stake truck crammed with long sections of irrigation pipe into the yard, and the others clambered aboard. The little caravan departed, the truck leading, and the tractor churning curtains of light tan dust behind its treads.

Gid turned to face a half dozen mounted men and addressed their leader, a tall, large-boned man sitting bolt upright on a big piebald horse with strong withers. The man's square, impassive face was weathered the color of saddle leather and cleft by a long aquiline nose. His iron-gray hair hung across one shoulder in a single long braid, intertwined with bright red ribbon. A tall black felt hat with a high crown and band of hand-worked silver and turquoise medallions sat squarely upon his head. He gazed straight down at Gid through wide-set eyes as dark as coal and listened to the foreman in flinty silence.

"Wolf, you take your boys up the mountain and find those doggies. Take that salve too. There's some cows up there that've got themselves tangled in the wire and they're all scratched up. Doctor 'em. And look out for any that have just calved. Any of 'em's got sores, you fix 'em, hear!" Gid concluded.

With a nod and grunt of understanding, Chief Gray-Wolf-Races-the-Wind and the other Pala riders ambled off raising little ecru clouds that hung in the air long after the sound of clopping hooves and jingling harness had died away. As the dust began to settle, Gid feigned seeing me for the first time.

"Well, I guess you must be Uncle Doc's nephew. We've been expecting you for over a week. Finally gave up waitin'. Thought you'd decided to stay back east takin' it easy with the other kids on vacation."

"No sir," I said, immediately on the defensive. "I'm sorry to be late, but I had to wait for a ride down here with my aunt. She came this weekend with supplies for Mr. Bill."

"Yeah, ain't it wonderful," mocked Gid. "All that old geezer's got to do nowadays is snooze in the sun and wait for his daughter to bring his eats. Sure is a tough life. Wish we were all that lucky! What's your handle gonna be, Doc's nephew?"

"Pardon me?"

"What's your handle, what're we gonna call you?"

"Oh, yessir. My name is Bob."

"Okay, Bob it is. Well, Bob, my name's Simpson, Gideon Simpson. You can call me Gid. I run Rancho Palomar for your Uncle Doc. I'm gonna start you off doin' something important. You're goin' huntin'—trappin' actually. You're lookin' to kill gophers—mean little bastards that live in underground burrows. There's thousands of 'em and they dig in our new-plowed fields. They wait until night an' then they just raise bloody hell with the furrows. They tunnel beneath the surface to connect their burrows, and the tunnels can carry off the water we're pumpin', sometimes as far as a quarter mile! The little fuckers are stealin'—stealin' water! Why, killing's too good for 'em! Y'unnerstan?"

"Yessir," I said, unwilling to question this stream of rising vituperation. As I would soon learn, Gid attributed sexual interest and proficiency to almost anything animate or inanimate that he found irritating or actually distasteful.

"Okay then. I'm gonna send you out with Hay Soos, here. You pay attention 'cause as soon as you learn the ropes, I've got somethin' else for him to do and you'll be on yer own." A short, wizened, extremely old Pala man, who had been squatting unobserved on the shady side of the foreman's back stoop, arose and padded softly toward us. He wore faded blue denims, shapeless moccasins, a beaded leather headband, and no hat. It was difficult to identify the slits of his eyes among the deep furrows strewn across his face.

"How," Jesus said, to my astonishment.

The foreman went inside his house and the old man beckoned me to follow him across the yard and into the tool shed. The contrast between the brilliant morning sunlight and the darkness within made distinguishing anything very difficult. Jesus pointed to the walls and said, "Take traps!" Having never laid eyes on a trap before, I was not prepared for the vast array of these devices that gradually materialized from the gloom, hanging from all the interior walls. The working part of each trap, two half-circular jaws that clapped together over a treadle trip, was attached by a length of heavy bailing-wire to a stout stake. Jesus was busy selecting as many traps as he could carry and I followed suit.

"You come," demanded Jesus and we trudged off, single file, Jeff following Mutt.

We followed the tracks that Pop and his crew had made, for what seemed an eternity. Although the morning was still young, the temperature was soaring under the harsh sun. My clothes were soon stained with perspiration and caked with light-tan dust.

"Stop here!" Jesus commanded, at last. We had come to a huge field of new growth that I guessed was corn, stretching away to the horizon, marked by trees at the river's edge. Looking carefully, I could see many stakes scattered widely about the field. Jesus swept his extended arm slowly from one side of the field to the other and said, "Set two day past."

Stepping into the unfenced field, the old man followed a furrow in the direction of one of the nearest stakes. Bending down beside it he observed, "Got him!" Then he began to scoop the sandy soil away from the wire that angled tautly downward. In a moment his swift strokes had revealed the burrow in which lay the trap mechanism that enclosed a motionless form. The animal, caught by its forepaws, had made a futile attempt to extricate itself. Its struggles were graphed in clawed hieroglyphs on the floor and walls of the tunnel. In the warm earth, decomposition was paced by dehydration—there was no odor. Nevertheless, the evidence of the small, painful drama that had taken place here shocked and revolted me. I remembered a time, years before when I had stared at the bloody, fluttering form of a pigeon that I had caused to die. As far as I could see, neither creature had ever caused me, or anyone else for that matter, any harm. To me, their deaths had been senseless; perhaps all such unnecessary death was senseless.

Jesus removed the gopher's corpse, cleaned the trap, and hung it over his shoulder. He shoveled the dead animal back into the burrow, thoroughly packing the tunnel closed with his moccasined feet, and picked his way forward to examine another staked site. This time the trap was empty, much to my relief.

Ahead, I could see a mound of earth that was darker than the previous two. Jesus said, "New pueblo. Set trap here." With that he knelt down beside the fresh mound, examining it carefully. He showed me by gesticulation and choppy phrases, the likely direction of the gopher's tunnel, and how to remove the covering earth without damage. He demonstrated the operation of a trap by tripping it with a stick, and I jumped when its jaws clamped shut with a sharp predatory report. Having established the danger to erring fingers more effectively by this example than with words, Jesus showed me how to bait, set, and place the trap within the burrow and how to cover the hole inconspicuously. His calm confidence and the deft swiftness with which he carried out these deceptions impressed me, but I was disgusted by the grim efficiency of the mechanized killing.

"You set trap," Jesus said at the same time pointing toward a freshly dug mound. I emulated what I'd been shown, and turned in a credible performance that needed only a few corrections. As the morning wore on we two odd colleagues continued to examine previously laid traps and to place new ones. If one counted death as success, I thought grimly, Jesus' success rate was about one kill in three traps set. The sun reached its zenith just as we arrived at the creek at the field's northern edge. Jesus squinted upwards and announced, "Sit here; eat." He squatted beneath the shade of a eucalyptus tree, removed a greasy bundle from beneath his shirt, and began to consume its contents. The old man had timed our work to arrive at this cool and shady spot for lunch and a siesta! With a start, I realized that I had not thought of this and would have to go hungry until night. I sat down in the shade and dozed.

The afternoon proceeded in the same fashion. Traps were set and corpses were retrieved in a macabre succession. If it were possible, the afternoon seemed hotter than the morning. I could taste the gritty saltiness of the perspiration that ran down my face, and into my eyes. I started to take my shirt off, but Jesus shook his head, emphatically.

"Hot sun burn white skin!"

At last, with its fiery finale hanging over the western foothills, Jesus headed for the ranch yard and I trudged home, exhausted and famished.

Bill was waiting supper when I arrived, too tired to care about the fuming and scolding over my lateness. The meal was palatable and eaten in silence, Bill having emptied himself of his irritation, and I wondered how I could ever face another such day. After the washing up I went to my room, undressed, and went to bed with only a cursory bath. Sleep came instantly.

After breakfast the next morning, I made myself some peanut butter and jelly sandwiches and a thermos of coffee, and placed this noontime repast into a brown paper bag. Bill reminded me that supper would be on the table at 6 o'clock sharp, bade me the usual warnings about being late, and lent me a cheap pocket watch from which the nickel-plating had long disappeared. I thanked my crusty benefactor, and vowed to be washed and seated promptly at 6:00 PM.

Once at the yard, the scenario of the previous morning was repeated with but minor variations. It was as if each man were an actor in a long-running performance of a mediocre play, his stage positions, lines, and expected responses having become completely mechanical. The old Pala man, Jesus, and I were sent out each morning to continue our rodent removal efforts, with the same mixed results. With conversation at a minimum and my experience with the work still limited, we never became friends.

The ranch workweek was six days; on the seventh, only essential tasks like milking the handful of Jerseys were carried out. After noon on Saturday, the Pala hands began to slip silently away from their assigned tasks, not seen again until early Monday morning. Sunday, a day of rest, they could remain at home with their families. Gid Simpson, who lost no opportunity to disparage his hands, insisted that they spent every weekend on a drunken spree.

When my second week began, I had lost much of my nervous inferiority, and settled in to the routine of ranch work. Jesus was given another task and Gid sent me out to make single-handed war on the gophers.

"Now, goddammit, Bob, you get your ass out there and kill them little fuckers. I don't want to see any traps hangin' in the shed! Unnerstan' what I'm sayin' to ya?"

"Yessir, you bet," I said, and trudged off.

From that day, however, the gopher death rate diminished. Whether this came about from the vigor of my ambushes or simply that they decamped for greener pastures, I cannot say. The fact was that fewer and fewer limp forms were recovered, fewer fresh mounds were pushed up in the fields and most of my set traps remained untripped. I was glad to have the guilt of their deaths removed in such a miraculous way. Once more, the tool shed walls hung heavy with unused traps. Gid was fit to be tied!

"Yer layin' down on the job, Bob. Dammit, if it weren't for you bein' Uncle Doc's nephew…" Gid never specified what the consequences might have been, but it was not hard to guess.

"But, Mr. Gid, I think I musta' got 'em all; there's no new mounds!" I cited in self-defense.

"Okay, Mr. Smart Guy! Let's find out if ya' got 'em all!" Gid snorted.

The next week, to my great relief, Gid sent me to work on the pipe gang. That was all right with me—the gang boss was Pop!

The creek that meandered through the ranch, the source of its irrigation water, had many faces. It bubbled through Eucalyptus groves, twisting and turning, wide and shallow. Elsewhere it stayed within its banks, and ran swift and deep enough to swim a few strokes. In sandy stretches it seemed to lose interest—just give up the effort, even sinking into the earth for a spell, to emerge again a few rods distant. Into its aquifer a number of shallow wells had been drilled.

Water was pumped from these wells through galvanized metal irrigation pipe, six inches in diameter. The pipe came in ungainly sections with openings along one side a furrow-width apart. It was laid on the ground at the edge of a field perpendicular to its furrows. Laying pipe was clumsy, backbreaking work, and demanded ingenuity and patience to join incorrectly aligned or damaged segments. As the day wore on, the segments became scorching hot, even through leather gloves. Pop taught me how to manhandle them without mangling my fingers.

After a line of pipe was laid, the openings in all but the first few segments were closed, and the tractor powered pump engaged. The number of furrows being watered depended upon the number of hands, who walked the furrows, shovels in hand, to direct the flow. When the furrows were saturated, the first pipe openings were closed and the next series of furrows were watered.

I leaned on my shovel that first morning, pleased with myself, a real ranch hand at last. As I scanned my furrows that were darkening with moisture, I was shocked to see that some seemed to stop short, the rivulet of water just disappeared! Worse, I could see geysers springing up, mysteriously, far down the field.

A chorus of guffaws from all the hands erupted all down the pipeline.

"Look there, Mighty Hunter, many gophers not yet dead!"

"Over here, Many-Gopher-Scalp, you miss one!"

"Never mind them, Bob! Git after them leaks! I can see Gid's pickup comin'," Pop chortled, and loped across the furrows to help me. Quickly, we plugged the gopher tunnels with earth, stomped them in and the geysers evaporated.

The ranch truck pulled up; the foreman emerged, and peered expectantly across the field. There were no geysers to be seen. "Keep your eye peeled for leaks, Pop. The kid here thinks he's caught all the gophers on the place. That's a laugh," he spat, with a contemptuous look in my direction. Then he jumped back in the truck and roared off toward the yard.

"Keep an eye out fer leaks!" Pop scoffed. "He must think we're all dumb asses!"

"I'm sorry, Pop," I said. "I really thought I'd trapped 'em all. Wishful thinking, I guess." I was embarrassed, ashamed, and guilty. I hated the trapping and knew I'd failed deliberately!

"Don't let it worry you, Bob. You could trap gophers ever hour in the day fer the rest of yer life and you'd still have gopher tunnels in the fields. I say, what's so ding-dang wrong with just pluggin' 'em as you find 'em?" After that, there was a live and let live attitude, as far as gophers at Rancho Palomar were concerned.

As the summer wore on and my skill and experience with the work increased, I was treated as an equal by all the Pala hands, even by Gid, who regarded everyone with contempt. There was a new aspect to the foreman's behavior however. Gid had always left the ranch on Sunday, sometimes even taking his family. Now, the weekends had lengthened, even to including his absence on workdays, when Pop had to issue orders. Gid's family no longer accompanied their father away.

Talk among the hands was that Gid headed south, and the name Tijuana was bandied about. Pop kept his silence, but when power tools came up missing he took action.

"I'm callin' yer Uncle Doc," he decided.

That weekend, Uncle Leo came down from Santa Monica with a generous supply of groceries. Bill's eyes lit up like a child's on Christmas morning.

"I'm doing the cooking tonight, Dad. We're having the best T-bones you've ever sunk your eyeteeth into! And some real Idaho bakers–home grown not those puny things you get in the grocery store! They were gifts from a patient. Caesar salad, too! What do you say to that?"

Bill was wild with delight. He even danced a few Polka steps, slapped his heels, and yelled, "Hot dawg!"

I rode down to the ranch yard in my uncle's Cadillac. He got out with the spring of a fighter in his step. "There's the son-of-a-bitch," he said to no one in particular. The firing was simple, direct, and its consequences immediate. Before sundown, Gid and his family drove off in his old car, towing a trailer full of raggedy belongings. Pop watched them go. No one waved.

After that, Pop became the ranch foreman. He didn't want the job. He even turned it down when my uncle offered him the post. But he promised that he would take the job temporary-like, until some one more qualified could be found. He did not move into the foreman's house, but continued to drive to the ranch each day from his rented room over the Pala General Store. The hands from the reservation were pleased as punch, so everything seemed to go on as before.

One Friday afternoon in late August, I was the last to leave a field that we had spent the day irrigating. The pipe had been disassembled and trucked to the yard, all the Pala hands riding in the back. I had disconnected the Caterpillar from the pump and was just ready to climb aboard and follow the truck.

"Come here, boy! Open the gate," someone shouted.

I turned to see a mixed group of riders, togged in the casually formal attire one might have seen on the set of *Sun Valley Serenade*—jodhpurs, burnished boots, pastel shirts and white hats. They were apparently weekend guests on the neighboring ranch that Uncle Leo had said was owned by screen star John Payne.

"Your master, Dr. Madsen, allows us to cross his ranch," the leader continued.

I opened the gate and stood aside, shirtless, with ragged jeans, while the effete crew rode past. The girls glanced at me and giggled. Someone simpered, "Oh, Marlene! His skin is like teakwood. I think they're such beautiful people. Don't you just love to look at them?"

The leader was the last to enter. I smiled, "I'll tell my Uncle Leo that you rode through."

Flustered, he said, "Be sure to give him our best, and thank you." He rode off.

I described the incident to my uncle when he came down from Santa Monica for the weekend, a few weeks later. He laughed uproariously. It was then that he made the surprising announcement that he was selling the ranch. The new owners were from Hollywood, perhaps the same crew I'd met earlier. They would need ranch hands from the Pala reservation and a foreman to run the place. Uncle Leo had given Pop a glowing recommendation. It appeared that everything would continue as before.

Another of his experiments in reconstructing the past had come a cropper. Like the fresh-eggs-from-our-own-chickens affair, it was never mentioned again. He did not tell Bill. He said he'd leave that to my aunt.

Uncle Leo took my cardboard suitcase and me back to Santa Monica with him on Sunday evening. As we drove into the gathering dark, he spoke of his concerns about the strained relations between the United States and Japan. He was certain there would open hostilities and took the pessimistic view that the West Coast could quite easily be invaded.

"Bob, I don't believe that you should enroll at Cal Tech this fall. With war a very real possibility, I don't want to be responsible for your safety. You will be safe at home with your family. In fact, I intend to send Car and the kids back there to live until it all blows over."

What is he saying! Not enroll in Cal Tech, I can't believe it! I looked over at my uncle and could clearly see the set of his jaw, silhouetted against the lights of passing cars. There was no doubting his seriousness. I would not begin the bright new future I'd envisioned on the trip out. I was devastated!

"Well, Uncle Leo, I guess you know best," I said without conviction. "I didn't listen to the radio much down on the ranch."

"Bob, if I'm wrong and there's no war, you can begin at Cal Tech next fall after you've graduated from high school. It's probably best to complete your senior year in Rochester anyway." The discussion was at an end.   .

As we turned into the driveway of my uncle's home, he returned to the subject of the summer's work. "I'm going to pay you for your time on the ranch, Bob. You'll have a check for $200.00, which is $50.00 per month as we agreed. And I'm sending you home next week on the *Super Chief!* How do you like that, eh?"

Wow, the new Santa Fe streamliner—gorgeous train, sleek silver cars and sharp looking locomotives, painted red and yellow like Indian warbonnets! Fastest train there is between Los Angeles and Chicago. Only sleepers, my own bedroom, no crummy coaches with people snoring in their seats and sandwich crumbs everywhere! Hollywood filmstars ride the Super Chief when they go to New York—it connects with the 20th Century Limited. Boy, what if I meet somebody like Carole Lombard and Clark Gable, or Jack Benny and Mary! Gosh, I wish the Super went through Rochester. Wouldn't the guys' eyes pop out if they saw Gary Cooper and me sitting together in the observation car! I was so excited that I had a hard time speaking. At last I said, "Gosh, thanks, Uncle Leo! That's just great!" I beamed with the thought of it happening to me!

Later in the week, my uncle flew to Chicago for a short course in post-surgical care at Northwestern University. My Aunt Carmen sent me home on a Greyhound bus!

GOING STEADY

When, I returned home in the fall of 1941, my friends welcomed me like the prodigal son, without recriminations. I was perplexed by their kindness that confused and embarrassed me. One of the first things that happened after I got off the Jefferson Lines bus from Kansas City was Jack Dallman's invitation to spend the weekend with him at Kamp Kahler, in a lean-to that he had constructed and thatched entirely of young willows. Jack, an Eagle Scout, was an accomplished camper, completely at home in the woods. He took great delight in the strictness and complexity that camping skills demanded.

The painul memories associated with my disastrous attempt to rescue our island clubhouse in the spring flood of 1938 had failed to dim the appeal of Scouting for me. Encouraged by Jack and inspired by his example, I struggled diligently over the next two years to acquire the merit badges that defined Scouting's higher ranks.

By the spring of 1941 I had done it, and on Mother's Day in May, our Chief Scout Executive presented me with the coveted Eagle insignia and a silver lapel pin that duplicated it in miniature. The ceremony included a touching Presentation of the Rose, when each new Eagle Scout gave his mother a red rose and an identical pin. Mother, eyes sparkling and moist with tears, smiled proudly at me as I pinned the rose to her dress. Loving her so much, I fumbled the pinning, succeeding only in bloodying my thumb on the rose thorns, but she showed no dismay.

My friend Jack and I were confined by continual rainfall to his lean-to's tiny interior that fall weekend. So we talked, each describing what had happened during the previous summer and examined the potential for an interesting and enterprising senior year. Jack's anecdotes were concise, straightforward and excited; mine, highly embellished!

"I really don't see how I can be interested in Rochester girls anymore, Jack! You know, dating starlets like I did is not the same thing as dating some ole Rochester girl!" ·

He was philosophical in the face of my disdain. "Aw, Bob, life is what you've got here now. You'll forget those Hollywood babes soon's you find somebody you like. There's plenty peaches on the 'ole RHS tree."

"Wanna bet!" I said. "Why, one night I had a date with Esther Williams. You know who she is, don't cha?"

"You betcha, and I wish I knew her better!"

"Yessir, I drove a big LaSalle." *Filled with chickens!* "Had dinner at the Ambassador Hotel, a huge, fancy place in LA." I sprinkled those initials around a lot for verisimilitude. "All the famous movie stars eat there. You can't believe the food, Jack. No sir, I don't suppose you'd ever find caviar and pressed duck back here—even in Minneapolis!"

"Gosh, what's that like, Bob? Why'd they want to press a duck?"

"It's to improve the flavor, o' course," I sniffed. "Well anyways, after dinner…"

"Didja have wine, Bob?" Jack interrupted.

"Of course! It was…a dry Sherry." *Isn't that the stuff Mother keeps in the decanter on the dining room buffet?* "Then we just danced the night away in the Coconut Grove."

"Out in the trees?" Jack asked.

"No, for gosh sakes! The Coconut Grove is a nightclub," I said, exasperated with his goofy interruptions.

"More wine, huh?"

"A glass or two, yeah. But it was champagne. You know a girl like that only settles for the best! And then I drove her home. She lives in a nifty, beach-front bungalow on Ocean Boulevard."

"Then what?"

"Whattya mean, then what?" I said.

"Did ya kiss her—or anything?" he asked.

"Just a goodnight kiss, that's all. We both had to get up early. She was filming and I had to go down to the ranch."

After a moment's silence, he sighed and said, "Well, buddy, you'll just have to play Casanova and teach these hometown girls the ropes. An' your first opportunity is next weekend. My girl, Connie, and her brother are having a party at their parents' house after the first football game of the season. I'm inviting you! Connie will find you a date. Okay?"

The girl that Constance Jewell found for me was her best friend, Patricia Eusterman, Dorothy's cousin. Pat was tall and slim, with shoulder-length, dark blonde hair. Her eyes, set wide under strikingly dark eyebrows, looked directly at me without wavering as she talked. Her slender nose turned up slightly, like a pixie's, a barely discernible cleft at its tip. When she laughed, her full lips parted to reveal even, dazzlingly white teeth.

Pat lived with her mother, dentist father, and many sisters in a rambling, brick home situated on the lower slope of Pill Hill. Victim of frequent remodeling in a vain attempt to keep pace with a growing family, the house was now too large for its narrow, hilly lot. The home's front entrance faced its neighbor to the south, and turned a cold shoulder to the street. Overall, and despite its size, the home was comfortable, understandably crowded, and appeared to the casual eye like an English country hall.

After a time, Pat and I became a steady couple, though not by an exchange of the usual tokens: the athletic sweater in school colors, the class ring, or the fraternal pin. Our companionship was more friendly than fervid, and I sought to remedy that in jealous imitation of many of my friends who were *going steady*. Throughout the fall, Pat and I attended movies, parties, and school dances together, but the relationship never seemed to come to a boil.

Each Christmas the Mayo Clinic arranged an extravagant party for its entire staff. In 1941, and despite the attack on Pearl Harbor that had precipitated our country's entry into World War II only eight days previously, the party went ahead as scheduled. Perhaps it was considered a last gesture to normalcy. Every available space, in the Mayo Civic Auditorium was utilized. There was an elaborate buffet supper, a program of music and comedy by nationally known entertainers, and dancing afterwards, with music furnished by the Russ Morgan orchestra, one of many popular swing bands of the day.

Pat and I attended the party together. She appeared to enjoy the program of choral numbers by the Fisk Singers and the Clinic Chorus, and laughed happily when the emcee, a well-known comic, impersonated the President and other famous people. When the program ended, Marty Adson, Jack Dallman and other friends of mine asked for dance exchanges. Harry MacLean, a new acquaintance from Canada, asked for two dances. He was finishing his last high school year in Rochester, and living with his older brother, a Clinic resident. Like all my high school acquaintances, Harry behaved as if Pat were my steady girl.

I intended to confirm that after the New Year's Eve formal dance given by the Job's Daughters. But first I had to receive an invitation. I could only assume that Pat would invite me. Time passed without the coveted envelope.

"Did I get any mail today, Mother?" became my anxious daily query.

"No, dear. I'm sorry, but there was nothing for you," she replied.

"Well okay, thanks." I left the kitchen in dejection.

At last, with only two days remaining, the invitation came. But there was little time to order a corsage from Ed Fiksdal, get my suit pressed, and wheedle transportation out of my parents! Any sensible suitor would have understood from this delay that he was not the preferred choice, perhaps not even the second, of the girl in question. But not me!

On the evening of the dance, I drove the green Olds up the long narrow driveway, hellish in winter, to the front door of the Eusterman home. Mrs. Eusterman opened the door, diaphanous material in hand, and a packet of pins in her mouth.

"Haffi noo yer, Bub," she said, with a twinkle.

"The same to you, Mrs. Eusterman," I replied.

"Mother, where in blazes are my shirt studs. I can't find them and now the damn collar and shirtfront are flapping 'round me like a broken umbrella. Of all the rotten inventions of the human race, the stiff shirt is the worst!" Dr. Eusterman stood in helpless disarray, while his tittering daughters flocked around him like variegated swans.

"Look in the top left hand drawer of your dresser, dear—the little one. They're in a box from Weber and Judd."

He marched upstairs, grumbling, "Women! Always putting things in the most ungodly places—in a drugstore box. My God!"

Mrs. Eusterman, busy with last minute adjustments to hems and straps, paid no more attention to her husband. "Patricia, your escort is here," she called upstairs. "Why don't you wait in the living room, Bob. I'm sure she'll be down in just a minute."

When Pat appeared, floating down the stairs in a creamy satin creation that was, like her sisters' gowns, the work of her seamstress mother, she looked lovely, even stunning. She was wearing my corsage from Fiksdal's, a great relief, since I should probably have botched the job of pinning it to her gown!

A masculine voice, like Moses from the mountain, boomed down from the landing, "Patricia, you look just beautiful this evening, radiantly beautiful, doesn't she, Bob?"

"Yessir," I chimed, with enthusiasm.

"Now, Patricia, your Mother and I have a dinner engagement, but will return home early. We will wait up for all of our lovely girls. The dance ends at midnight, Bob, and I want my daughter home no later than twelve-thirty."

"Yessir, you can count on me. We'll be here on time. You bet," I said, playing the toady.

"Oh, Daddy, you're heartless!" Pat said, without feeling.

The Masonic Temple ballroom sparkled with silvery crepe paper and balloons. On the bandstand, the Lee Williams orchestra, a local band, tootled in warm-up. Lee's white tie and tails, smudged and grimy, shone at elbows and knees. He stared out over the dancers' heads, raised his baton, and the lackluster outfit began to blow the old standbys: *Stardust, Serenade in Blue, and Begin the Beguine.*" Girls filed in from the restroom after a last minute breathless exchange of gossip, and joined their partners.

Our dance card was filled in an astonishingly short time. Perhaps Pat had asked her girlfriends for help. At any rate, she and I had surprisingly few dances together. And then it was midnight. The band played its theme, couples danced slowly cheek to cheek, confetti fell and swirled, and then we jostled our way to the coatroom. After the overly warm ballroom, laced with the peculiar aroma of crushed flowers and stale perfume, the night air was sharply cold, cutting through the frothy formals and thin-soled shoes. With the slamming of car doors, and noisy good-byes, the couples left the Temple. I gunned the motor, hoping to have as much time for those goodnight kisses as possible.

I managed the driveway obstacle course leading to her house, thanks to chains, stopped before her door, turned off the engine, and set the brake. I had only a few minutes before the cold, and the inevitable rap on the upstairs window, put an end to all romance. So, I made my pitch immediately.

"Pat, we've been dating now for four months—going together really! I like you a lot, Pat, and I want all our friends, everyone, to know that. I wish you would wear my Eagle lapel pin to show that we are going steady. That way, other guys, would lay off, because they'd know you belong to me." *Boy, how was that for getting to the point in a hurry!*

"Oh Bob, I wish you hadn't asked me that. We're such good friends and all. I've gotten to know you and like you over these last months.

And it was sweet of you to ask me to go steady, but I just can't accept your pin." She ended in a sad-sounding whisper.

"Why not, Pat? If you think we're good friends? Why can't you wear my pin?" I was thunderstruck!

"Well, you see, it's my father. He has told all of us not to take anyone's pin, or ring, that such a pledge is a serious step, like being engaged!"

"We could be engaged—engaged to be engaged," I replied, surprised by my lightning wit.

"No, Bob, I just can't..."

"Why don't we think it over for a while?" I wheedled. "I'll put the pin up here on the sun visor, and we can talk about it another time. I'd *never* offer it to another girl!" I stabbed the pin onto the cloth with angry frustration. The air in the car was now frigid. I started the motor, but there would be no further action this evening.

"Thanks for a wonderful evening, Bob. I'm sorry if it had to end this way. I've got to go in. I can see Father at the window!" True or not, she got out of the car, ran around the rear and was inside before I could even stumble out of the driver's side to escort her.

◆   ◆   ◆

Grim rumors, describing our losses in men and materials in the first days of the war, filtered in from Hawaii and the Philippines. These were confirmed over the next several months, bringing Americans to understand that this would be a long and costly struggle. That knowledge and the tightened restrictions on transportation occasioned by gasoline rationing put a damper on all normal social activities and entertainment. The diminutive Eagle pin remained jammed into the visor of the Olds, and for the most part the Olds remained in the garage.

Meanwhile, the problem of Pat's reluctance remained—her father. I decided to overcome his antagonism toward me with the same weapon that had always worked on the Edison School bullies—my wits. I had read an announcement, posted outside the principal's office, of a state-wide essay contest sponsored by the American Legion. The subject, Patriotism Promotes Good Citizenship, was right down my alley, and the grand prize was a cash award toward tuition at the college of the winner's choice. The deadline for submission of each applicant's entry, not to exceed 2,500 words, was less than a month away! *Hot diggity dog! This is it. I'll show him how smart I am. I'll write the winning essay and prove it!*

For the next two weeks I busied myself in the public library, rapidly scanning the lives of the patriots in American history. I sought the advice of the librarian, and my civics and history teachers. At home I ground my way through countless Ticonderoga #2 pencils that I had purloined from diverse sources and consumed an amazing number of pages from spiral exercise tablets. These overflowed the wastepaper basket giving it the appearance of a reject container in a popcorn-ball factory. The muse struck without warning and I wrote at odd moments, sometimes jumping out of bed to jot down a phrase.

"Bobby, dear! What are you working on so hard? It isn't right for you to lose sleep, dear. You could get sick!" my mother said one evening.

I was non-committal at first. "Oh, it's just an assignment, about citizenship," I said.

When I had finished, I told my mother about the essay contest, emphasizing the college tuition award for all it was worth. Then I read the essay, a cliché-laden travesty that only a mother could love.

"That was nice, Bobby," she said with a smile. She had always smiled, even when my project was half-baked. I needed to prove myself to my girl's father!

"I think I'll drive over and show my essay to Dr. Eusterman," I said. "He's a member of the American Legion. He'd be a good judge."

"Of what?" my mother said, indignantly. "Of the whiteness of your teeth! Why, when your father served in the First World War, that man was still a fresh kid. Didn't it ever occur to you that your father was a member of the American Legion? Bobby, I'm surprised at you. Why don't you go in the living room and ask him for advice?"

"Well, gee!" I was totally unprepared for her vigorous demonstration of marital fealty.

Mother strode into the living room, dripping soapsuds, holding her dishrag. "Nels, Bobby has written an essay for an American Legion contest. He's going to take it up to Eusterman for advice!" she sniffed. "What do you think of that?"

Dad looked up from his newspaper, glanced at me, and spoke somewhat sadly, "Oh, Stella, let him go. What difference does it make?"

I felt like a sap. I had not thought of my father's feelings—only of myself. Ashamed, I could only say, "Well, I guess I'll be going, then." Dad turned back to his paper. Mother said, with fierce feeling, "Hmmph!" and went into the kitchen.

Driving to Eusterman's I tried to put my feeling of shame aside, but it kept bobbing to the surface and I rang the bell with little eagerness.

"Come in Bob," said Mrs. Eusterman in greeting. "I'll call Pat. She's in the garden," she hesitated.

"No ma'am. I'd like to see Dr. Eusterman."

She brightened. "Well, of course. He's in the living room, Bob. Won't you go right in?"

The head of the house was seated, reading his newspaper, just as I had left my father. "What is it, Bob?" he said, without enthusiasm.

I showed him my essay, explaining the reason for writing it, and alluded to its noble content. "I'd like to get your advice, sir, before I send it in. You can be most helpful, being an American Legionnaire and all! May I read it to you, sir?"

"Why of course, my boy, of course," he said, flattered. "Begin whenever you're ready."

And so I read the piece, fumbling and mispronouncing at first, then warming to the subject, and misreading his attention as enthusiasm.

When I finished and looked up from the still trembling pages, he said, "That was nice, Bob." He turned again to his paper.

Just then I heard bantering and laughter from the hallway. Pat, cheeks flushed and radiant, came into the room, quite out of breath. Her smile faded when she saw me. "Oh, hi," she said.

Harry MacLean was with her. His handsome face broke into a crooked grin, "Hi there, Bob. I just walked Pat home. We were throwing snowballs," he added, as if in expiation. There was no snow on either of their coats.

Pat's father put his paper down and rose from his chair. "Good evening, Harry. Thank you for bringing Patricia home."

"I was glad to, sir," Harry said, flashing his smile. Turning to me he asked, "Can you give me a lift home, Bob? I'd be much obliged. I rode over with my brother and he's making hospital calls."

"Sure, Harry. I was just leaving, anyways. Goodbye, sir," I said to Pat's father, "and thank you for listening."

"Oh, think nothing of it, my boy."

"Bye, Pat, see you later."

"Goodbye, Patricia," Harry said. He turned to her, bent his extremely long frame from the waist and took her hand. I thought he was going to kiss it. He looked like an angular English butler.

"Bye, and thanks," she blushed, with a smile.

In the car, on the way to his house, Harry looked through the windshield at the road ahead. "Bob, my parents died in an automobile accident when I was young. Since then I've lived with my brother and his wife. But it's not the same as a family. We're more like roommates. Ever since I came to Rochester, the Eustermans have been like my family. I like them all, but Mrs. Eusterman is my favorite. The girls are like my sisters." He lapsed into silence.

"Gosh I'm sorry, Harry. I didn't know," I said. "It's wonderful that they can be your family!" *Well that's a relief. A guy sure can't go steady with his own sister, or pin her either for that matter.*

◆　　◆　　◆

Winter sputtered to a close at last, and doddered off in grimy slush. As the days lengthened, with touches of warm sunlight, tokens of spring, most of the senior students struggled to retain their interest in schoolwork. For the boys, war held an uncertain future. Even so, everyone desired to graduate with the very best record they could earn. Yet there were still extracurricular activities to divert one's attention.

At an all-school assembly in April, merit awards were presented to teams and individuals that had been involved in basketball, football, swimming and gymnastics. Several, including Jack Dallman and myself, came forward to receive the coveted red and black school letter from Coach Bruno Beckman. Most recipients sewed the letter onto a sweater or jacket; some conferred these upon a girlfriend.

I was so happy to have a team letter that I could hardly contain myself. It was Jack who had urged me to try out for gymnastics, a sport that demanded agility, grace and perfect timing. I had proved to myself that I could compete in varsity sports as well as the next guy; the diffidence that had dogged me since Edison had vanished! I burst with invincibility when I walked back to my seat, and I searched for Pat in the crowd. She wasn't looking at me but appeared to be searching the audience.

Early in May I was appointed emcee for the senior farewell breakfast that would include a program of entertainment. The traditional Senior Farewell formal dance was held later in the same week. Pat, Jack Dallman, his girlfriend Constance Jewell, Harry MacLean, and many other friends volunteered to help with both events. Connie and Pat planned to have a picnic supper for all the volunteers the Saturday following farewell week. It was to be at the Jewell's cottage on a quiet bay at the north end of Lake Zumbro; Pat asked me to take her.

The morning of the picnic, a wonderfully warm and beautiful Saturday in mid-May, I rose early, came into the kitchen, and asked,

"Mom, when will breakfast be ready? I'm starved. Can I make the toast?"

"Breakfast is almost ready, Bobby. Your father is cutting the grapefruit. Sit down, dear. The toast is already in the oven."

"What's all the fuss? This is Saturday. You got no school today!" Dad said, puzzled by my early appearance. Nancy was still asleep.

"I've got an awful lot to do today! Connie Jewell and her brother are having a picnic supper out at their cottage for all the people that worked on the senior farewell. I've got to get the car slicked up before I pick up my date. I can take the car, can't I, Dad?" I asked. I had already sounded him out the night before.

"Yes," he replied. "Now quit yumping around. Sit down and eat. You can't do nothing on an empty stomach."

After breakfast, I centered the Olds on the wash rack, adjusted the water temperature and went at it, hammer and tongs! She was soon sparkling, thanks to the heavy coat of wax I had applied late in the fall. Drying her off, cleaning the windows, I whistled happily with the thought that Pat and I would spend the evening together. *Tonight I'm going to ask her to be my steady girl. Now that we're graduating she might say yes. We could have so much fun this summer, and then there's college. I wonder if she'll be going to the U. Anyways, how could she refuse a groovy guy like me?*

The wash rack had a wall access to the same central vacuum system that served the mansion. I attached the long, cumbersome hose and its steel nozzle, manipulating as deftly as possible so as not to damage my mirror finish. Seats, door panels, ceiling, the works! I had passed over the visor before I had even given the pin a thought. Dumfounded, I winced when I saw the telltale hole where it had been. For a minute or two, I could only stand, hangdog, and listen to the angry hissing of the long vibrating snake that had swallowed my token of affection! When I pulled the switch the snake died with a laugh on its steely lips.

I quickly moved the car to a dry stall, hosed down the wash rack, coiled both the vacuum and washing hoses on their holders, and rushed to the garage basement. There, in the dim recesses, the business end of the central vacuum system stood beside the now silent oil furnaces. Standing several feet taller than me and a good deal fatter, the battleship gray monster proclaimed itself to be TORNADO—Whirls the Dirt Away! In front, at floor level, was a large, oval door, secured by a half dozen lugs. From its open maw, John Tewes removed the vast quantities of dirt that had been whirled away from the mansion.

Spurred by necessity, I gathered several steel bushel baskets in a circle before the door. I had to use a wrench to turn the lugs. *Good God Almighty!* The chamber was full. I sat on my haunches and started through the gunk bit by bit; revolving the dust and grit through my fingers to make certain the pin wasn't there. The examination took several hours, filled my lungs and hair with dust—and was fruitless! I emerged from the basement empty handed, and dejected. No pin! What could I do?

Later, thoroughly scrubbed and dressed in casual correctness, I emerged from the bathroom.

"Gosh Bob, what took so long? You don't need that much improvement anyway! Is your date worth all that primping?" Nancy exclaimed in mild heat. She had a date, and now would be late. But I didn't dare use the vacuum cleaner as an excuse.

"I'm sorry, sweetie. Just daydreaming, I guess. I'll make it up to you later. Anyways, it'll do your guy good to cool his heels. Take it from me. I know!"

"Yeah, yeah! Beau Brummell speaks!" She smiled and disappeared with a swirl of her chenille robe.

"You won't be late now, will you, dear?"

"No, Mother. G'Night." I ran down the stairs two at a time.

"Drive careful, you hare!" Dad called after me.

When I arrived, Pat was all ready. Her parents had gone out for dinner and then a movie, thank God. So I zipped out of her driveway, the car dazzling in the late afternoon sun.

The Olds and I in 1942

"You must have worked on your car all day, Bob. It looks really neat!"

"Thanks. I like to keep her looking spiffy for the folks," I boasted, modestly.

For the rest of the drive out Highway 52 toward the cities, we talked about the past school year, our favorite teachers, and our plans for the future. To my dismay, I discovered that Pat wouldn't be going to the University at all. She was going east to college in the fall! *Well, damn, what's the point, if she's going that far away—practically to the moon? We'll only get to see each other on holidays!* My hopes for going steady in college slid down into my shoes. I felt as flat as a day-old banana peel on a hot sidewalk.

When we reached Jewell's cottage, I detected a smell like burning Keds coming from under the car; it was the rear brake drums. In my excitement I had driven the whole distance with the hand brake on. *Holy mackerel! What will Dad say? I'll have to tell him. Good gosh, what a dumb jerk I am! How could I do such a stupid thing?*

Pat had gone inside to help Connie. Only Jack Dallman noticed. "What d'ya do Bob, forget to take off the brake?" He grinned, good-naturedly.

"Yeah, you guessed it. How dumb can you get?" I said, and we walked to the cottage together.

Connie's mother had helped Connie and Pat prepare the picnic supper. To put it bluntly, other than put up crepe paper and bunting, and run errands to the grocery, the two girls had done little. But Mrs. Jewell's fixings were quite surely the best of the genre: sliced ham, hot dogs, hamburgers, two kinds of potato salad—one served hot, Dutch apple pie for desert. Most of the kids drank coffee, but there was soda pop on ice.

We ate outside, on the porch, the steps, folding chairs, and leaning on our elbows on the lawn. The conversation naturally turned to farewell week and the formal dance that we had all enjoyed. I thanked all my friends for their help with the senior breakfast, and they clapped in return. One of the girls proposed we play charades. There was some support, but most of us had come with dates and were looking for a more promising game that could safely be conducted in the gathering dusk. Just then the electric yard light came on. Powered by current from the generating station at the dam, the lamp yielded an anemic yellow glow that barely extended to the landscape shrubbery and, of course, the outhouse.

"Let's play motion," cried Jack, with barely contained eagerness.

"Oh, yes, let's," echoed Connie.

It was hardly surprising that there was general concurrence to Jack's idea. The game would have been considered childish, had it been suggested in the light of day. It was simply a form of "tag," with the variation that those tagged were jailed, and could be released by a signal from one of the hidden players.

In due course, I had become "It." Standing at the base of the yard light pole, my forehead against my arm, I began to count. Jack Dallman stood near me, taunting.

"You'll never catch me, four eyes!" He wore glasses himself! "Even if you see me, you'll never touch me."

"57, 58, 59..."

"Notice how I've never been tagged—not once tonight. Yaah, yaah, yaah!"

"85, 86, 87...Jack's taunting ceased and I heard his light steps slipping away. I peeked under my forearm and saw the door of the outhouse close silently.

"97, 98, 99, 100. Ready or not, here I come."

I'm going to get that guy first thing. I'll show him! I strode quietly across the intervening yellow-lit space to the outhouse and tore the flimsily hooked door open, at the same time yelling, "Aha! Gotcha!"

High-pitched girlish screams blew away my gleeful grimace. The dimly lit interior revealed two seated forms, and the unmistakable realization that I had exposed Pat and Connie with their undies down around their ankles.

I started backwards, confused, embarrassed, and shocked! Titters that turned to guffaws came from the surrounding darkness. Soon everyone was laughing at my idiotic error.

I walked quickly away, the blessed darkness closing around my shame. Past the boathouse, out to the end of the dock, where I sat down and stared at the still, black water. The moon, in new quarter, sent an accusatory finger of light across the mirror calm surface.

Oh how awful! I opened the door on my own girl. What a fool thing to do. Now her folks will really hate me. And she already hates me! No point in asking her to be my steady girl now. Oh, hell! I wish I could just jump in and never come up—never!

I felt a hand on my shoulder. The voice was Jack's. "Come on back, Bob. It's Okay! They'll all forget about it."

"You know that isn't true. I'll never live this down. I've lost her for good."

Silence. Then, "Wellll...there's other fish in the lake!"

DOWN AT THE DEPOT

A mong my earliest recollections, certainly the most vivid are of
trains—hot black steam locomotives thrashing by crossings, tracing the horizon with giant smoke plumes, whistling a diminishing
cadenza in the distant nighttime. I was drawn to the steam locomotive,
so magnificent and powerful, by a desire that was never sated. Everything related to that wonderful machine attracted my interest: the station where it waited, bridled for the race to the great cities of my
imagination, the roundhouse where it slumbered, even the steel rails of
their coming and going. As I grew older, the love for trains and railroad
travel became a fixture of my being.

There were two railroads serving Rochester, the Chicago and North
Western Railway and the Chicago Great Western Railroad. Though
the names had a ring of similitude, these roads differed in their history,
size, service, and public image. The main lines of the Chicago and
North Western fanned out from Chicago to Milwaukee and upper
Wisconsin, Omaha and the west, and the twin cities of Minneapolis
and St. Paul. It served industry, but had extensive rural branches, and
was primarily a granger road. In contrast, the Chicago Great Western
had been cobbled together from short lines, failed to reach its namesake terminus, and was forced to rent trackage from its competitor in
order to attain that destination. Launched much later than the North
Western, it was disadvantaged from its earliest days in the competitive
race for business.

The North Western traced a determined path across Rochester from
east to west, crossing Broadway, and its erratic competitor, six blocks
north of the Clinic. *The Minnesota 400*, its premier train on the line
that led trains from Chicago all the way to the Black Hills of South

Dakota, raced into town, paused for less than a minute, and dashed on. In addition to the *400's* twice a day appearance, once in each direction, there were a pair of slow locals and two night trains with Chicago sleepers.

The Great Western line meandered through town like a stumbling drunk. From its depot, a block east of Broadway, and only three blocks from the Clinic, one could take the cars for the Twin Cities, Omaha, Kansas City, or Chicago. A map of its lines resembled an inverted maple leaf, the stem ending at the Twin Cities, the veins intersecting at Oelwein, Iowa, where the railroad's shops were located. In earlier years the road had identified itself as *The Maple Leaf Route* but had substituted *The Corn Belt Route* to reflect its bread and butter commodity. The railroad ran trains between its several termini like a spider scurrying across a crooked web. Oelwein, Iowa became a frenzied center of activity at train time, when the inefficient process of shuffling cars between trains compromised any notion of speedy travel on the six trains that stopped at the Rochester depot.

In addition to these dozen passenger trains, a goodly number of freights trudged into and through town so that a gritty, moving finger of coal smoke was rarely absent from Rochester's skyline. From my earliest childhood, those fingers beckoned me to come and experience the thunder and might of the belching giants.

I was scared, excited and delighted whenever my father took me to either depot at train time. Sometimes, he would hold me high on his shoulders so that I could better see the engineer in his cab. I waved and smiled and felt grand when the engineer deigned to return the wave, even on occasion to speak.

"Hello, sonny. What do you think of her, eh? You'd better stand back now; we're getting ready to leave."

Dad set me down beside the wondrous, resting locomotive. I grabbed his hand, and we waited, listening and watching. Steam rose from the stack in a steady roar, the innards gurgled and hissed, and the air pumps high on the boiler's side hammered in a rhythmic ka-thunk, ka-thunk. Fire flashed from the great engine's belly and the heat scorched my face. When the safety valve popped I jumped with fright, and almost jumped out of my skin. Then the conductor gave his high sign, called "Boooard," and the bell began its regular dang, dang, dang. The engineer eased the great locomotive forwards with mighty sounds of swoosh, swoosh that accelerated and soon mingled into a throbbing urgency. I was dizzy with joy.

Whenever my parents took my sister and me riding in the family car, I maintained a sharp lookout for signs of a train. The telltale appearance of smoke on the horizon never failed to energize my plea for a detour.

"Oh, look Daddy, there's a train! Can we go see it?"

"Goss, that ware yust a little teakettle. What you want to see that for?"

"Oh, please, Daddy, let's catch him." I quickly learned that despite my father's verbal condescension for steam transport, the thrown gauntlet could goad him.

"Aah, we catch him, easy." And Dad would hunch over the wheel like Barney Oldfield, and we'd bounce off the highway onto some gravel lane that would lead to the tracks.

"Nels, do we have to go so fast?" Mother always asked, at the same time raising her hand slightly as if to hold onto her hat in the fierce wind of our going.

The train, when sighted, usually proved to be an accommodation, threading its way along a weedy branch. A coach and a combine trailed a smallish, asthmatic ten-wheeler. Dad was right; this was no *Twentieth Century Limited.* My pleasure was undimmed by his disdain; often I was rewarded by a wave from the cab, or from the lanky baggage man in vest and shirtsleeves, doffing his striped cap in the open combine door. They were as amused by the chase as my father was.

◆   ◆   ◆

When I was 13, in the summer of 1937, my parents bought new bicycles for Nancy and for me. They were Hendersons, with balloon tires, coaster brakes, and steer-horn handlebars; they were beauties! Mine was a royal blue; Nancy's maroon. These magnificent conveyances were a vast improvement on the used, hard tire bikes that many kids in the neighborhood possessed. Riding luxuriously on the big, wide tires, the new bicycles gave us access to a much larger Rochester than shoe leather had. In my case, that also included transportation to the various jobs that I held during the remainder of high school, and of my life at home.

My frequent destination was either of the town's railroad depots. At the Great Western station, the more significant trains from distant cities arrived and departed at inconvenient times, but the North Western's *Minnesota 400* steamed away for Chicago at 2:30 in the afternoon!

"Nels, where is Bobby?" my mother would ask from the doorway leading up to our family's quarters in the carriage house.

Dad, at his bench, or probing an automobile's gizzard, would reply, "Oh, down at the depot, I suppose." He'd straighten himself, throw his left arm forward to reveal his worn Elgin and say, "You listen, Stella, you'll hear that *400* tootle."

"Why is he off watching a train? I want him to run the vacuum cleaner for me."

Now it was time for him to voice her line. "Oh, Stella, leave the boy alone. Does that yob got to be done now? He always comes back. You wait and see."

At the depot, I leaned my bicycle against the big, sliding door to the baggage and express office. Inside the dim cavern, I could see my friend Arnie Engstrom, the baggage agent, bent over tagged milk cans and crates of fresh eggs.

"Hi, Arnie. Keep an eye on my bike for me, will ya?"

Arnie's overalled bulk straightened. He brushed the frowzy, straw-colored hair from his eyes with a dirty left hand, and his moon face broke into a wide grin of recognition. "Well, if it ain't the cinder sniffer. Sure, I'll watch it. Don't you worry, buddy!" He turned back to his express shipment that would go out on the afternoon *400*, now whistling at the yard limits about a mile to the west.

I dashed down the platform toward the telegrapher's bay window from which Ray Vogelstad, the telegraph operator, was peering down the tracks. He gave me a nod of recognition and a friendly wave with his left hand, but kept the right hand fixed upon his clattering key. His green, celluloid eye-shade was a constant fixture; it kept his wispy salt and pepper hair in place when he was handing orders up to a passing train crew. He wore a blue-striped broadcloth shirt, gartered above the elbows, which was a cut above Arnie's denim, and denoted a higher order of responsibility. Ray also doubled as ticket agent.

The Chicago and North Western depot

The depot eaves extended out over the platform, clear to the arrival track, and provided a shady haven for the waiting passengers as well as the curious train-watcher. I spotted an empty baggage cart, green body and stakes, red-spoked wheels, standing at trackside, and I climbed aboard what I deemed to be a splendid vantage point. Holding firmly to the cart's frame, I shaded my eyes and searched westward where smoke and a moving headlamp declared the swift approach of a train. The crossing guards had already halted automobile traffic, allowing the locomotive to steam majestically past the depot, cross Broadway, and come to a stop with a loud squeal of brake shoes. The head-end cars blocked Broadway; the rear Pullmans lay across First Avenue.

Arrival and departure for the *400* were each listed in the timetable as 2:30 PM, which meant that the agents and train men had to load and unload passengers and any express items as rapidly as possible. Meanwhile, the conductor, watching his pocket watch, provided a clear sense of urgency to the scene. As I watched, a fat man in a brown suit, bowler hat, cigar and newspaper got down from the parlor car. The black Pullman porter, whisking non-existent dust from the man's lapels, grinned, cackled meaningless pleasantries and held out his hand. The fat man, without looking into the porter's imploring eyes, dropped a coin into the extended palm. I noticed the fat man's princely bearing, the gold watch chain, and the trail of cigar smoke and decided that he must be someone important, even famous. *Someday I'm going to be famous too!*

One Saturday afternoon in the fall of 1939, shortly after I had entered the tenth grade, I rode my bike to the North Western depot to take in the *400*'s arrival. Arnie beckoned from the interior of his cave. He looked like a troll on holiday, trying to keep a happy secret.

"Ray wants to see you, buddy. Get your behind right up there, toot sweet," and he chuckled with glee.

"What's he want, Arnie?"

"That's his secret. Now beat it, or I'll be late fer the hot shot." The last was a common designation for *The Minnesota 400* among all the North Western's employees, track workers, trainmen, or clerks.

"Hi, Ray. Arnie says you want to see me," I said when I reached the bay window that was open to catch the Indian summer breeze.

"Bob, my boy, you're not going to believe this, but there's a change in the *400's* consist today that'll dazzle your eyes."

"What is it, Ray?"

"Just wait. Here she comes now."

The familiar whistle of number 1617, a light Pacific type, whose eccentricities were well known to me now, sounded at the throat of the west yard. By this time I was able to distinguish the finesse of each whistler, and recognized Carl Odegaard's hand. I picked a good spot, next to the Broadway crossing gate that was now lowering with an insistent high pitched ding, ding, ding. In less than a minute the train pulled in, with what I judged to be the same set of coaches that I had seen repeatedly over the years.

And then I spotted it. Between the aging green coaches and the two first-class cars on the rear, a low yellow and green streamliner coach gleamed in the bright afternoon sunlight. It had wide windows, and its all green roofline, lower than that of the other cars, was smoothly rounded. Curving metal sides that extended close to the tracks hid the undercarriage where I would normally have seen air brake reservoirs, battery boxes, and braces. Surprised and please, I failed to close my mouth until I heard Ray's voice behind me.

"That's what the whole train will look like soon, Bob. Isn't that spiffy? That coach matches the running gear of the Twin Cities train." *The Twin Cities 400* that ran from Chicago to the namesake metropolises was a high-speed diesel-powered streamliner.

"Wow! Won't she be beautiful when all the coaches match that car, Ray?"

"You bet, my boy! You bet! And we sure could use something new around here!" He turned and walked briskly to the head end, his Y-shaped order pole holding a folded flimsy for the engineer.

The streamlining of my *400* was a slow process. The new equipment, released from service on the *Twin Cities* when that train received new coaches, arrived in fits and starts giving the Rochester train an odd, irregular roofline. Since most patrons chose the new cars they were always full. The green cars continued to grow old gracefully, as my mother had begun to say of her and Dad.

By the time of my return from California, in the early fall of 1941, most of the older cars had disappeared from the train's consist. However, the steam locomotives, always the same pair of elderly, light Pacific types, soldiered on unchanged.

During my last year of high school I had far fewer occasions to hang around either of the two Rochester depots. In addition to the ordinary concerns of schoolwork there was the added question of just how I might go on to college. With my uncle's support now withdrawn, I did not see how that was possible. I had worked at various part-time jobs ever since my *St. Paul Pioneer Press* days, and had accumulated respectable savings. Nevertheless, I realized it was nowhere near what a college education would cost.

My parents never discussed the matter of college with me realistically. When I sought their advice, I could readily sense that I had outstripped their knowledge and competence. My mother would assume an anxious tearful look, and turn to my father, who ducked the conversation, literally and figuratively. Hunching his shoulders, gazing at his worn shoes with a beaten expression that seemed to be begging forgiveness, Dad clutched at straws, and suggested that I go see the Doctor for advice.

My own thoughts vacillated between an idiotic optimism that *something would turn up* and the gloomy realization that I could not afford to go on to school. That notion became ever harder to bear as the year advanced, and more and more of my Pill Hill buddies discussed their college plans and questioned me about mine. Having no concept of student loans, scholarships, and tuition awards, I could only dissemble.

"I guess it's the U for me," I'd say. "Dad has always wanted me to be a mechanical engineer, but I'd prefer chemical engineering myself." Happily for me, their self-centered conversations turned elsewhere.

I found better paying jobs: ushering at the Civic Auditorium, and finish worker at the Model Laundry. Both paid more than anything I'd previously done and strangely, I found myself the youngest employee at either place. The Mayo Properties Association owned both institutions, and I suspected that Dad intervened on my behalf.

I even made a vain attempt to secure a college scholarship. *Time* magazine announced a nationwide college scholarship contest that carried out the massive early elimination through weekly "current events" tests given in high school civics classes. The odds of winning a Harvard scholarship by this method were about equal to those for winning the Lottery, or a Publishers Clearing House drawing. Even so, the competition became a healthy intellectual diversion and deflected the anger that I harbored toward Uncle Leo.

For many years during winter, the Parks Department and the city Fire Department combined forces to maintain an outdoor public ice rink on land adjacent to the Chicago and North Western line east of Broadway. Though there was an indoor rink at the Mayo Civic Auditorium after1939, the purists, the hardy, and those who could not afford the Auditorium fee continued to use the outdoor rink. Nancy and I, and sometimes my father, invariably skated there. Dad enjoyed it because it reminded him of his youth in Norway, when the easiest way he could reach school in winter had been by skating across a frozen lake. Nancy and I liked it because all of our friends came there, one could meet members of the opposite sex in the warming house, and if lucky, you might walk them home.

On a gray afternoon in 1942, I heard number 1617 whistling for the Broadway crossing; it was Carl's touch on the cord. I skated north as fast as I could without bumping into anyone. The North Western track to the east ran directly parallel to the north edge of the rink, and curved gently around the entrance gate to the Oakwood Cemetery. Eliciting little notice from the other skaters, I clung to the fence, looking off westward for the oncoming *400*.

Accelerating out of town, Carl was forcing the draft, to get a hot fire and a good head of steam. The column of smoke and steam from the engine's stack belched forth like Vesuvius, and the noise was deafening. Carl whistled for the cemetery crossing, the engine entered the curve, and then I saw that #1617 had been given a shroud of green and yellow metal plate to hide the fact that she was just an elderly Pacific, and conform her to the remainder of the cars. She looked like a dowager got up for Mardi Gras in an overly tall eccentric headdress. Looking top-heavy, the engine charged past, teetering round cemetery curve and away. I was too dumbfounded at first to wave, but then got my voice and yelled after, "Hurray, for you old girl. You look good!"

Look at you, old 1619, you've got a new coat and you're setting out to give the first string diesels a run for the money. But you look like a queen to me! And if you can do it with nothing but a 1910 set of wheels, a gutsy whistle and a new coat—so can I. I turned away, and skated off to find Nancy. It was time to head for home.

NERVES OF STEEL

During the time that I was growing up, the Mayo Clinic utilized two principal buildings that occupied an entire block on Second Street, SW. The original structure was of a restrained classical design, faced in red brick, and trimmed in marble. Only five stories high, appearing squat and compact, it was a premier medical facility when it opened in 1914.

The Mayo Clinic

A newer building of yellow brick with limestone trim, was the only tall structure in Rochester, and was directly integrated with the 1914 building. The basic structure of the new Clinic, dedicated in 1928, was a thirteen-story, heavily ornamented box, above which five more floors were stepped back to support a 23-bell, carillon tower. Essentially fantasy Romanesque, the new building had decorative brick roping on each corner, pilasters and balconies at upper windows, and a richly crenellated cornice. There were griffins, and gargoyles, eight larger than life statues of nurses guarding the carillon tower, and numerous bas relief plaques placed in the south and west walls. At the main entrance were huge, heavily carved, two-story bronze doors, mindful of the Pantheon. They had only been closed twice in my lifetime—when Dr. Will and Dr. Charlie Mayo each died in 1939.

Atop the new building that was named for its designing genius, Dr. Henry S. Plummer, one of the six original Mayo partners, there was a tall pylon with a revolving beacon for aircraft. When we were children, Nancy and I had accepted the pylon as a mooring mast for dirigibles, according to our vivid memory of *King Kong*.

In a series of innovative moves that would alter the operation of their medical partnership, Drs. Will and Charlie created a foundation, managed by a board of governors, to operate their institution. Following the retirement of the two brothers from active participation on the board, Dr. Donald Balfour, my father's employer, became the next chairman.

The original Mayo partnership, six physicians in addition to themselves, had expanded to an association of several hundred. Many of these were permanent staff members, but the majority were residents on a three-year advanced training program. There was no dearth of applicants to these residencies, with the result that Mayo selected the very best graduates from internships throughout the world.

When my father told me, shortly before my high school graduation, that I might join this heady mix of professionals, I was surprised and hesitant. Until then, my whole energy had been focused on schoolwork and the final tests that confirmed my competence.

"Bob, I want you to come down to the Clinic with me this morning. We need to get you a yob," Dad said one morning at the breakfast table.

"Whaaat? How can I work there? I'm not a doctor."

"There ware plenty working there who aren't doctors!"

"But, I'm only a high school kid. What could I do?" I asked, with some reluctance.

"Now quit your argying, and go put on your suit. I'll be leaving with the Doctor when he calls, and you better be ready!"

There was no mistaking the emphasis in this last. I got up from the table, went to my room and quickly changed clothes. I was so nervous that I couldn't get my tie straight and, for the first time in some years, asked Mother to help me with it.

"Hello," I said into the receiver when the telephone rang.

"Bob, tell your father I'm ready," said the voice I had heard repeat those words a thousand times before.

"Yessir," I answered, replacing the phone, and repeated the now familiar message. "It was the Doctor. He's ready."

My father already had his coat and hat on. I told my Mother good-bye, and she said, "Now Bobby, you mind your P's and Q's!"

Oh for gosh sake! The same old thing. How's that 'sposed to help me now? "Yes, Mother."

In an odd turnabout on the usual routine, I rode in the rear seat of the limousine. Dr. Balfour sat in the right front seat with my father. He was a big man with a square jaw and a hint of jowls, balding, with a circlet of well-brushed white hair beneath the brim of his light gray homburg. Sitting directly behind him, I could easily detect the gentle to-and-fro motion of his large head.

"Good morning, Nels."

"Good morning, Doctor," replied my father. There was a short silence. "I thought I'd take Bob to see Harry Bennett this morning."

"Good idea, Nels, just the place for him this summer."

Soon we had reached the main entrance where Joe Fritsch, the head factotum, stood at curbside in every kind of weather, welcoming all comers. He was probably more the embodiment of the Mayo Clinic and its compassionate attitude toward patients than any other individual in the institution.

Touching his cap in acknowledgment, Joe smiled broadly, opened the passenger door wide, and helped Dr. Balfour to alight. "Good morning, Doctor. How are you this fine morning, sir?"

"I'm very well, thank you, Joe. Yes, excellent weather, like to be out in it, myself." A nod of his head, and he turned toward the huge, always open, bronze doors.

Joe looked snappy in his sparkling shirt, dark blue uniform and cap. The words Mayo Clinic were embroidered discreetly on the band of his lapel pocket. After closing the car door, he bent over and looked in. "How are you, Nels? What brings you down this morning, Bob?" Joe knew everyone in Rochester, and remembered his or her names like a magician.

"Bob's come to see Harry Bennett, Joe."

"Well, good luck to you, young fella. Hope to see you join the team." Then the man whom most everybody called Joe Clinic turned to greet another arrival.

Dad parked the Cadillac a short distance north, in front of the 1914 building, and beside a brass Clinic sign that said NO PARKING. "Come on Bob," he said. I got out and followed him into the marble magnificence of what had been the first building's waiting room, but was now a registration area.

Registration, harried on Monday, diminishing through the week as patients were taken through examinations, was packed with worried, uncomfortable people. They were seated on padded wicker sofas and armchairs, surrounding a large elaborately ornamented ceramic tile and marble fountain, now filled with plants. Registration clerks sat opposite them at a long similarly decorated marble counter, looking like ticket agents at Grand Central Station. As names were called, patients walked, shuffled, or were pushed in wheel chairs toward the registration counter, clutching their medical referrals in nervous fingers.

On the other three walls of the registration hall there were doors leading to the offices of support services at the Clinic: language translators, hospital representatives, and housing agents. One door bore a label reading: GENERAL SERVICE. H. Bennett, Head. We went in.

Mr. Bennett's secretary, a middle-aged woman who considered herself more attractive than a revealing neckline and marcel wave warranted, looked up through tortoise-shell frames and twittered, "Good morning, Nels. I haven't seen you around in ages. Who's this with you?"

"Hello, Essie. This is my son, Bob. Is your boss in?"

"Yeah. He's expecting you." Her face drooped as it always did when people ignored her.

A big, muscular man sat behind the desk in the inner office. His hair was brown, cut short and parted on the side. He wore a coffee-colored, pin stripe suit and vest, beige shirt, and striped, tan tie. His chocolate-brown eyes looked directly at Dad.

"Morning, Nels. Sit down. I understand your son wants to work with us. Is this the boy?" He turned toward me, and his dark gaze seemed to uncover all my weaknesses in an instant.

Dad looked at me and said, "Well, Harry, Bob's a good boy and minds his parents. I think he should mind you, too."

"Is that right, young man?"

"Yessir. You can count on me." *For what? Gosh, what can I do for this guy?*

"I'm glad to hear that, Bob, because we have team spirit here at Mayo Clinic and that includes the General Service as much as it does the doctors. We work together; we don't carp when the going gets steep. Do you think you can work with other men, older than you, without complaining?"

"Yessir. I've been a ranch hand, and an usher—and all the others were older than I." I didn't mention the laundry, where most of the workers were women! "What'll I be doing, sir?"

"We do just about anything the doctors want us to do, Bob, except operate, of course," and he laughed from his belly—sharp but short. "General Service is a patient support system. We welcome them here; you know Joe Fritsch, of course. We check coats and packages, push wheelchairs, run elevators, and carry urgent materials between the Clinic and the hospitals. We are an essential component in the Mayo system," he said, with pride.

He looked me up and down, assessing my appearance. "You look very neat and smart today, like a man should. We will expect you to report for work like that every day; your hair washed and combed, clean fingernails, and a fresh, starched shirt. Wear a brown suit and always polish your shoes!"

He turned back to his desk and said, "See my secretary. Fill out all the employment forms, including your fingerprints, and come back Monday morning prepared for work. You'll be paid $60.00 a month."

"Thank you, Harry," Dad said, and suddenly I realized that they had already talked the whole thing over.

"Thank you, sir," I said.

Walking back to the car, Dad and I said little. I thought, *wow, 60 bucks a month! At that rate, I could live at home, no expenses, save it all—well, maybe keep out a little for a movie now and then. Maybe in a year or so I could even go on to college! A year's not too long. They're going to fingerprint me, too—just like the FBI. Boy, this job must be important!* My head was spinning like a top.

I owned two suits; the green gabardine, considered my "good" suit, and a brown, wool serge. The latter had belonged to my father, a heritage from the '20s, and had been altered in an attempt to give it a more acceptable contemporary look. It possessed neither, had thin lapels, shiny elbows, and a pinch back. I thought that it made me look like a rube; it more likely resembled the outfit of a numbers runner. I wore the suit when I was ushering at the Civic Auditorium, dolling it up with a poetic handkerchief, a collar pin, and cufflinks.

"Do I have to wear this old thing, at the Clinic, Mother?" I asked with resentment. "Gosh, look how shiny it is. All the doctors will know it's old-fashioned."

"Yes, dear, it will be perfectly all right. No one will think anything of it."

From the living room, "What else you got? It's brown. You wear it like your mother says and be quiet about it."

On Monday morning, I found a card with my name on it, in a large rack next to the time clock. The rack did not discriminate; professionals and non-professionals were all arranged alphabetically. A tall, hawked nosed man with a thin face that drooped to a pointed chin walked towards me. His shoulders slumped and he had a slight stoop; he looked like a vulture on the prowl.

"Hello, Bob, I'm Clyde Crume," he said with a laconic smile. He held out a limp mitt and we exchanged the manly greeting. "You'll be working under me for a while. I'd like you to start out today up in the main lobby, as a greeter."

"Yessir, Mr. Crume."

"Call me Clyde, Bob. Everyone else does," he said.

"Yessir, Mr…. er, Clyde."

Inside the huge bronze doors that served as a main entrance to both Clinic buildings, there was a grand staircase of green marble that led up to the main floor of the new Plummer building. In the wall to the immediate right and left of the top step there were Dutch doors, one a coat checkroom, and the second a receiving room for the urine specimens that most patients were asked to bring for laboratory examination. Small paper bags holding waxed, paperboard containers were given to each patient for this purpose.

Clyde explained that my first job of each day was to stand on the receiving room side of the top step, and discreetly approach each patient that I saw carrying a specimen sack. "Tell the person that you are from General Service, and will take their specimen and deliver it to the laboratory. Be polite, speak quietly, and whatever you do don't use the word urine. We are not here to cause a Clinic patient any embarrassment. You got that."

"Yessir, polite, quiet, and no pee."

"And no jokes either, kid."

Clyde left and I assumed my post, feeling like a palace servant assigned to announce guests arriving for a ball. Patients began to arrive, and I was suddenly entirely occupied, nearly overwhelmed, with retrieving the specimens. Dashing discreetly to and fro, I gently snatched each small sack to the safety of a special cart, positioned just inside the Dutch door. After perhaps an hour, when patients had gone to their respective departments for examination, the rush let up as abruptly as it had begun.

I began to arrange the specimen sacks on the cart and discovered, to my dismay, that one of them did not contain the expected waxed container. Formless and soft, the contents, when I peeked, turned out to be…peanut butter sandwiches. Clyde's words of admonition came crashing into my consciousness, *not here to cause a Clinic patient any embarrassment*. I could see someone opening what they thought was their lunch, in the company of others, offering them a bite. *Good gosh, now what'll I do? How could this happen—and on my first day? I just know I'll be canned! I can't do anything right! Now I'll never go to college! Never!*

Undecided quite how to proceed, I examined the alternative courses of action. Should I own up at once, and hope to be given a second chance. What about just throwing the sandwiches in the trash and claiming ignorance of the whole affair?

A small rustling caught my attention, and I turned to look into the soft, gray eyes of a worried face. The woman had wispy white hair, pulled tight in a bun. Her dress of gray calico had seen many washings, its pattern nearly invisible, and hung from her thin shoulders like a bed sheet on a pole. Even on this warm day, she wore a crocheted shawl.

"Sonny," she said, "I'm afraid I've made a terrible mistake. I meant to give you my 'spesmin, but gave you my lunch instead. I'm so sorry. I wonder if you could let me have my lunch back. I didn't mean anything by it. This here's my true sample." She handed me a familiar small brown sack whose neck had been twisted into a tight rope.

Hot diggity dog! I'm saved! Thank you Lord! I thought, and retrieved her sandwich sack, which I had placed on a counter behind the door.

"Yes ma'am," I said. "I have your property right here. It would have been safe with General Service here at Mayo Clinic, Ma'am," I said self-righteously.

"Thank you, Sonny, and God bless you." With tremendous relief, I watched her walk towards the elevators.

As time passed, I managed to avoid egregious error, my regular duties increased, and I reveled in an inspired self-importance. If asked to carry envelopes containing patients' X-ray films from Radiology to an examination floor, I would rush off, a picture of life and death, emergency in action. Affecting an out-of-breath attitude helped to convince the uninitiated that here was a truly important figure, perhaps a surgeon, hurrying to a consultation.

Should the duty require that I transport radium vials, safely placed within a lead canister suspended at the end of a three-foot chain, I did so with flair. I held the chain at arm's length, with nerves of steel, glancing occasionally at the canister, while continually assessing my pathway ahead. Pedestrians gave me a wide berth, and though I thought this was in deference to my authoritative demeanor, it was most probably because they knew an idiot when they saw one.

I was often told to take patients to their destination by wheelchair. With the exception of St. Mary's Hospital, located a mile to the west, all other hospitals, and some hotels, were connected to the Clinic by a network of pedestrian subways. Wide and level, these presented no obstacles to the wheelchair bound. At the Worrall Hospital, however, there was a downward ramp between the subway and the ground floor of the building.

"Bob, go up to South 9, and take a wheelchair patient to the Worrall," Clyde Crume said one morning.

"Okay, I'm on my way, Clyde."

The Ninth Floor waiting room glowed in the bright-yellow light that streamed through the tall leaded glass windows. Brilliant rainbows of color fell from the heraldic devices in their upper panes. All the chairs were occupied by patients who were reading, dozing, and waiting to be called for their appointments. The room resembled the lobby of a luxurious resort hotel.

Mr. Elmer Dougherty sat in his wheelchair beside the front desk. I had practiced a purposeful stride and confident bearing in order to reassure patients, but it was *my* confidence that vanished when I saw the man. His bulk filled and seemed to spill over the chair's arms. He wore an examination gown that barely covered his knobby knees and a terry cloth robe that would not close about his abdomen. His legs, blue-veined and white, looked like he was wearing a too-large suit of long underwear. When he saw me coming, his eyes lit up like neon signs, and his face, florid except for his forehead, broke into a happy grin.

"Howdy, Sonny, you think you can handle this here cargo?" he drawled, meaning himself. Some of the waiting patients laughed with him.

"Yessir, I'll get you there safe and sound," I said. *Good gosh, how the dickens could a guy get this big. I don't think he's missed many meals lately. He must weigh a ton!*

I made sure that both Elmer's feet, encased in worn corduroy carpet slippers, were firmly set in the foot rests, unlocked the wheels, and leaned into the handlebar at the back of the chair. The tires made a tormented squeal as they rolled forward on the cork floor. I got us to the elevator lobby and pushed the button.

"Excuse me, please. Wheelchair coming in," I said to the knot of passengers when the elevator doors opened. Ted Mertz, a small man, was operating the car. He gulped and rolled his eyes upward when he saw my predicament, and helped me position Elmer in a rear corner. Ted closed the doors. *Oh Lord, is this guy too heavy for the cable?* I thought. But we arrived safely at the subway level.

Ted gave me a shove and off we went, Elmer and me, at a snail's pace. I walked upright at first, but soon had to bend forward, elbows bent, chest against the handlebar, to keep momentum. Elmer seemed oblivious to my struggle and chattered on, happily, about his *spread* in Texas.

"I got me a right nice little place down there, it's on the San Paducky River, and there's no want 'a water for my shorthorns, none a tall! You should see it, Sonny, from the verandy, I mean. Far as you can see in ever direction is good Texas dirt, and good for grazin'."

I was fading fast when we reached the Worrall ramp. It was longer and steeper than I had ever noticed before. *Look at that slope! I can't do this. What if I spill him and he gets hurt?*

"Think you can get this here buggy down the slope, Sonny?"

"I've pushed patients to the Worrall before, sir, but…".

"Well, dagnab it, let's give 'er a try then." He waved a heavy right arm in a circle near his ear and yelled "Yippee!" which was enough to set us in motion.

As the weight tore at my arms, I braced myself, flatfooted against the forward motion. My rubber heels shrieked, and I tried desperately to aim the chair toward the doorway into the building. The door was closed! *Oh God, help me please!*

Our descent ceased abruptly, and I collapsed on the handlebar. Elmer had brought us to a stop by extending his legs against the door.

"Well, sir, that was a right smart bit of pulling, considerin' all you had to pull. I got to hand it to ya', son. You've got spunk!"

Ted Mertz resigned from General Service to marry a Black Jack hostess in the game room of the Diamond Cufflink in Las Vegas. Clyde put me on elevator duty as Ted's replacement.

A bank of cars rose from their terminus in the ornate main lobby of the Plummer Building. They were always operated manually, with an eye toward patient safety. The operator closed his door, announced the floors called, and then started the car. Permission to leave the main floor was under the command of the elevator dispatcher, often Clyde himself. Armed with information from a large position-light board, the dispatcher paced authoritatively through the lobby crowd, calling out, "Next Car Up," and releasing cars by clicker-augmented hand signals.

After careful and thorough training in the procedures and diplomacy of car handling, I was let loose upon the innocent world of patients. My reassuring poses, protective arm motions, authoritative conduct, and quasi-religious announcements, were a model of Clinic decorum. Sometimes I wavered from doctrine.

The operator called out the general area of expertise at each floor. General surgery, pulmonology, rheumatology, were permissible identifications, as was gastroenterology at North 7. By a slip of the tongue during my first days on the cars, I called out "proctoscopy," before opening the doors at Seven. No one stepped forward; I threw the handle and rose to Eight, calling "ophthalmology." Several men without spectacles got off! I peered around the open car door to see if there was anyone for Up, and chuckled to myself to see the selfsame men opening the stairwell door to descend. I was careful not to repeat the blunder.

A single elevator was operated until 9:00 PM on weekdays and 12:00 noon on Saturdays to benefit staff physicians who wished to use the twelfth floor medical library. Elevator operators were assigned the after hours duty on a rotational basis. Trips to and from the twelfth floor were sporadic, so the night operator was instructed to park his open car on the main floor, and await calls.

I loved the night duty, and spent most of my time reading in one of the deep leather armchairs that lined the walls of the main lobby opposite the elevator bank. The library calls gave me an opportunity to meet the senior Clinic doctors in a more friendly and intimate atmosphere. Men that my father had known for years began to address me by my first name.

On Wednesday evenings I had no time for reading. Staff meetings were held from 7:00 until 9:00 PM in Plummer Hall, an auditorium on fourteenth floor. In between the rush before and after the meeting, there were the usual library calls. Even so, I often managed to park my car on fourteen and sneak in to the darkened hall to listen to the papers being delivered. I had taken science courses in high school, was able to comprehend some of the material, and began to ply my physician acquaintances with questions. Some were dismissive, but most treated my inquisitive interest with kindness and encouragement!

One Wednesday I was listening to a speaker describing a comparative evaluation of treatment methods for seasonal allergies, when I heard the elevator call bell. Slipping out of the hall, I dropped quickly down to the main floor. When the car door opened I saw my father.

"Vare ware you?" Dad said, a little too loudly, his voice echoing up and down the cavernous lobby. "I thought you ware supposed to sit hare waiting for customers!"

"I just took someone up, Dad, and then I peeked in to listen. I can hear the elevator bell—easy!"

"Well, you better not let Bennett find you away from your post," he warned, mildly.

"What brings you down here, Dad?"

"Oh, your mother sent me to the drugstore. She always got to have something. I thought maybe I would come over and give you a ride home."

Then I had an inspiration. *I'll bet Dad would like to hear the allergy paper! He'd understand it and be interested! Maybe we could talk about science and he'd see how eager I was to go on to school and learn how to do this kind of work.*

"Dad, come on up to Plummer Hall. There's a talk on allergies right now. You'd be interested, Dad, and you'd find out more about your hay fever. It's dark in there, and you can just slip in and sit down. No one will notice. Come on, Dad. Please."

"Say, what you think I am, a doctor? I don't know that kind of stuff, Bob."

"Please, Dad."

Reluctantly, my father stepped aboard the car and we rose quickly to the hall. I found him an aisle seat and then heard the bell. The physician in the lobby was Dr. Horton. "Good evening, Bob," he said in his fine Virginia accent. "Take me up to the library, please. There are some papers on migraine that I must read before tomorrow."

"Yessir, right away. Watch your step, Doctor."

Dr. Horton began to speak about the difficulties of treating migraine and about the complex causes of the complaint. Even when we had reached the floor, he stood in the door of the car. I was a captive audience for his speculations. He enumerated and weighed dietary, hereditary, and emotional contributions. I couldn't get away. Finally, he walked into the library, head down, hand stroking his chin, still musing.

I ran the car on up to fourteen. Inside, it was apparent that the speaker was concluding his presentation. "May I have the last slide, please?" It was a bar graph of some sort. I found a seat on the aisle and turned to scan the audience.

Dad sat across the aisle, two rows behind me. In the light from the screen I could see him clearly. He sat straight, facing front. His hands were folded beneath his hat that lay in his lap. Unblinking, he looked straight before him, and his eyes betrayed the sadness of having the intelligence, but not the training, to comprehend. He seemed to understand that for him it was too late to be other than what he was, a servant to one of these men. I was overwhelmed with contrition and sorrow. Then the lights went up.

"Hello, Nels, glad to see you here tonight." Dr. Melvin Henderson, a senior staff member and a contemporary of Dr. Balfour and the Mayos, had come up to my Dad. They shook hands and Dad smiled.

"Well, thanks, Doctor. I came down to pick up my son, Bob."

"Oh, yes. Bob's working General Service this summer. He's a smart boy, Nels. You must be proud of him. I look for him to make a mark in this world one day."

"Nels, what brings you down here tonight?" asked Dr. Thomas Magath, head of Clinical Laboratories. "You hoping one of these young fellas have found out something that can help your hay fever?"

They all laughed together. My father was relieved and happy amongst his long time friends.

THIEF IN THE NIGHT

After my egregious, outhouse blunder at the Jewell's cottage, my social life had gone on vacation, the victim of a severely damaged ego. It was just as well, what with the new job at the Clinic. I told myself that I needed to focus all my attention on work, be promoted, and earn more money.

Reverting to type, reading became my off-duty activity. Fortunately for me, Mother did not concern herself with my newfound voracious reading habits, and Dad didn't seem to notice.

Coming into the kitchen one evening after work, I found Mother setting out the plates for dinner. She seemed preoccupied, and was humming *Rescue the Perishing* softly to herself. Remembering the words, I thought, *oh, oh, she's got someone's problem on her mind. I wonder who needs rescuing this time.*

When she saw me, she said, "Go wash your hands, Bobby, dear. Dinner is all ready. I'm just waiting for your father."

I returned to the kitchen table and took my usual place.

"How did work go today, dear?"

"Fine, Mom, 'bout the same. I did meet Miss Helen Keller, though."

"You did! Bobby, she is a fine woman. A famous woman! Tell me about it."

"Not much to tell," I said. "I was standing on the sidewalk talking to Joe Fritsch, and Dad pulled up in the Cadillac. He was waiting for the Doctor, and I got in the front for a moment to say Hi! Dad turned toward the rear seat. It was kind of dark, because the rear and side window blinds were drawn. Dad introduced me."

"He did? What happened then?"

249

"Strange! The first women repeated Dad's sentence while the second one, Miss Keller, held her hand up to her friend's lips. Then Miss Keller turned toward me, her eyes were clouded over, and I could tell she was blind. She put her hands on my face, Mom, and moved them all over my head. They were so soft, just like downy feathers!"

"Oh, Bobby, how thrilling!"

"Then Miss Keller spoke to her friend. Mom, her words were so odd, so garbled, I couldn't understand a thing. Then her friend said, 'Miss Keller says that you have a strong, intelligent face and she knows you will be an important worker for good in this world'."

"Oh, Bobby, what a nice thing for her to say. I'm so proud of you, dear."

"Thanks, Mom. What are we having for supper?"

"Mock chicken legs, mashed potatoes and peas, with prune whip for dessert. How do you like the sound of that?"

"Boy oh boy, mock chicken and prune whip, two of my favorites!"

"Bobby, I want to ask a favor of you."

I knew it. I knew it. Oh well, there's prune whip for supper. "Sure, Mom, what is it?

"I went to Ladies Aid meeting at the Church today, and my dear friend Gladys Mitchell was there. We had the longest talk, and Bobby, she is having the hardest time since she and her husband have separated. You know her daughter Helen; she's in your Sunday school class."

"Yeah, I know Helen, all right. Everything she says is a wisecrack. Boy, you don't want to get on her hate list. Once she starts on you, she never lets up!"

"Never mind now, it's her mother I'm talking about. Everything her husband used to do, she now has to do by herself, or hire someone to do it for her. And Bobby, she can't always find a handyman, or they want too much money. Oh, she's having such a time of it. I feel so sorry for her, poor thing."

"For crying out loud, you'd think Helen could help her! What's Mrs. Mitchell need done, Mom?"

"Well, it's her hedge, dear, along the driveway. It's grown like Topsy, she says. Now she's unable to get her car into the garage! Bobby, dear, would you mind going over there on Saturday and trimming her hedge?"

"Heck, no, sounds easy as pie to me," I said.

The Mitchell house was a smallish bungalow, with sloping walls of green shingles, yellow shutters and trim. Its roofline drooped over two half-moon dormers, and curved under at the eaves. There were flower boxes packed with droopy petunias under the front windows. The blotchy front walk curved tipsily through the small lawn and died at the front stoop. A daintily arched roof sheltered a yellow front door with a single round window near the top. The house looked like a fading '20s flapper with bangs. Behind, and to one side, there was a one-car garage in the same cutesy green, and from it to the front sidewalk grew an enormous buckthorn hedge, dense and unyielding. Near the garage, in the shade of a large maple, it was as tall as I was; toward the front, where it had continuous sunlight; it was nearly eight feet high! I rolled up on my bike, jammed on my brakes, and just sat there in the street gaping. *Holy cow! No wonder old Helen hasn't laid a hand on that brute. That's the Goliath of hedges, all right!*

I tapped on the front screen door, and a breathy, sing-song voice called out, "Just a minute, please. I'll be right there."

Gladys Mitchell, a plump blonde woman, with rosy cheeks, a porcelain complexion, and a warm, motherly smile, came to the door, drying her hands on her apron. "Oh hello, Bob," she said.

"Good, morning, Mrs. Mitchell. Mother said that you needed your hedge trimmed," I said, hoping that she'd already hired someone else.

"Oh, gosh, yes. Aren't you the nice one to offer to help me," she gushed. "The tools are in the garage, Bob, and there's a ladder, too."

No escape now, boy, you might as well get to work. The sooner you start, the sooner it'll be over! I nosed around in the garage, found a ten-foot wooden stepladder, a rusty pair of hedge shears, and a file. After putting a workable edge on the shears, I started to work at the front.

Morning wore on, Mrs. Mitchell coming out at lunchtime with lemonade, which I really hated, and peanut butter sandwiches! *Just melts in your mouth, huh!* The clippings mounted, as I brought the monster to its knees, but it was slow, hot going, and the cut ends of the darn hedge had produced decorative stripes on my arms.

I did not hear the bicycle approach from the street. Suddenly, the stepladder began to lurch and sway; I had nothing to hang on to and crashed through the hedge to the ground.

A grinning, impish figure, straddling her bicycle in an *I dare you* stance, was holding the ladder as if to say *I threw you to the ground and what are you gonna do about it?* Her hair was thin, combed on the side and ended in curly puffs that hid her ears. Her forehead was high and broad; above cupid lips there was a sharp, skinny nose.

"For gosh sakes, why'nt you warn somebody when you're gonna dump 'em," I said.

She laughed, "What's the point? You could never dump anybody then."

I knew it, just knew it! A wiseacre!

Helen and I became good friends. Though she had been a picnic guest at the Jewells' cottage and witness to my outhouse faux pas, she didn't condemn but thought it a hilarious twist of fate. I was so relieved; it was reason enough to admire her.

For most of that summer, we went swimming, danced to swing records at friends' houses, played cards, or went to the movies. Most of our dating was conducted by bicycle, except for infrequent occasions when we double-dated with a friend who had a car.

Often Helen would meet me after work and we walked to her house, spinning idle fantasies about our lives. It was difficult conversational ground, for she was already enrolled at the University of Minnesota, with an eye toward a future in fine art, and I had no idea that I would ever make it to college. I wished so much that I had the opportunity, the good fortune, that so many of my friends took for granted. Not knowing whom to blame, I resented my parents for not making better plans.

One evening, Helen and I had gone to the movies. I had persuaded Dad to let me have the Olds. After the movie and the ice cream soda that was de rigueur fare for such an occasion, I took Helen home. The Mitchell's house backed up to Kutzky Park. A short distance beyond her house, with only a few homes in between, lay the grounds of the Rochester Tennis Club. This evening, by implicit mutual consent, we drove past Helen's door toward the Tennis Club drive. Prompted by restless hormones and a shared desire for callow clutchings, I drove onto the gravel drive in total darkness, having doused my headlights.

I drove slowly, in mounting excitement, until the car gradually lost momentum and refused to go forward. Surprised, I reversed gears to no avail. The usual rocking procedure that every Minnesota driver learns early failed me. I got out of the car to find that I had driven off the end of the gravel, merely a service road, and that the Olds had sunk to the hubcaps in the lush, green, freshly watered lawn of the Club.

Helen laughed hugely. I was appalled at my stupidity, and at the spectacle that the car would present in the morning. I could already imagine the denunciations. *Isn't that the Twedts' car over there? I know Nels Twedt wouldn't have gotten stuck like that. It must have been that boy of his. What reason would he have to be out there last night? With some girl, I suppose! Hasn't he been going around with Gladys Mitchell's oldest girl—isn't her name Helen?*

I had seen my friend Ronald Schultz at the movies with Geraldine Schlitgus—he had his Dad's car. I wondered if they were still parked up in front of her house.

"Helen, we've got to get you home," I said. "After that I'm going to run up to Schlitgus's to see if Ron can come down and help me pull the car out.

"Whaaat?" Ron said, when I presented my predicament. More prudent, less venturesome than I, Ron was wearing a white shirt, collar covered in lipstick, a horrid looking tie, worse in the dark, and a pin-stripe suit. Gerry hurried into the house.

"Get in," Ron said, feigning vexation, but on the verge of laughter that was stifled out of consideration for my pale, hopeless look, made more pathetic in the glare of the street lamps.

While we drove, I unburdened my fears on him. It was thoughtless, selfish, but Ron was understanding and listened. "What a stupid jerk I am. I must have been out of my mind. Why didn't I just park in front of her place? Oh Lord, Ron, what will Dad say? And Mother—it's really her car you know," I said, shaking with anxiety at the specters I'd raised.

The unspoken terror, one that I couldn't discuss with Ron who had sent in his application for Engineering School already, was the effect on my nebulous chances for any help from my folks for college.

Going down Second Street, Ron slowed when I pointed out the service road to the Tennis Club. Swinging the car lights down the gravel, we could see the red reflectors on the green Oldsmobile.

"My God, Bob, where the heck did you two intend to go? Into the club house looking for a sofa?" Ron queried. He slowed and stopped well short of our car, but still safely on the gravel.

"What do you think, Ron?" I asked, hopefully, searching his face for a miracle.

"No hope, my friend. Get in, we're getting out of here." Grimly he backed onto the street and took me home.

I went upstairs as usual, locking the doors and turning out the lights behind me, and undressed quietly in my darkened room. Once in bed, sleep would not come. My conscience held me under scores of indictments. *Helen's mother will confront her daughter with searing questions about her relations with you. She will speak to your parents about the consequences. You will probably be forced into marriage and never see the inside of a college—never amount to a hill of beans. The Tennis Club will certainly sue your parents for damages, and the car will require costly repairs. You will, of course, have to foot the bills yourself, using up your savings and making all thoughts of college impossible.*

Early the next morning, I was awakened from these fitful nightmares by the tinkling of the telephone.

"Hello. Nels Twedt speaking," I heard my father say. "Yah, Bernie. Whaaat! No! Wait and I'll see." There was a silence and then, "No, Bernie, she's not in the garage. I'll be right there."

"What is it, Nels?" I heard Mother say from the kitchen.

"It ware Bernie Lunde, the Police Chief. He says your car ware stolen and he has found it, out at the Tennis Club. The thief got stuck in the mud and had to leave it."

"Oh! Lord help us!" I heard her say.

Then Dad was gone. He went downstairs and I could just make out two voices, probably he was speaking to John Tewes. The truck backed out and zoomed off. I stayed under the covers.

By the time I got up later to get dressed for work, Dad had returned with the car that John and he had rather easily pulled free with a long log chain. The only damage was a good deal of mud on the undercarriage, which I volunteered to wash off after work.

"Thank you, dear, you're very sweet," said Mother with a smile.

NIGHT TRAIN

As the days of summer wore on, and July became the prophet of August heat to come, the daily temperature rose inexorably. Mother called the days sweltering and the nights sultry!

I chaffed at the inhospitable weather, and what I now began to recognize as imprisonment in a job with a very low ceiling. *There's no better job to advance to. Nothing, that is unless old Bennett were to drop dead in his tracks. Even then I'd still be a flunky—just head flunky, and a little better paid!*

The heat transformed my restyled brown suit into a thermal straitjacket. I detested the thing, and avoided leaving the cool confines of the Clinic with paranoid dedication. The pedestrian subway became my preferred route, even when to go outside might have been much shorter. If the subway were not possible, I clung to the shady side of the street, skipping from shadow to shadow like Liza crossing the ice.

I saw Helen occasionally. She talked of school; I listened without interest. We no longer went swimming, and my tan was fading almost as fast as our relationship. *Soon I'll look like all the professionals at the Clinic, ethereal and pure.*

One Saturday in early August I trudged home with my jacket slung over my shoulder. Hot and tired, the few blocks I had to walk seemed like miles, and the jacket like a millstone. Or was it just the jacket? I remembered *The Rhyme of the Ancient Mariner* that I'd read in English 12. *It's the darn job! That's my albatross!* Feeling sorry for myself, indeed, I went into the shade of the garage.

Upstairs, my sister and my parents were seated at the kitchen table having lunch. My mother looked at me with a bright smile and said,

"Sit down, dear, you look tired. We're having tuna salad sandwiches and iced coffee. There's watermelon for dessert."

"Thanks, Mom," I said with a sigh and sank into my chair.

Nancy was wearing her *I know something you don't know* smirk.

Dad ate steadily, and then wiped all the globs of spilled salad from his plate with bits of bread. "Goss, Stella, this ware good fish salad!"

"Pass the watermelon," Nancy said. Black seeds were floating about in juice on her plate that she tilted toward Dad.

"Pass the watermelon, *please*," repeated my Mother.

"Yeah, please!" Nancy said.

Dad forked another triangular piece of melon onto her plate and a larger slice to his own. "There, now be quiet," he said. We all ate melon, slurping and spitting.

Dad finished eating, stacked his dishes at the side of the sink, and said, "You kids wash up." He went into the living room, and I could hear the rustling of his newspaper.

"Bobby, dear, when you and Nancy have finished cleaning up, come into the living room, please. Dad and I have something to say to you."

Oh, oh, they must have found out who the Tennis Club thief is.

Nancy smirked, "Well let's get started. Sooner we get finished, sooner I can get out of here and go swimming." Her near platinum-blonde hair was striking against her skin that was tanned to the color of teakwood. In just a few days, she would be 14 years old; I had never seen another girl quite as beautiful!

When we were belly-up to the sink, ready for the *you're not getting 'em clean, I'll tell Dad* game that we played each time, she winked at me—a big slow wink.

"What's going on?" I said in a whisper.

"I don't know, Bob," she replied in a way that said she did.

"Well, why all the winking then? Come on, you must know something!"

"Just keep your shirt on! You'll know soon enough—and you're gonna like it. Now get those hands in the suds, I'm in a hurry!"

Puzzled, still anxious, and not put at ease by Nancy's mysterious white lies, I scrubbed away in silence. When we had finished, Nancy bolted down stairs, two steps at a time.

"Nancy! Stop that running on the steps," Dad called after her.

"Yes, dear, it's certainly not ladylike," Mother agreed, but wisely left the business of laying down the law to her husband.

"Okay! Okay! No running!" she replied with mild exasperation.

"You wanted to talk to me?" I said to the air in the living room. I hoped the answer might come back, *No, it ware nothing.*

"Yes, Bobby, your father has something serious to say to you. Sit down, dear."

The afternoon paper hid all of Dad but his long trouser legs, noticeably thin at the knees, and his work-callused fingers, curled about the margins like a shield. He seemed to be defending himself against the inevitable consequences of what had already been decided.

"Nels, talk to your son!"

He closed and folded his paper, set it aside slowly, thinking about his words and then looked into my worried face.

"Bob, right after you ware born, while your mother ware still in the hospital, I called up Svein Rasmussen and bought a life insurance policy for you. We paid on it ever since. And you know there ware some mighty skimpy times around here—but we always managed to pay every week."

"Yessir. I've seen him up here, a thousand times, I guess, and always with his receipt book!" *Whew, what a relief, this isn't about the car stuck in the Tennis Club lawn at all. It's about insurance, of all things. What does he want me to do, I wonder? Pay it myself, I suppose.*

"Your mother and I thought we would turn it over to you to pay the premiums when you got a yob and ware settled. By taking it out when you ware little we got the sheepest rate, and it wouldn't change when you ware able to make the payments."

"Yes." *Rats! I knew it. Just another albatross.*

"But that policy ware a twenty-year annuity. So we thought maybe we could give you the money instead!"

"But I'm only 18, Dad!"

"Listen, will you! I went to see Harry Harwick up in Administration, and he told me the Clinic would lend me money against the policy, with no interest until you graduate! If that still isn't enough, and you run out of money, your mother and I will find some way to help you. But you got to use all your own money first!"

I was incredulous. I had $998.00 in the bank. With the insurance, there would be nearly two thousand dollars! "Gosh, I'm speechless. Wow, I can't believe this! What a gift! I really don't know what to say, except thank you both—from the bottom of my heart, thank you!"

"We want you to get your education, dear," Mother said. "You've been a good student at Edison and in High School, Bobby, and we just know you'll do your best in college, too!"

"I sure intend too! I'd like to go the University, that is, if you think it's a good idea, too! It's a first-rate school, but the tuition, for state residents, is much cheaper than at a private school, like St. Olaf." I knew my father had a great respect for this Lutheran, Liberal Arts College in Northfield. He listened to their Sunday morning church service on the radio and was a firm champion of F. Melius Christiansen, Director of the St. Olaf Lutheran Choir.

"Couldn't you go to Rochester Junior College, Bobby? You could live at home and save on room and board," Mother suggested. Her hands lay tightly restrained in her lap, knuckles white as snow, lest they reveal her sadness and anxiety.

"Well, I was thinking about engineering, Mom. That's what Ron Schultz is going to do—chemical engineering. Factories making war material employ all kinds of engineers; mechanical, electrical, and especially chemical engineers. The need for engineering students will shoot up and maybe draft boards will give 'em deferments. RJC doesn't even have an engineering program!"

It was a reasonable argument, and I felt that Dad was my unspoken ally. He had always been a vociferous critic of "those enyineers" in the automotive industry, yet I suspected that he envied them their calling. Still, the tenuous nature of any future plans in the face of wartime uncertainties was obvious. The draft age, still 21, might be lowered at any time. Some of my friends were volunteering out of fatalism, and to secure what they thought was a safe, even prestigious, branch of service.   .

"Stella, I think he should make up his own mind. Bob, you go see the Doctor for advice." When he sensed that he was getting into deep water, Dad always deferred to others whom he felt were more competent. He reopened the paper, Mother smiled happily, and I was on cloud nine.

The rest of August was a hectic time, but I was so elated, I didn't have a care! Even the heat, which continued torrid, no longer concerned me. My friend Ron Schultz had already reserved a double room in the men's dormitory, Pioneer Hall. The guy from northern Minnesota, whom the University had selected to be his roommate, had written Ron to say that he couldn't get the tuition money together and would enlist in the Navy instead.

"Ron, I'd really like to share that double with you! Do you think the U has found someone else?"

"Are you kidding! I just got the letter from the guy yesterday. I'll call him and ask him to hold up canceling with the U, until we can send in your request to room with me. It'll be okay! I think it'd be great to room together—you old stick-in-the-mud," Ron said. He looked sideways at me and grinned, reminding me of my mishap on the Tennis Club lawn.

"Aw, cut it out, or I'll tell!

"Tell what?"

"Tell how you had the hots for ole Rita Wilbur before you and Geraldine became a twosome." The ensuing playful scuffle confirmed our dorm decision. I was pleased as punch to be sharing with a schoolmate from Rochester, and to be saving money as well.

Mother had made a critical survey of my meager wardrobe. She showed the green suit, worn thin in the seat and knees, trousers too short, to my father one evening.

"Nels, I hate to send Bobby off to the University with nothing but this thing. Look how worn it is. Bobby, put this suit on and show your father," she said, turning to me."

"Okay, Mom!" *Boy is he going to get a surprise!*

I returned to model the suit, wrists and ankles showing plainly, looking like an elfin Honest Abe.

"You ware right, Stella. Those are certainly high-water pants," Dad observed, and then burst out laughing. He bent over with the humor of my appearance, face reddening with mirth. "I think we got to get him a suit for school. It will be a going away present."

Mother looked away, her shoulders slumped, and she said, "Yes, for going away."

Dad, Mother and I went to Hanny's. Though it was supposed to be a pleasant occasion, there was little talking. When Hanny brought out a dark brown herringbone tweed that he thought was stylish, we agreed that it was fine. Hanny took measurements with the usual friendly banter about my having *shot up there!* Then Dad talked with Hanny about paying for the suit on time, and we left.

In the car, on the way home, Mother said, "I think the suit looks very nice on you, dear."

"Thanks, Mom and Dad. It's a really swell suit…and ought to last a long time."

My last day of work in General Service was Friday, the twenty-fifth of September. I had already said my good-byes to each of my coworkers. Most knew that I was leaving for college, and wished me good luck. At nine that morning, I went to see Mr. Bennett.

"Hi, Miss Teslow," I said to Essie, when I entered the outer office. "I have an appointment to see Mr. Bennett."

Essie slipped the crossword puzzle page in the morning *Minneapolis Tribune* under her desk blotter and said, "Good morning, Bob. Please have a seat."

Over the intercom she said, "Mr. Twedt is here to see you, sir." Indistinguishable grunts and burbles, like a faraway train announcer, came from her speaker.

"You may go right in," she said, and flashed a perfunctory smile.

"Come in, Bob," Mr. Bennett said, extending a firm hand for the heavy handshake of the successful manager. "So, this is your last week at the Clinic."

"Yessir, and I've come to thank you for hiring me. I learned a great deal and I have a lot of good memories. Every one of the men was helpful and friendly. But I want to further my education and am going up to the University of Minnesota."

"A good choice, Bob. Many of the men on my staff came to work right after high school. Not all of them are as bright as you, but they are sober, good workers. Unfortunately, most of them don't have the opportunity to finish their education. When Nels first came to me and asked me to hire you, I thought that might be true for you as well, Bob. I'm glad I agreed then to take you on, and after meeting you, I was sure I'd made the right choice."

"Thank you, sir."

"But now you're leaving, and for a brighter future. Good luck, Bob. You will always get a good reference from this office."

"Thank you again, sir. Goodbye."

Clyde Crume was in the outer office talking to Essie, and he followed me out into the registration area. "Sit down for a minute Bob, I'd like to talk to you," he said.

We found a place in the rear, away from Bennett's office, and out of earshot of the patients. Clyde was relaxed, acting far more friendly than I had ever seen him.

"I wanted to tell you, Bob, that I really enjoyed having you work here at the Clinic this summer," he began. "I didn't expect you'd amount to much, but you've certainly proved me wrong."

"I'm glad I did, Clyde," I said.

"Bob, you're one of the best workers I've ever had on General Service. You've been courteous and calm, even with difficult patients—and we've seen some cranky and hysterical ones, haven't we?

"Yes, Clyde," I chuckled, "we certainly have."

"You always got the job done, Bob. Many patients have come to tell me how polite and helpful you were to them. I appreciate your work, but I also respect your decision to leave us."

"Thank you for telling me, Clyde," I said. "I'm proud that you changed your mind about me."

"To tell you the truth, Bob, I went to Harry earlier in the spring and argued against his hiring any high school graduates. I thought young men like you would be irresponsible and unreliable. He agreed with me. Then one day, when I was in Essie's office, your Dad came to see Harry and I overheard Nels asking him to hire you. I felt sorry for Nels then, having to go hat-in-hand to Harry Bennett. But your father won him over, Bob. Nels has guts and determination, that's for sure."

"Yessir, he has," I agreed. I felt humbled, hearing what my Dad had done. *I don't have that kind of guts.*

I worked the late shift that evening, running the library car. Shortly before quitting time I ran the car up for a call, and the person waiting on Twelve was Mr. Harry Harwick, head of Administration.

"Good evening, sir. Going down?" I said.

"Evening, Bob. Yes, I'm through for today," he said. "Your Dad tells me that you're going up to the University, Bob. Going to take up engineering, are you?"

"Yessir, chemical engineering."

"A wise choice. Chemistry is essential to all biological science. It's certainly essential to the war effort. When do you leave, Bob?"

"I need to be on campus next Monday, sir—for registration!

"We'll miss you around here. Mr. Bennett has told me that you were an excellent worker."

"I've enjoyed working on General Service. Everyone was very helpful to me."

The car doors opened at the main floor dim now with only a few sconces lit. Mr. Harwick turned to me and said, "I'm glad that we could help you financially, Bob. Mayo Clinic has not had any educational loan program before, but your father made quite a case for you, and I think we'd better consider making such a program permanent. Nels spoke very highly of your abilities; he is really very proud of you. Don't let him down! Well, goodnight Bob, and good luck!"

When I unchained my bike from its accustomed spot behind the Clinic, I glanced at my watch. Just after nine o'clock. Still, if I hurried, I could watch while the sleeper for Chicago was switched into the night train from Rapid City. A special Pullman car was used for the Rochester service; it had side doors that would accommodate patients traveling to and from the Clinic on a stretcher. The car was handled overnight, remaining in the Rochester coach yard during the day.

I arrived to find the night-shift telegrapher already at his post—a new man, whom I did not know. Sitting astride my bike with one foot on the western end of the platform I could see the agent, under a green-glass shaded bulb. He was bent over his order book, writing furiously as the repeater clattered out railroad business. The single bulb sent a sad yellow light out over the arrival tracks. The man looked like a lighthouse caretaker, spending out the strand of his life at the far reaches of the electric clacking.

Down eastward, I heard a metallic screech followed by the tap of metal against metal. Dimly I could see the car tonk, checking the journal boxes, and tapping the wheels of the night Pullman, listening for the hollow sound that signaled a crack. In railroad denim, bent over his tasks, I could only make out his movements by the eccentric motions of his lantern.

In a moment, an ambulance arrived, red lights flashing, but without the siren. I could see by his slight stoop that Clyde was the driver. Two other General Service guys were with him, and they opened the rear doors; the interior was lighted to reveal a seated figure, which stepped out into the dark. The men removed a stretcher, and with great gentleness, carried the patient to the wide side door to one of the Pullman's bedrooms. *Another patient going home after surgery.* A woman entered to sit besides the patient, all doors were shut with slamming sounds, and the ambulance left.

Whistling for the west yard limits, the Night Express arrived, bell clamoring, and brake shoes squealing loudly at the indignity of having to stop short of its destination. Conversations ensued, between the train crew, the night trick telegrapher, and the crew of a yard goat that shuffled out of the shadows, leaking water and steam. The yard engine shunted the Rochester Pullman off the siding and placed it, without the slightest jar, at the end of the Chicago-bound train. The air hissed, to announce successful connection, there was a muffled *Booard*, and the Night Express pulled off.

I had watched this scene so many times from my privileged seat in the dark that I knew every motion, each speech, and all the sounds. The red lanterns at the end of the train swayed off in the distance. Sadly, I clapped my hands in lonely appreciation. I knew that I was leaving a play before its run had ended, and that I should never return to this place again.

TO HAVE YOUR CHANCE

We spent a hectic weekend. Mother and Dad were in constant discussion about the potential need for, and the advisability of packing, various items of clothing and accessories. There was, after all, only a limited amount of drawer and closet space in the double room in Pioneer Hall that Ron Schultz and I would share. The same could be said for the carrying capacity of the Olds. It had long been decided that only Dad and I would be making the trip to the campus, thus freeing up the back seat in addition to the trunk of the car.

Dad was a seasoned packer, having spent more than thirty years at it for Dr. Balfour. He went about finding space within space, sorting, analyzing, and arriving at ingenious solutions. When he had about reached optimal success, Mother would think of some overlooked item.

When I had left home the previous year, headed for California, I only carried a modest suitcase full of summer clothing. My parents assumed Uncle Leo meant what he said about sending me to Cal Tech and that not only board and tuition but clothing needs were included in the offer. I traveled light; Mother and Dad really had little idea what clothes I would need in Pasadena anyway.

Now, all was different. I would have to bring all the clothing and accessories that I would need for a four-year stint in Minneapolis, and my parents were absolutely convinced that they knew everything there was to know about *that* subject. At first, I bowed to their suggestions, but as the items filling every available space in the Olds began to mount, I balked.

Mother handed me a cardboard box containing footwear to load: two pairs of dress shoes, sneakers, corduroy slippers, buckled overshoes, and a pair of rubbers with tongues. *Good Lord, does she think I'm going to pitch manure?*

"Motherrr! I'll never wear all this stuff," I complained.

"Bobby, there's not a thing there that you won't need at some time, up there."

Looking at the rubbers, I objected, "But I have a raincoat!"

"Yes, dear, and an umbrella. Now I want you to promise me that you'll wear your rubbers."

I could just imagine the comments I'd get if I wore 'em! *Does your mommy make you wear your rubbers when you go out with a girlie, Bob?* And the roar of laughter that would accompany them.

"Yes, Mother." I put the box in the trunk, promising myself that the rubbers would never again see the light of day.

Suddenly I understood that the underlying reason for these trivial exchanges was simply the desire we each had to prolong the time together. Mother and Dad knew that we would never talk to each other in quite the same way again. They were saddened, and inwardly afraid, that their schoolboy son would return, transformed into an adult whom they would love and respect but might not like.

Sunday we all went to services at the Congregational Church. On the front steps, we met many of my parents' friends. Gladys Mitchell came over, looking like an ecstatic daffodil in her wide-brimmed straw hat and pale green chiffon dress. It was a warm day yet her costume did not seem appropriate for a Sunday service in September. Her daughter was not with her.

"Good morning, all you Tweet folks," Mrs. Mitchell said, still mispronouncing our name. "Isn't it a perfectly beautiful morning?" She sang the words, like an ingenue in *Oklahoma*.

"Gladys, how nice you look," said Mother, who just hated to hear herself described like a bird. She preferred, and always used, Tweed. "Where is Helen this morning?"

"Oh, she's already gone up to the University," Mrs. Mitchell laughed. "She just had to go up an meet her new roomy. They've already become good friends on the telephone. Helen makes friends so easily," she said, looking at me.

Nancy and I remained silent during this dippy exchange, and then we all went in to find our regular pew. The entrance hymn was "Holy, Holy Holy," which my mother sang, clearly and beautifully. Sharing a hymnal, Nancy and I made a passable duet, while Dad, bending close over his, followed along with his finger on the lines.

After the Invocation, we sang "When I Survey the Wondrous Cross," a favorite of my mother, and one that my sister and I had often sung with her while doing the dishes. The lovely music and inspiring words remained with us through the Collection, and the special musical offering of the quartet dominated by the imprecise warbling of Mrs. Knapp.

The Rev. G. P. Sheridan took his Sermon text from 2 Timothy 3: 14-15, "Stand by the Truths You Have Learned," largely in consideration of the many young people in the congregation who were leaving home to continue their studies elsewhere. Expanding upon his theme, the minister leaned heavily upon the words *Remember from whom you have learned them.*

I looked at my parents. Dad was listening closely, nodding slightly, in agreement. Mother, with less restraint, returned my glance, smiled encouragement, and nodded toward Dr. Sheridan, as if to say, *Listen to his words, Bobby. Don't forget them—don't forget us!*

We paced the crowd, out of the sanctuary, to greet our minister. He stood at the top of the staircase, sun glancing off his dark hair, combed straight back, divided in the center.

"Goodbye, Bob, remember to pray daily, ask the Lord for guidance, and do your best, always," he said.

"Yessir," I replied without really appreciating the full meaning of his advice.

We had dinner at home, Dad saying the Grace. *"I Jesu navn går vi til bord, å spise og drikke på dit ord. Dig Gud til aere, oss til gavn, så får vi mat i Jesu navn Amen."*

We talked about happy times, laughing together. Nancy's blue eyes, appearing cerulean in her tanned face, were anxious and moist with tears. "You behave, you hear," she said, with a small smile.

"Sure will, honey," I said, "same to you."

We all went down stairs to the loaded car. Dad had brought his camera, a relic of the 20s, with foldout bellows. The posed snapshot, taken to freeze the passage of time, was a tradition in our family that frequently left my father, the invisible photographer, out of the picture. The time required to arrange these shots, often taken when we were all dressed fit to kill, caused Nancy and me discomfort and impatience. We usually cooperated with difficulty.

"Come on, Bob, let's take your picture. Stella, come hare with your son. Nancy, stand next to Bob," Dad said.

Nancy rolled her eyes in feigned exasperation. I looked at her and shook my head slightly. "Okay, Dad, here we come," I said.

Dad prompted our placement, motioning left or right, commanding the exchange of places, all the while gazing down into his viewfinder. "Goss, why can't you smile, Stella." There was a faint click of the shutter release and he straightened, satisfied.

I looked at my father, folding his camera, winding the straps, his worn suit, hanging loose about his tall frame. He had sealed my childhood, releasing me with hope and his blessing. I could see the wear of years on his face and the concern in his eyes.

Then I kissed Mother and Nancy, and we spoke our good-byes again. Mother began to cry.

"Well, Bob, are you ready?"

"Yessir."

Dad and I got into the Olds, backed out, everyone waving, and turned toward Highway 52 North.

It was Indian summer weather, sunny and warm for late September. We rolled down our windows to claim the breeze, and I felt once more the heady sensation that I had experienced a year before—of leaving the static and the humdrum behind to begin a great adventure. Dad must have sensed my feelings, for he began to talk about himself.

"When I was your age, in 1905, I came to America with a friend, and we ware so excited. We thought America was the land of milk and honey, streets ware paved with gold—so foolish we ware. Larson and I, we worked our passage," he said.

"How did you do that? Were you sailors?"

"We went to the captain of a freighter anchored in Bergen harbor, and told him that we had part of the money for tickets, could we work off the rest. He said we could. The ship ware carrying horses, so we shoveled horse dung all way 'cross the Atlantic." He laughed good-naturedly at the memory.

"Did your father give you part of the money?"

"No, nothing from him! Ole Bårdson Tvedt hated the Amerikaners—the people who ware leaving for the New World. It ware a gift from my half-sisters. I had one sister and three half-sisters. Your grandfather, *bestefår* in Norwegian, married twice. He had three sons and three daughters by his first wife, Johanna—she was a Fammestad from across the fjord. When Johanna died, my father married again. She ware Oline Askeland, and they had four children, my dear sister Elisa, and we three boys: Ole, Henrik and me.

"How did your half-sisters have money then?"

"Well, Johanna willed her silver breastplate that ware part of her native costume to her daughters. It ware good sized, and worth a lot of money. The three girls sold it and divided the money. Kari used her share to help pay for a ticket to America in 1901. Johanna and Karolina both stayed at home, and they gave me their money for part of my ticket in 1905."

"Golly, Dad, that was quite a nice gift, I'd say."

"Yah it certainly ware. Otherwise, you never would have existed," he grinned at his own joke.

"Were you and your half-sister Kari the only ones to come to America?"

"Oh, no! The first one ware my half-brother, Bert—Bård in Norwegian. He left home when he was 24, in 1899. I think you met him once, Bob. Yah, Bert came to Rochester in the summer of 1937."

"I remember him, Dad. We all went over to eat at the Fish House in Winona. He looked just like you, and his wife was kind of dumpy—with a bun."

"Yah, that ware the man. Well, Bert wrote home to his sister Kari, painting a rosy picture of America, how easy it ware to get work hare, how everyone was rich, and they all wanted to hire Norskie women for maids. Boy that ware a hot one!" Dad laughed uproariously and slapped the steering wheel with glee. I joined his laugh because it was good to see him enjoy himself. He acted like a boy!

I thought of Mrs. Seaman, Bob's mother, and said, "Working as somebody's maid doesn't sound like a reason to leave Norway!"

"Noooo, it ware not," Dad said, his tone becoming serious. "But, there ware reason enough at home. My father ware not an easy one to get along with. The boys, in particular, could not wait to leave home. After Bert, Kari, and I came, my half-brother, John, and my brother Ole came over. John married a widow lady and went to farming around Sioux Falls. Ole went to Washington State, joined Bert, and they both went on the gold rush to Alaska."

"Gosh, did they strike it rich?" I asked.

"No, they got enough to open a bar in Dawson Creek, but it ware a wild place and they sold out and went back to Seattle."

We sat silent for a time. Dad was thinking about his siblings, I suppose. I was trying to sort out all these people, about whom I had learned more in the last few minutes than I had ever known in my entire life.

"Dad, was there anyone left at home?"

"Yah, there ware Ivar. He ware the oldest son left in Norway, so he got the farm, but he had to take care of the old man for the rest of his life in the bargain. And Ivar lived always with his knees knocking."

"Why?"

"Well, if Bert had come home, he could nudge Ivar out of the line of inheritance and off the farm. Those ware poor times in Norway. Without the farm, Ivar would have had to hire out as a hand, or go to sea. Neither one ware very good choices for a family man."

"What about your sisters?"

"Oh, the lucky ones got married to men who owned farms. The unlucky ones ware spinsters all their lives—yust sit in the chimney corner and knit socks for their keep—or they died young!" I knew he must have been thinking about his own sister. Dad had always said that Nancy looked like Elisa, and now that name had assumed an identity.

"Dad, did your sister Kari, or any of your brothers ever go back to Norway?"

"No, no one."

"What about you, Dad? Don't you want to see your father?"

"No, I don't want to see him. I won't go back there." He sat rigid, arms straight before him, gripping the steering wheel.

"Why not?"

He said nothing for many minutes. When he answered, in a strangely low, pitiful voice, he said, "He ware mean and spiteful! He ware cruel to all of us, but he beat me one time too many!"

"Oh," I said, not knowing what else to say.

Dad began slowly at first, and then with words tumbling more rapidly, "It seemed like we were always getting a licking, sometimes for small things, sometimes for nothing. He whipped me for letting a calf get loose, and for letting the goats stray too far. Once he beat me for falling out of a tree! I ware hurt, and Ivar helped me to get to the house. Instead of getting patched up, I got a whipping for climbing in his tree!"

"Gosh, Dad, that wasn't right!"

"Noooo, it ware not. So, none of us boys wanted to stay there with him, except poor Ivar." He thought for a moment, brightened, and said "That ware why I was as excited to sail away as you are now. You got to go away from home to find your future."

"You're right, Dad."

"I ware glad to get away from that man's meanness, and I worried that I carried his terrible temper inside me. Sometimes when I ware upset about something, I felt it boiling up inside me and I always tried to keep it in check—but that time you went out in the canoe at Balfour's farm, I yust couldn't control it. I'm sorry that I beat you, Bob; I thought I killed you!"

"Dad, you told me not to go out there. I did a dumb thing. I don't blame you for giving me a licking; I deserved it! Don't worry about it. You don't need to feel sorry!" As I spoke, Dad's hands relaxed, he exhaled softly, and tears trickled down his cheeks.

"Thanks Bob! You ware a good son," he said.

"I want you to know that I am very thankful to Mom and you for helping me. I know it must have been hard for you to go see Mr. Harwick and Mr. Bennett."

"I wanted you to have your chance, Bob."

We continued to talk during the rest of the journey, but now it was of things that two good friends might discuss. We spoke of the war, how long it might last, and how the effort to defeat the Nazis would alter our lives. Each of us knew that the draft might make swift and drastic changes in my education, but we didn't talk about that. We remembered driving to the Cities for Christmas shopping, when Nancy and I were little, and I described how we much both of us had anticipated and enjoyed these outings.

Finally we pulled up in front of Pioneer Hall. Ron was there to meet us, and we began unloading the car and carrying my stuff to our dormitory room. We puffed up two flights of stairs with each load. For a time we worked in silence. My father was dressed in an out-of-date black suit, worn fedora, and scuffed brown shoes, and I recognized nobility. All too soon we were finished.

Dad walked to the car, opened the glove compartment and retrieved the Kodak. Unlimbering its bellows, readying the aperture, he said, "Ron, will you take a picture of my son and me?"

"Sure, Mr. Twedt, I'd be glad to!"

Dad and I at U of M, 1942

The resulting snapshot shows two old friends seated together, while lives that rush on in separate directions are stilled for a moment. Then we stood facing each other and Dad said, "Well, Bob, I think you can handle it from here on."

I understood his meaning and replied, "I'll do my best, Dad!"

We shook hands, and then he pulled me to him and hugged me.

0-595-23927-7

Printed in the United States
772700005B